"With a keen eye and deft hand Allen plunges into the ever-changing discussion of the biblical teaching on God's justification of sinners, practicing a truly intersubdisciplinary examination that draws upon exegetical, historical, and dogmatic studies, addressing contemporary cultures and the life of the church with his insights. Agree or disagree, readers will be challenged to address 'forensic' and 'participatory' views of justification from perspectives gathered from Allen's own Reformed tradition as well as from Luther and a variety of historic and contemporary Lutheran and Roman Catholic theologians. This volume will fire fresh exchanges regarding the nature of the gospel and the definition and application of God's justifying action in Christ Jesus."

—**Robert Kolb**, Concordia Seminary, St. Louis

"In this extremely learned book, Michael Allen performs a dual service for Christian theology. First, by applying the lens of dogmatic analysis to a topic largely dominated by exegetical and ecumenical concern in recent decades, he exposes the shortsightedness of many contemporary approaches and debates and enables us to perceive a more capacious domain of possibilities. Second, by means of compelling argument and well-chosen examples, he demonstrates that historic Protestant teaching regarding God's gracious justification of the ungodly retains its status as a hinge upon which many doctrines turn and a wellspring of theological and spiritual vitality."

—**Scott Swain**, Reformed Theological Seminary

"The new debate on justification is getting interesting! Allen provides a lucid scholarly guide to the controversies. He intervenes in the debate on behalf of divine immutability and forensic imputation. How little the classic fault lines still apply! How much less can the matter of justification be regarded as passe."

—**Paul R. Hinlicky**, Roanoke College;
Univerzita Komenskeho, Bratislava, Slovakia

# JUSTIFICATION
## *and the* GOSPEL

### UNDERSTANDING THE CONTEXTS
### AND CONTROVERSIES

## R. MICHAEL ALLEN

**B**
**Baker Academic**
*a division of Baker Publishing Group*
Grand Rapids, Michigan

Published by Baker Academic
a division of Baker Publishing Group
P.O. Box 6287, Grand Rapids, MI 49516-6287
www.bakeracademic.com

Printed and bound by CPI Group (UK) Ltd, Croydon, CR0 4YY

Library of Congress Cataloging-in-Publication Data is on file at the Library of Congress, Washington, DC.

ISBN: 978-0-8010-3986-7

13   14   15   16   17   18   19        7   6   5   4   3   2   1

For Wesley Hill

# Contents

# Contents

# Acknowledgments

Several persons helped in the preparation of this volume. A number of friends were willing to read through material and offer comments: Todd Billings, Scott Swain, John Webster, Wesley Hill, and Jonathan Linebaugh. The book is surely improved by the wisdom of each of these friends. At Baker Academic, I am grateful for the help offered by Bob Hosack as well as B. J. Heyboer, Bryan Dyer, Jeremy Wells, and Trinity Graeser.

My family encouraged me throughout the writing process. Emily and Jackson have celebrated the project and never begrudged it. I am grateful. My institutional family at Knox Theological Seminary has also been supportive during the time needed to produce this volume. I am thankful especially to Luder Whitlock and Warren Gage for protecting my schedule and ensuring that institutional responsibilities did not crowd out time for research and writing. I should also mention that Jonathan Linebaugh has endured more random interruptions regarding the doctrine of justification than any academic should expect from the person in the office next door. That he is still talking to me, and that he has proven so helpful throughout the writing process, is a great gift.

A slightly edited version of chapter 3 appears in the *International Journal of Systematic Theology*, and a version of chapter 4 appears in the *Journal of Reformed Theology*.

I dedicate the book to Wesley Hill. We have been friends for more than a decade now. That friendship has involved a theological journey that began with serious thinking about the doctrine of justification and has led both of us together to a commitment to being catholic and Reformational theologians for the church. Over the years and across the continents, he has remained a steadfast and joyful friend even as he has become a remarkably capable theologian. The book surely would not exist without our shared journey.

# Introduction

For decades now, the doctrine of justification has been revised, reshaped, and reformed. From ecumenical and exegetical angles, the traditional Protestant consensus has been altered by joint declarations and new perspectives. The new consensus is simple: the classic articulation of justification by faith alone—prized by the Reformation theologians, espoused by their church confessions, and expounded by their dogmatics—will not cut it today. What might be left in its place is up for grabs, with a number of suggestions, but this deconstructive consensus seems to hold.

How extensive is the rethinking? Dawn DeVries describes the state of discussion regarding this doctrine in her entry to the *Oxford Handbook of Systematic Theology*.[1] She notes that four shifts have occurred in historical, exegetical, and ecumenical quarters, requiring massive reformation in the systematic realm. First, Hans Küng's study of justification in *Barth and Roman Catholicism* has shown that each emphasized one side of a double grace, without denying the importance of the other's concerns. Second, the so-called new perspective(s) on Paul have redefined the nature of first-century Jewish religion and, thus, the status quo to which Paul polemically responds with his justification doctrine in Galatians and Romans. No longer do we view Paul offering a rebuttal of Pelagian works righteousness with his gospel of grace; now we see him proclaim the correction of an ethnocentric religion by the Abrahamic promise of blessing to the nations. Third, Tuomo Mannermaa and his "Finnish interpretation of Luther" present a new portrait of the first Reformer: one interested just as much in sacramental life and participation in God as in justification and

1. Dawn DeVries, "Justification," in *The Oxford Handbook of Systematic Theology*, ed. John Webster, Kathryn Tanner, and Iain Torrance (New York: Oxford University Press, 2007), 197–211.

imputation, perhaps even interested in the former matters to the neglect of the latter ones. The double grace described by Küng can be found in the Finnish Luther, with differing emphases apparent in various phases and texts. Fourth, the *Joint Declaration on the Doctrine of Justification* by the Lutheran World Federation and the Pontifical Council for Promoting Christian Unity has suggested that the condemnations of the Reformation era no longer need apply to today's Lutherans and Roman Catholics. Each of these moves—somewhat discrete, yet no doubt mutually reinforcing at times—seems to provide one more nail in the coffin of the Protestant doctrine.

In the face of such seismic shifts in adjoining disciplines, DeVries advocates some major adaptations to the doctrine of justification. Indeed, she offers no criticism of any of these developments; rather, she suggests ways to maneuver in light of them. Her article is a microcosm of the larger debate. Though justification has been a hotbed of ecclesial and scholarly contention in the last few decades, systematic theologians have played a decidedly marginal role in such discussion. Ecumenists and exegetes have dominated the debate with discussion circling around Paul's view of the law or Luther's view of union with Christ. A theological malnourishment has occurred wherein biblical scholars define and debunk certain "Lutheran" or "Protestant" views by means of interpretive argument, all the while engaging very little with broader, systematic implications and connections. One frequently gets the impression that academics trained in their own discipline (e.g., Pauline studies) lack familiarity with Reformation theology, discern textual meaning in biblical texts that seem to conflict with catchphrases or present-day practices rooted in the Protestant tradition, and, therefore, argue against the doctrine of justification *sola fide*. But do they actually find textual support for overturning the authentic teaching of the Reformation or simply some textbook caricature of the same? One wonders.

I offer this book as a missive, an exercise in conceptual, exegetical, and historical reconsideration and, simultaneously, a challenge to existing paradigms and the perspectives of this new consensus. I wish to suggest that several new emphases should be embraced and celebrated, while other revisions ought to be questioned and in fact rejected. As I hope to show, many of the supposed problems with the classic Protestant doctrine of justification by faith alone are alleviated when it is viewed in its proper dogmatic location, adjoining other crucial loci (e.g., participation, Christology, sanctification). Many of the blind spots of the contemporary scene are addressed by the full breadth of the gospel, as described by the confessions and dogmatics of the Reformation era. To put it bluntly, I hope to inject a bit of dogmatic reasoning into a debate beholden to contemporary exegetical and ecumenical inclinations.

Dogmatic theology is meant to aid biblical exegesis. At this point, John Webster's reflections on the two forms of "biblical reasoning" prove instructive:

> Dogmatic reasoning produces a conceptual representation of what reason has learned from its exegetical following of the scriptural text. In dogmatics, the "matter" of prophetic and apostolic speech is set out in a different idiom, anatomized. Cursive representation leads to conceptual representation, which abstracts from the textual surface by creating generalized or summary concepts and ordering them topically. This makes easier swift, non-laborious and non-repetitive access to the text's matter. But, in doing this, it does not dispense with Scripture, kicking it away as a temporary scaffold; it simply uses a conceptual and topical form to undertake certain tasks with respect to Scripture. These include: seeing Scripture in its full scope as an unfolding of the one divine economy; seeing its interrelations and canonical unity; seeing its proportions. These larger apprehensions of Scripture then inform exegetical reason as it goes about its work on particular parts of Scripture.[2]

Exegetical reasoning—direct reflection on the words of Scripture—is aided by dogmatic reasoning. Indeed, recovery from the disciplinary myopia bred by so much overspecialization and the mass pains of our biblically illiterate culture would be aided more by dogmatic reasoning than might otherwise be the case. As Webster argues, though, this is not to say that some systematic a priori belief (whether a "first principle" or "central dogma") is then teased out and employed as an exegetical trump card. Rather, it is to say that "dogmatics is the schematic and analytical presentation of the matter of the gospel. It is 'systematic,' not in the sense that it offers a rigidly formalized set of deductions from a master concept, but in the low-level sense of gathering together what is dispersed through the temporal economy to which the prophets and apostles direct reason's gaze."[3]

The following chapters address the doctrine of justification *sola fide* from a number of angles: the location of justification within the broader scheme of Christian dogmatics; the relationship of participation and justification to the gospel of Jesus Christ; the coherence and necessity of the Christ's faith; the claim to hold a "christocentric" theology and the issue of imputation; the link between justification, freedom, and obedience; and, finally, the light shed on ecclesiology by this doctrine. The book comes in three parts: a broad consideration of the link between justification and the gospel (the place of the doctrine in Christian theology; justification and participation as ground

2. John Webster, "Biblical Reasoning," *Anglican Theological Journal* 90, no. 4 (2009): 750.
3. Ibid.

and goal of the gospel); a look backward at recent debates regarding the work of Christ for us (the faith of Christ; christocentricity and imputation); and a look forward to underappreciated theological vistas involving the way in which the work of Christ for us takes operative form in the work of Christ in us (justification, freedom, and obedience; justification and ecclesiology). As this book focuses on debated points, each time it (re)locates them in wider dogmatic scope and with a fully canonical perspective. It does not address every question or theme related to justification, but it sketches a way forward largely by reexamining the past—both biblical and ecclesial.

# PART 1

# JUSTIFICATION AND THE GOSPEL

# 1

# The Place of Justification
# in Christian Theology

In this chapter and the next, we will consider a thesis: *the gospel is the glorious news that the God who has life in himself freely shares that life with us and, when we refuse that life in sin, graciously gives us life yet again in Christ. While participation in God is the goal of the gospel, justification is the ground of that sanctifying fellowship.* As we unpack this thesis, we will begin with the twofold subject matter of Christian dogmatics: God and all things in God. Thus, we will trace out the external works of God that are known as the gospel—God's gracious giving of life to us. We will argue that the doctrine of justification is the key doctrine for expressing certain facets of the gospel, though it does not engage every pertinent question and cannot be called, without qualification, "the article of the standing or falling of the church." While it is absolutely necessary, it is not altogether sufficient for the Christian confession. We will then consider two ways in which the doctrine of justification does shed light on other doctrines, exercising sway across the dogmatic spectrum (though not independently) by speaking into our doctrine of God and doctrine of humanity.

## Thinking Dogmatically: God and Fellowship with God

The subject matter of Christian dogmatics is the life of God and others in him: *the gospel is the glorious news that the God who has life in himself freely*

3

*shares that life with us and, when we refuse that life in sin, graciously gives us life yet again in Christ.* As we begin to consider the scope and sequence of the gospel, we do well to describe the very practice of theological knowledge and rational testimony to the gospel.

In the first question of his *Summa Theologiae*, Thomas Aquinas addresses the object of theological knowledge: "All things are dealt with in holy teaching [*sacra doctrina*] in terms of God, either because they are God himself or because they are relative to him as their origin and end."[1] In his concern to address the question of theology's subject, Thomas notes a potential objection: "Besides, all matters about which a science reaches settled conclusions enter into its subject. Now sacred Scripture goes as far about many things other than God, for instance about creatures and human conduct. Therefore its subject is not purely God."[2] Indeed, Thomas notes the way other medieval theologians speak of the subject matters of theology: of reality and its symbols (Augustine, Lombard), the works of redemption (Hugh of St. Victor), or Christ and his body (Robert Kilwardy and others). He does not dismiss the topics they raise as if they were unfitting for theological reflection, though he locates them as always subordinate to God: "All these indeed are dwelt on by this science, yet as held in their relationship to God." Later: "All other things that are settled in Holy Scripture are embraced in God, not that they are parts of him—such as essential components or accidents—but because they are somehow related to him."[3] Other things exist not in themselves, but in God's power and by his will. Other things prosper and flourish not by their own mettle, but by the provision and grace—the life-giving promise—of the triune God. Indeed, this is the promised end of the gospel: "Behold, the dwelling place of God is with man. He will dwell with them, and they will be his people, and God himself will be with them as their God" (Rev. 21:3). Human life exists for and is defined by fellowship with this living One.

This gospel is good news precisely because it is a promise of life from one who has life in himself. Pledges are only as good as their author. Indeed, the apostle Paul shows concern for this question in his writing to the Roman Christians. After recounting the great divine promises of assurance in Romans 8:31–39, he then notes that a doubt may arise in his audience's mind. They could be remarkably enthused by the pledges given there—who would not be?—and yet wonder if God is able and/or willing to come through on these promises. After all, God promised great things to Israel and seems not to have

---

1. Thomas Aquinas, *Summa Theologiae*, trans. Thomas Gilby (London: Blackfriars, 1963), 1a.1.7, reply.

2. Ibid., obj. 2.

3. Ibid., *ad* 2.

kept his word. He had pledged that they would be his people, and yet, most recently, the vast majority of Israelites had rejected the Messiah. Thus, Paul must launch into a discussion of the truthfulness and trustworthiness of God's Word (e.g., Rom. 9:6). Paul's reflection on the election of God and the story of Israel demonstrates the importance of the doctrine of God for the gospel to be *good* news (see Rom. 9–11). The reliability of one's word matters a great deal for those who would bank on it. The God of the gospel is the one of whom it is said, "For from him and through him and to him are all things" (Rom. 11:36). God's Word called the world into being from nothing and creates new life just the same. It makes all the sense in the world to cast our cares upon him.

The Gospel according to John presents a similar concern for the theological basis of the gospel itself, rooting the incarnational mystery (John 1:14: "the Word became flesh") in the story of the God who was alive and gave life to all things (see John 1:1–4). Repeatedly, the Gospel points backward to the full life from which the Word comes to give life; the Prologue accents this point lest the reader miss it. Indeed, knowing the fullness of God generates faith in his gospel. For this very reason, Thomas argued that knowledge of the Trinity was important for Christians.

> The knowledge of the divine persons was necessary to us on two grounds. The first is to enable us to think rightly on the subject of the creation of things. For by maintaining that God made everything through his Word we avoid the error of those who held that God's nature necessarily compelled him to create things. By affirming that there is in him the procession of Love, we show that he made creatures, not because he needed them nor because of any reason outside him, but from Love of his own goodness. . . . The second reason, and the principal one, is to give us a true notion of the salvation of mankind, a salvation accomplished by the Son who became flesh and by the gift of the Holy Spirit.[4]

Knowing the self-sufficiency of the triune life demonstrates the divine freedom (from external need or compulsion) and, thus, the gratuity of God's external works, both creation and new creation. More recently, John Webster has focused upon the importance not only of knowing the triunity of God but also of grasping the aseity of God as the necessary backdrop and launching pad of God's gospel.[5] In an era dominated by historicist approaches to

---

4. Ibid., 1a.32.1, *ad* 3.
5. On the importance of an operative doctrine of God for understanding creation, see John Webster, "Trinity and Creation," *International Journal of Systematic Theology* 12, no. 1 (2010): 4–19. On the link between an operative doctrine of God and the gospel, see Webster, "'It Was the Will of the Lord to Bruise Him': Soteriology and the Doctrine of God," in *God without Measure: Essays in Christian Doctrine* (London: T&T Clark, forthcoming). On the doctrine

God, reflection upon God's life in himself has not been given great prestige in contemporary theology. Such reflections upon the "immanent Trinity"—that is, God's life in himself—are viewed suspiciously as being prone to speculation that is separated from or opposed to God's revelation of himself in Jesus Christ. Yet careful consideration of the biblical witness points us back behind the divine economy to its roots in God's eternal life in himself, from which his movement toward us, in creation and new creation, is generated.[6] It is thus decidedly unhistorical to limit our theological reflections to the events experienced by the prophets and apostles in the name of historical concern and, perhaps, a christocentric epistemology, precisely because Jesus and his ambassadors constantly point backward to the one who commissioned and sent them (see, e.g., John 5:19, 26, 30).[7] Discerning the eternal roots of the gospel is essential to maintaining the genuine gratuity and the unimpeachable reliability of that same news. And this is crucial for understanding the place of justification in Christian theology. Justification describes a crucial event in the divine economy. Yet it remains an event in the history of God's external works, which range from creation to consummation.

John Webster has raised the question of distorting the doctrine of justification by asserting that it is the "ruler and judge over all other Christian doctrines."[8] As I have described above, Webster argues that the gospel speaks of the God who has life in himself and then gives that life to others. In other words, there are two parts to Christian doctrine—God and the works of God—of which it can truly be said that "there is only one Christian doctrine, the doctrine of the triune God," for this God does these things.[9] What, then, of the gospel and, specifically, the doctrine of justification? Webster argues that there are two ways in which they are made relative.[10] First, all the works

of aseity, strictly speaking, see Webster, "Life in and of Himself: On God's Aseity," in *God without Measure*.

6. This movement behind the divine economy is not a speculation upon the hidden God, precisely inasmuch as it is not only impelled but is also guided by Holy Scripture, itself a gift in the divine economy.

7. In chap. 3 I will argue that the biblical portrayal of the Christ's faith, exercised by the incarnate Son during his particular sojourn upon the earth, flowed out of his eternal relationship to his heavenly Father (most poignantly described as his eternal generation). Scholastic theologians would say here that the external works of God are patterned after and express the inner works of God—this maxim simply serves to unpack the claim that Jesus really is "the image of the invisible God" (Col. 1:15) and that, though "no one has ever seen God," Jesus really "has made him known" (John 1:18).

8. John Webster, "*Rector et iudex super omnia genera doctrinarum*? The Place of the Doctrine of Justification," in *What Is Justification About? Reformed Contributions to an Ecumenical Theme*, ed. Michael Weinrich and John P. Burgess (Grand Rapids: Eerdmans, 2009), 35–56.

9. Ibid., 37.

10. Ibid., 39–42.

of God are relative and subordinate to the being of God—there was a time when he, and he alone, was; all else flows out of this triune fullness. Second, the works of God include creation and providence, as well as the gospel and justification. In other words, soteriology is not the sole external work of God.

We could add a still further relativization: within the work of salvation, justification is not the only divine act. The God who declares the ungodly righteous also makes them holy and upright. The God who suffers in our place also sanctifies our persons. The Bible is not stingy in its description of God's saving work: justification is a glorious part of this jewel, but it is a many-splendored beauty that exceeds God's justifying work alone.

In light of these reflections regarding the nature of theology's object and the scope of the gospel, then, we can ask what use might be made of some Protestant insistences that justification by faith alone is the cardinal or primary piece of Christian doctrine. Among a number of contemporary Lutheran theologians, and especially in the American movement known as Radical Lutheranism, justification becomes not only a doctrine but also a principle and maxim. We will consider three such approaches, two European Lutherans (Eberhard Jüngel and Oswald Bayer) and one Radical Lutheran (Mark Mattes). For example, Jüngel argues,

> In the justification article all these statements come to a head. The decision is made here first of all as to who this God is, and what it really means to be creatively active. Next, it says what it means to die for others and to bring forth new life in the midst of death: a life that imparts itself through the power of the Spirit to our passing world in such a way that a new community arises—the Christian church. The justification article brings out emphatically the truth of the relationship between God and people and in so doing the correct under-standing of God's divinity and our humanity. And since the Christian church draws its life from the relationship between God and people, and only from that relationship, the justification article is the one article by which the church stands and without which it falls. So every other truth of the faith must be weighed and judged by that article.[11]

What does Jüngel mean? "It is only when explained by means of that doctrine [of justification] that Christology becomes a materially appropriate Christology at all."[12] Jüngel's concern is that justification alone unfolds the name of Jesus in a specifically Christian way. Just as ancient theologians, in the courses charted by Arius and others, had to insist that there were un-Christian

---

11. Eberhard Jüngel, *Justification: The Heart of the Christian Faith*, trans. Jeffrey Cayzer (Edinburgh: T&T Clark, 2001), 16.
12. Ibid., 29.

ways of talking about Jesus, so Jüngel suggests that any Christology that does not describe the justification of the ungodly misses the mark in testifying well of Jesus. As he argues later, the *sola gratia* simply unfolds the *solus Christus* in authentic fashion.[13] But it is not merely authentic; it is autocratic: justification is "the hermeneutical category of theology," inasmuch as it brings all doctrine into the realm of the legal dispute.[14] Jüngel suggests that thereby justification proves its mettle and its primacy—but he has yet to argue for the superiority of the legal metaphor. And many who have gone through judicial proceedings in various facets of life would consider them barely tolerable, much less good, and only good on the basis of instrumental value in making other things possible. Surely a claim that the legal dispute is lord and ruler of doctrine requires argument.[15]

Bayer's approach is particularly notable when it comes to this issue. He argues that there is real breadth to the doctrine of justification in Martin Luther's theology, inasmuch as it affects social and anthropological reflections. "Justification is not a separate topic apart from which still other topics could be discussed. Justification is the starting point for all theology and it affects every other topic."[16] Bayer argues that justification uniquely identifies humanity as being curved outward, defined by that which is outside of it rather than internal to it or fashioned by it. Thus it has implications for the self (not self-created or even self-shaped, but given being and gratuitously created) and for society (not the project of human progress or the occasion for anthropological achievement). In every aspect humanity is marked by gift: justification offers the fundamental articulation of life by gift.

Bayer agrees with Luther, then, about the subject matter of theology. In his comments on Psalm 51, Luther says: "The proper subject of theology is man guilty of sin and condemned, and God the Justifier and Savior of man the sinner. Whatever is asked or discussed in theology outside this subject,

13. Ibid., 174.

14. Ibid., 47, 48. Surely Jüngel's suggestion at this point draws on the argument of Karl Barth: "The doctrine of justification not only narrates but explains this history. It is the attempt to see and understand in its positive sense the sentence of God which is executed in His judgment and revealed in the resurrection of Jesus Christ" (*Church Dogmatics*, vol. 4/1, *The Doctrine of Reconciliation*, ed. G. W. Bromiley and T. F. Torrance, trans. G. W. Bromiley [London: T&T Clark, 1956], 516).

15. Oswald Bayer has, in many ways, attempted to rethink justification in a creational and not strictly legal fashion. But this approach raises its own questions, including the question of why such matters as anthropology should be viewed exclusively under the heading of justification, since the term is inherently legal.

16. Oswald Bayer, "Justification as the Basis and Boundary of Theology," in *Justification Is for Preaching: Essays by Oswald Bayer, Gerhard O. Forde, and Others*, ed. Virgil Thompson (Eugene, OR: Pickwick, 2012), 32.

is error and poison."[17] It is clear that Bayer intends the doctrine of justification to identify the word of law and the promise of gospel, both spoken in divine-human exchange. Theology reflects on that conversation: confession of sin, assurance of pardon. God speaks only these two words; therefore, the doctrine of justification is the subject matter of theology. Thus, Bayer says that justification is not only the "starting point" but also "the basis, boundary, and the subject matter of theology."[18]

Mattes has gone so far as to suggest that justification must be the criterion for every theological statement, or else one has fallen into system-building and the theology of glory. He clearly worries that theological reflection will easily follow the presuppositions of the sinner; only justification puts the sinner on his heels and hallows the Word of God. Justification serves as a second-order epistemic principle, shaping every statement made by Christians in their first-order claims (their prayer and praise, worship and witness). Like Jüngel and Bayer, Mattes clearly thinks the hiddenness of God is a danger to any approach that does not treat justification as a sieve for theological speculation.

Webster catalogs a number of similar references, all of which try in some way to express the classic affirmation of many Protestants that justification is the article by which the church stands or falls (articulus stantis et cadentis ecclesiae).[19] Webster finds these varying approaches wanting, inasmuch as "it is simply not possible to maintain the unqualified claim that of itself justification suffices to answer the questions: 'Who or what is a really divine God? Who or what is a really human being?'"[20]

Now three options are before us: (1) justification is the central doctrine and principle by which all other doctrines are judged; (2) justification is simply one among many doctrines and holds no privileged place in the dogmatic corpus; or (3) justification is the central doctrine and principle in addressing certain questions and confessing particular aspects of the gospel, though it is not meant to answer every question and must be located in a wider analysis of God and his gospel.

The first option cannot be maintained in its strict form. Justification requires other doctrines to make any sense. In his suggestion, Webster goes on

17. Martin Luther, "Psalm 51," in Selections from the Psalms I, ed. Jaroslav Pelikan, Luther's Works 12 (St. Louis: Concordia, 1955), 311, quoted in Oswald Bayer, Martin Luther's Theology: A Contemporary Interpretation, trans. Thomas H. Trapp (Grand Rapids: Eerdmans, 2008), 37n21. See also Gerhard Ebeling, "Cognitio Dei et hominis," in Lutherstudien Band I (Tübingen: Mohr Siebeck, 1971), 221–72.

18. Bayer, "Justification as the Basis and Boundary of Theology," 32, 48.

19. For reflection along these lines, see the various studies of Jüngel, Pannenberg, Moltmann, Jenson, and Bayer in Mark C. Mattes, The Role of Justification in Contemporary Theology, Lutheran Quarterly Books (Grand Rapids: Eerdmans, 2004).

20. Webster, "Rector et iudex super omnia genera doctrinarum?," 49.

to describe a host of crucial tenets related to, though not fully described by, justification: God, divine-human fellowship, law, sin, the incarnation, and the gospel declaration of restored fellowship in Christ. While Webster can look back on this dogmatics in brief as a gloss on Psalm 11:7—"the Lord is righteous; he loves righteous deeds; the upright shall behold his face"—he shows that further canonical reflection is required to flesh out this text so that it is good news. Neither sin nor the incarnation is mentioned in Psalm 11:7, though both, of course, cohere beautifully with the premise and the promise of the text. Similarly, the declaration that God justifies the ungodly requires numerous other articles to make sense.

Bayer does demonstrate that justification affects other doctrines. But demonstrating this point is distinct from showing that no other doctrine does so as well or, at least, that justification does so in a manner superior to or privileged before all others. And the claim that justification is "the basis and the boundary of theology" requires that precisely that comparative claim be made. Bayer begins his essay on justification by saying that "justification is not a separate topic apart from which still other topics could be discussed. Justification is the starting point for all theology and it affects every other topic."[21] But we must note that he has juxtaposed two options that allow for an excluded middle. He wants to oppose the notion that justification is unattached and separated from other doctrines. Yet his counterclaim is not merely that justification is attached to other doctrines and that "it affects every other topic"; rather, he goes still further to suggest that "justification is the starting point for all theology"—that is, it has some peculiar primacy across the theological board. Bayer is not only claiming that it has systemic import and universal effect but also that it has hermeneutical primacy in theology. Justification is the ruler of all other doctrines.

But this is precisely what Bayer never argues. His essay is a wonderful demonstration of glorious success alongside abject failure. In what he does, he succeeds wildly, demonstrating the social and personal implications of justification. Yet in what he says he will do, not only does he fail, but he offers no argument whatsoever. The reader has much to be grateful for at the end of the day but can only say that the article is poorly titled and headed by an inaccurate thesis statement. If it made a more modest claim, its true brilliance would be seen.

Building on the work of Jüngel and especially Bayer, Mattes complicates matters and confuses the project of system-building with the error of deflating the gospel proclamation of the church. In his study of contemporary approaches to justification, he finds Jüngel, Pannenberg, Moltmann, and Jenson

---

21. Bayer, "Justification as the Basis and Boundary of Theology," 32.

all guilty of toning down the promise of Jesus. "Theologically speaking, the greatest peril of the university, with all its various disciplines, is the attempt to establish—by whatever means—an encyclopedic 'God's eye' view of reality, walking by sight, not by faith."[22] But this assessment mixes matters that must be kept distinct. Why must efforts at discerning the full scope of God's reality be encyclopedically declared to be "walking by sight, not by faith"? That there is a natural theology—what Luther would rightly call a "theology of glory"—cannot be denied. Nor can it be denied that much of the contemporary university's profile lends itself to human attempts to chart the better course of wisdom apart from the killing and making alive that the gospel brings by God's grace. Yet there is surely no reason to employ the bombastic statement that justification is the criterion of all theological knowledge to make the claim that all theological knowledge must speak of the crucified, justifying Christ given for sinners. As with Jüngel and Bayer, Mattes can show that justification is necessary as a criterion for theology; unfortunately, he also suggests that it is a sufficient criterion. The two are not the same thing. Against these Lutherans, and even against similar claims made by Calvin himself, we must say that justification is not the sole ruler of Christian doctrine.[23]

However, the second option proves of no more use than the first. It simply will not do to suggest, as some have, that justification is merely one among many such images employed to talk of God's life with us or of the divine economy. Justification does strike a spiritual nerve and serve to testify to a leading edge of the gospel account. Furthermore, when it is articulated in the form of imputation, it reminds us that God in Christ assumes our place and we in him enjoy all spiritual blessings. That notion of exchange or interchange is pivotal to the exposition of God's being and our own. While other biblical idioms may suggest it (e.g., sacrifice or penal substitution), justification has served historically to make this crucial point.[24] Jüngel, Mattes, and especially

---

22. Mattes, Role of Justification, 179.

23. John Calvin, Institutes of the Christian Religion, ed. John T. McNeill, trans. Ford Lewis Battles, Library of Christian Classics (Philadelphia: Westminster, 1960), 3.11.1 (where Calvin says this is the "main hinge on which religion turns").

24. In Roman Catholic theology, the notion of "initial justification" would serve this role (as in Thomas Aquinas, Summa Theologiae 1a2ae.114.5, reply, ad 1). For reflections on the distinction between this initial dispositional movement of God and the ongoing transformative work of God in justification (according to the Council of Trent), see Bruce D. Marshall, "Beatus vir: Aquinas, Romans 4, and the Role of 'Reckoning' in Justification," in Reading Romans with St. Thomas Aquinas, ed. Matthew Levering and Michael Dauphinais (Washington, DC: Catholic University of America Press, 2012), 216–37; and the account of Thomas's doctrine of justification as involving (1) forgiveness, (2) sanctifying grace, and (3) guidance for life, found in Charles Raith II, "Aquinas and Calvin on Romans: Theological Exegesis and Ecumenical Theology" (PhD diss., Ave Maria University, 2010), 52–94.

Bayer are surely right to insist that the doctrine of justification plays a cardinal role in pointing to the axiomatic status of the first commandment.[25] Whether individual or social, human being is the result of gift; furthermore, the divine character is marked by the self-sacrificial love displayed in the gospel story: God is a gospeling sort of being. Thus, we cannot treat justification as simply one doctrine, untethered or disconnected from others.

While justification is relativized by the other ways in which God's work of salvation is described, it does hold a systematic place that shapes other doctrines. As justification is further relativized by the other works of God (for example, creation and providence), we see that it nonetheless portrays a divinely determined focal point of the whole divine economy. And as justification is still further relativized by the doctrine of God's own life, we continue to see that the very God who has life in himself freely wills to share that life with others, even the ungodly whom he will justify in Christ. Understanding any of these other doctrines, then, cannot be done in a specifically Christian way apart from the confession that the justification of the ungodly is an essential ingredient within the whole. In other words, this is a claim that justification is not merely a discrete component of the whole, but that it is a constituent aspect of the whole.

Here it is crucial to highlight that Mattes and these Lutherans have not framed the debate well. Their proposal suggests either that justification of the ungodly serves as one doctrine, hermetically sealed off from all others, or that it is the hub that holds together all others and puts them in their place.[26] Notice the metaphors used: the first option entails no systematic effect of justification on other doctrines, while the second possibility suggests, by definition, that justification is *the* center of Christian teaching—a wheel only having one hub. In the foreword to Mattes's book, Klaus Schwarzwäller presents precisely this dichotomy. One can either promote something as "the major article" or demote what is essential. "So the question here is whether or not the faith itself is at stake with one article among others. If it is, this article is obviously much more than one article among others. In this case, the 'article,' as it were, stands for the creed."[27] This kind of juxtaposition of extremes leads Mattes to suggest that the necessity of the doctrine of justification intrinsically requires its sufficiency for theology. At times the way he uses the language of this doctrine

---

25. See Mattes, *Role of Justification*, 182. For historical approaches that emphasize the axiomatic nature of the first commandment, see Martin Luther, "Treatise on Good Works (1520)," in *The Christian in Society I*, ed. James Atkinson, Luther's Works 44 (Philadelphia: Fortress, 1966), 15–114; and Karl Barth, "The First Commandment as a Theological Axiom," in *The Way of Theology in Karl Barth: Essays and Comments*, ed. H. Martin Rumscheidt (Allison Park, PA: Pickwick, 1986), 63–78.

26. See Mattes, *Role of Justification*, 4, 10.

27. Klaus Schwarzwäller, foreword to ibid., viii.

as a *discrimen* suggests that there might be an opening to consider it a hermeneutical grid for doctrine writ large, though amid others. Yet he continues to refer to it as "the" *discrimen*.[28] In their arguments for the sufficiency of this doctrine as the *discrimen* or "center and boundary" of all theology, Mattes and Jüngel continue to cite Luther.[29] Yet all the quotations from the great preacher point to the doctrine's necessity, not its sufficiency as a hermeneutical filter for theological analysis. For their claims to be grounded, they would not need to prove that Luther believes justification is the only doctrine, but they would need him to say that it is the only doctrine that serves as a *discrimen*—that is, a center, basis, or boundary. While Luther clearly believes it does serve in such ways, and while he does refer to it as a primary doctrine, he does not speak of it as the only such doctrine. Luther knew that the creed says more than this, even though it must speak this word of "forgiveness of sins."

In light of the argument thus far, then, the third approach must be followed: justification is the central doctrine and theological rule with respect to particular theological questions. In saying this, of course, we celebrate the doctrine of justification in its particular place (and nowhere else). It does not answer every question. For example, one would be hard pressed to begin with the statement "God justifies the ungodly" and go on to unpack a fully trinitarian theology or a doctrine of creation. Yet some essential questions—the character of God's love, the nature of the divine-human fellowship, the stance of the creature before God, and many more—are answered most fully in God's justifying word.[30] Where it speaks, it does so essentially and beautifully. But we would be asking too much to expect it to address our every need or whim. In fact, to do so would be to turn from dependence on God and his address and instead to demand doctrines that say what we wish and speak to whatever we might desire.

In this vein, Webster helps point to this crucial role for justification. Even as he seeks to relativize the doctrine, he does affirm that "among these different articulations of God's saving work, the idiom of justification has an indispensable place for at least four reasons."

1. "Justification is a primary theme in some of the key texts of one of the major New Testament witnesses; an 'apostolic' soteriology loses its claim to the title if it diminishes the importance of *dikaiosunē theou*."

28. Mattes, *Role of Justification*, 11.
29. Ibid., 5–6nn8–9; Jüngel, *Justification*, 17n4, 18n6. For language of justification as the "center and boundary," see Ernst Wolf, "Die Rechtfertigungslehre als Mitte und Grenze reformatorischer Theologie," in *Peregrinatio*, vol. 2, *Studien zur reformatorischen Theologie, zum Kirchenrecht und zur Sozialethik* (Munich: Chr. Kaiser, 1965), 11–21.
30. See Barth, *Church Dogmatics*, 4/1, 520–21.

2. "Justification is inseparable from many other themes in the economy of salvation (covenant, sin, law, the death and resurrection of the Son, and God's holiness and the sanctification of the people of God) and so has greater scope than more narrowly focused concepts such as ransom or penal substitution."

3. "The idiom of justification lays particular emphasis upon salvation as historical encounter."

4. "Justification—especially a radical notion of *iustitia imputata*—is especially suited to convey the anthropological entailments of the sheer gratuity of God's work. Again, as Jüngel puts it, 'The *articulus iustificationis* reminds us that God's grace is the fundamental and all-determining dimension of human life.'"[31]

I would add a fifth point—related to Webster's fourth point—regarding the importance of justification: justification, especially as understood via imputation, is particularly fit to convey the theological entailments of the sheer gratuity of God's work. God truly is—all the way down in the triune life—a God of glorious grace. Hence, writing to the Ephesians, Paul celebrates the gospel not merely as revelation of human flourishing but also as a manifestation of the divine fullness (Eph. 1:23). Because the gospel shows us who God is, Paul announces repeatedly that it is "to the praise of his glory" (1:12; cf. 1:6, 14). We will come back to this link below (under the heading "Justification and the God of the Gospel").

I also wish to expand Webster's second point in such a way that even his first point must be extended. Justification as a dogmatic idiom serves to gather together and make sense of a host of biblical terms and concepts, but Webster does not mention perhaps the most crucial: namely, sacrifice. This conceptual relationship will be discussed in chapter 2. It and other terminologies (ranging from "salvation" to "reconciliation" or "making peace") describe the basis of our acceptance before God, while we were yet sinners. This is standard and necessary fare in good dogmatics. Our theological terminology is meant to help us read biblical language well, though it need not simply stick with or restrict itself to the biblical terms as such.[32] The same kind of synthetic work that led to the doctrine of the Trinity in the fourth century took shape in later thinking regarding the doctrine of justification in the sixteenth and later centuries: a host of texts, employing various biblical concepts, were found to express certain

31. Webster, "*Rector et iudex super omnia genera doctrinarum?*," 46–47.
32. On the nature of biblical and dogmatic language, see the discussion in chap. 2 under the heading "The Forensic Entryway of the Gospel" as well as Michael Allen and Daniel J. Treier, "Dogmatic Theology and Biblical Perspectives on Justification: A Reply to Leithart," *Westminster Theological Journal* 70, no. 1 (2008): 105–10.

unified judgments of immense importance. These texts ranged from Romans 3 to Exodus 12, from Genesis 22 to Galatians 2, from Ephesians 1 to Hebrews 8. Thus, the biblical idioms that pour into our doctrine of justification extend far beyond those mentioned by Webster, and, therefore, the range of prophetic and apostolic texts that is tied to this doctrine is far greater than some select portion of the Pauline corpus.[33] Indeed, the sacrificial imagery of the Old Testament alone proves of immense worth in teasing out a doctrine of justification, and the Epistle to the Hebrews reflects on this massive biblical witness in light of the Christ event in a way that, though it does not employ the idiom of justification, should inform our theological reflection on the doctrine of justification.

Certain key tenets of soteriology and of the life of the Trinity are especially manifest by way of the idiom of justification. It accents the gratuity of God's life-giving work and the *ek*-centric nature of human existence in Christ. Yet it does not say everything we are called to confess. Justification says little of the goal of the gospel.[34] We must turn elsewhere to speak of that. In chapter 2, we will see that the notion of participation in God proves essential at just this point (albeit rightly rendered as covenant fellowship rather than deification). Indeed, Paul does exactly this at the conclusion of his discussion of justification in his Epistle to the Romans: "Therefore, since we have been justified by faith, we have peace with God through our Lord Jesus Christ. Through him we have also obtained access by faith into this grace in which we stand, and we rejoice in hope of the glory of God" (5:1–2). Justification brings peace and grants access, but it is the glory of God that is the hope of the Christian. Thus, Paul declares the glorious news that the gospel is based on a justifying word of Christ, but he simultaneously points to its participatory *telos*, the hope that we shall behold the glory of God. That justification does not tell us every aspect of the gospel could be further accentuated by the subsequent statement that, moreover, it does not say everything about God (who not only makes all things new in Christ but also first made them in creation and, in both cases, does so for the purposes of both reconciliation and glorification).

While justification does not say everything, it does say certain essential things. Dogmatics must say this and honor this function of justification, or else

33. Thomas Aquinas argues for such practice, for example, in his comments on Eph. 2:8, where he discusses Paul's phrase that "to be saved is the same as to be justified" (*Commentary on St. Paul's Epistle to the Ephesians*, trans. Matthew Lamb, Aquinas Scripture Commentaries 2 [Albany, NY: Magi, 1966], chap. 2, lect. 3, 95; cf. Daniel Keating, "Justification, Sanctification, and Divinization in Thomas Aquinas," in *Aquinas on Doctrine: A Critical Introduction*, ed. Thomas Weinandy, Daniel Keating, and John Yocum [London: T&T Clark, 2004], 142).

34. It does tell us that the goal is sure and fixed: in Christ, not in and of ourselves. Thus it is not completely silent regarding the end of the gospel. But, nonetheless, it does not itself tell us of the beatific vision, the presence of God, the resurrection of the body, the renewal of the kingdom, etc.

it risks being incapable of following the apostle Paul's writing to the Galatian Christians. As Paul addresses the churches of Galatia, he quickly expresses to them that he is "astonished that you are so quickly deserting him who called you in the grace of Christ and are turning to a different gospel" (Gal. 1:6). The pedigree or profile of a teacher matters not. Even if an apostle or angel from heaven were to present a different gospel, it must be rejected (1:8–9). But, apparently, this rejection has not happened among the Galatians. Instead, they had embraced the "gospel of Christ" and have since been troubled by those who distort that message (1:7).

Nowhere else in all his writings does the apostle speak with such stridency. In fact, this point was worth public confrontation with Peter in Antioch, when Paul observed that Peter, the Jews there, and even Barnabas refused to enjoy table fellowship with their gentile brothers and sisters in Christ. "I saw that their conduct was not in step with the truth of the gospel" (Gal. 2:14). An ethical and ecclesial misstep is the presenting issue, to be sure, but Paul notes that this is a gospel concern. As he seeks to explain the roots of this issue, he immediately turns to the doctrine of justification: "We ourselves are Jews by birth and not Gentile sinners; yet we know that a person is not justified by works of the law but through faith in Jesus Christ" (vv. 15–16). It is precisely this contrast—between justification "by works of the law" or "through faith in Jesus Christ"—that Paul calls an astonishing "turning to a different gospel" (1:6).

Galatians surely points us to the existential energy tethered to the doctrine of justification. It has an intimate relationship to the assurance of the Christian. Herman Bavinck locates the issue this way: "What is the way that leads to communion with God, to true religion, to salvation and eternal life: God's grace or human merit, his forgiveness or our works, gospel or law, the covenant of grace or the covenant of works? If it is the latter, if our work, our virtue, our sanctification is primary, then the believers' consolation ends, and they remain in doubt and uncertainty to their last breath."[35]

Galatians, too, highlights the harrowing result of relying not solely on Christ but also on one's own work or fitness. Heinrich Bullinger notes that though the Galatians "still confessed the name of Christ," they were "said to have turned away from him." How could this be so? "It is those who do not acknowledge the benefit of his grace or who do not attribute all the glory to him who are said to have turned away from him."[36] Paul ruminates over the

---

35. Herman Bavinck, *Reformed Dogmatics*, vol. 4, *Holy Spirit, Church, and New Creation*, ed. John Bolt, trans. John Vriend (Grand Rapids: Baker Academic, 2008), 205.

36. Heinrich Bullinger, *Commentary on Paul's Epistles*, on Gal. 1:6, quoted in Gerald Bray, ed., *Galatians and Ephesians*, Reformation Commentary on Scripture (Downers Grove, IL: IVP Academic, 2011), 23–24.

pathway to righteousness: a gift in Christ rather than a gain through law. So, he says, "I do not nullify the grace of God, for if righteousness were through the law, then Christ died for no purpose" (Gal. 2:21). As he returns to his stinging personal rebuke of the Galatians, he likens the instrument of faith to "hearing," a totally receptive activity over against the approach of the "works of the law" (3:2, 5).[37]

The pathway of "works of the law" fails inasmuch as it cannot be fulfilled. Paul is concerned about their "advantage" and suggests that exclusive religious rites (the pathway of "works of the law") lead to destruction. Why? "I testify again to every man who accepts circumcision that he is obligated to keep the whole law" (Gal. 5:3). Such persons are described in brutal fashion: "You are severed from Christ, you who would be justified by the law; you have fallen away from grace" (v. 4). While the Judaizers certainly were not denying any role for Christ in salvation, they were practically (if not also principally) dismissing his sufficiency for justification. Luther and Calvin remind us—later readers of this epistle—that all other attempts at justification by religion are sure to be far worse, inasmuch as the Judaizing approach is the best possible form of "works of the law": at least it suggests that works once commanded by God are required, whereas later laws are merely human proposals (e.g., late medieval Roman sacramental practice or, we might add, the moral projects of fundamentalist withdrawal or modern liberal inclusion, both of which can be equally enslaving).[38] The Reformers saw the Epistle to the Galatians not as denying the place of the law (or the divine commandments as such) for the Christian, but as repudiating any suggestion that they are essential for being in Christ and enjoying peace with God.[39] Against this particular form of law, Luther would repeatedly speak of the need to "kick it out of the conscience."[40]

37. J. Louis Martyn, *Galatians: A New Translation with Introduction and Commentary*, Anchor Bible 33a (New Haven: Yale University Press, 1997), 281–89.

38. Martin Luther, *Lectures on Galatians (1535), Chapters 1–4*, ed. Jaroslav Pelikan, Luther's Works 26 (St. Louis: Concordia, 1963), 23 (1:7), 34 (1:14), 36–37 (1:15–17), 42–43 (2:1), 46 (2:3), 144–45 (3:10), 285 (4:27), 289 (4:27); cf. John Calvin, *The Acts of the Apostles 1–13*, ed. David W. Torrance and T. F. Torrance, trans. John W. Fraser and W. G. J. McDonald, Calvin's Commentaries (Grand Rapids: Eerdmans, 1965), 170. Calvin's and Luther's comments are clearly contrary to Douglas Campbell's claims that "justification theory" requires an extreme legalism ignorant of historical differences between late medieval Roman Catholic religion and the first-century experience of the Pharisees and Judaizers (*The Deliverance of God: An Apocalyptic Rereading of Justification in Paul* [Grand Rapids: Eerdmans, 2009], 121).

39. Luther, *Lectures on Galatians (1535), Chapters 1–4*, 45–46 (2:3).

40. Ibid., 24 (1:7); see also Luther, *Lectures on Galatians (1535), Chapters 5–6 (1519)*, ed. Jaroslav Pelikan, Luther's Works 27 (St. Louis: Concordia, 1964), 4 (5:1), 15 (5:3). See similar comments in Luther, *Selections from the Psalms I*, 27–28 (2:5).

Galatians does not merely point to justification's link to assurance but also reminds us that the doctrine is designed for doxology.[41] The God who justifies is the God who will be boasted in fully. Bavinck is suggestive here as well in showing the results of forgetting this truth: "If our work, our virtue, our sanctification is primary . . . then Christ is violated in his unique, all-encompassing, and all-sufficient mediatorial office, and he himself is put on a level with other humans, with ourselves. Then God is robbed of his honor, for if humans are justified on the basis of their works, they have reason to boast of themselves and are, partly or totally, the craftsmen of their own salvation."[42]

Christ is relativized—God is minimized. To misread or misapply justification in Christ is not primarily to mistake our existence (though it is that); it is fundamentally to mischaracterize the God of the gospel. And Galatians makes precisely this point in its conclusion: when drawing together all that he has celebrated and commanded, Paul says that he wishes only to boast in his crucified Lord (6:14). Mattes makes the point in perceptive fashion: "From the perspective of Reformation theology, the quarrel about the gospel's distinctiveness is less a dispute about how to secure anxious consciences and more a matter of how to honor God properly. Can *more than* faith be offered by humans to give God the worship that is God's due?"[43]

Galatians is also appropriate to mention at this point, because in the book Paul is addressing a polemical situation. In the modern era, Karl Barth has noted that talk of justification as *the* word of the gospel has occurred rightly in certain times. He lists four such occasions: Augustine's opposition to the Pelagians, Luther's attack on the sacramental practice of the late medieval Roman Church, the early nineteenth-century rejection of a secularized version of salvation in Enlightenment thinking, and in Barth's own day, he proposes, when "humanistic religiosity" threatens in various ways. Against each ideology, the justification of the ungodly is a "fully developed weapon with which to meet all these things." However, Barth suggests a sense of proportion and order: "In the Church of Jesus Christ this doctrine has not always been *the* Word of the Gospel, and it would be an act of narrowing and unjust exclusiveness to proclaim and treat it as such."[44] While "there never was and there never can be any true Christian Church without the doctrine of justification," this is not the same as saying that it is always the pressing matter of the moment.

41. G. C. Berkouwer wisely points to the links between *sola fide* and *soli Deo Gloria* (*Faith and Justification*, trans. Lewis B. Smedes, Studies in Dogmatics [Grand Rapids: Eerdmans, 1954], 55–57).

42. Bavinck, *Reformed Dogmatics*, 4:205.

43. Mattes, *Role of Justification*, 13.

44. Barth, *Church Dogmatics*, 4/1, 523.

Suggestions that one must be all in or completely out present a false middle and fail to recognize the unique glory of this doctrine. "It has its own dignity and necessity to which we do more and not less justice if we do not ascribe to it a totalitarian claim which is not proper to it, or allow all other questions to culminate or merge into it, or reject them altogether with an appeal to it, but if we accept it with all its limitations as this problem and try to answer it as such."[45] As in Paul's presentation of it in Galatians, Barth sees the doctrine as of the essence of the gospel without calling it the entirety of the gospel: "The problem of justification does not need artificially to be absolutised and given a monopoly."[46]

Justification serves as Christian language in three forms. In first-order discourse of praise and proclamation, we speak of God's justifying the ungodly: we thank him for it, we present this good news to others, and we have the joy of hearing these words of assurance declared to those who confess their sin and need. In second-order discourse of Christian doctrine, we analytically reflect upon the biblical truth that God does justify the ungodly. Yet as we follow the witness of Scripture, we find that justification also functions in third-order discourse by shaping our thinking about theological thinking. Justification affects our theology proper and our anthropology; thus, it affects our approach to theology itself, that is, to theological method.[47]

We now turn to ways that it functions in this third level, that is, as a theological criterion giving shape and structure to other doctrines. We will consider two such instances in the remainder of this chapter before returning to some more extended case studies in the third part of this book. First, we will consider the way the justification of the ungodly informs our understanding of the character of God. Second, we will reflect on the anthropological implications of the divine justification in Christ alone. This anthropological reflection will be fairly brief, inasmuch as the last two chapters of the book extend it in the direction of ethics and ecclesiology. In these case studies, I do not argue that justification is a sufficient criterion for thinking well about God and humanity, but we do see that it is a necessary criterion for any such attempt to do theological reflection about the God of the Christian confession, that is, the God of the gospel. We will tease out some of those systematic implications here before they are extended in part 3.

45. Ibid., 528.
46. Ibid.
47. Mattes refers to this methodological work as "second order" precisely because he mixes the work of theology and proclamation. However, a distinction between first- and second-order discourse is essential, if one is to preserve the difference between the performative statements of Christian liturgy and witness and the theological analysis rendered by the creeds, confessions, and dogmatic tradition of the church.

## Justification and the God of the Gospel

Jesus Christ truly reveals God. As John the Evangelist tells us, "No one has ever seen God; the only God, who is at the Father's side, he has made him known" (John 1:18). This revelation of the divine mystery occurs in the Word becoming flesh. With these verses in mind, Bernard of Clairvaux proclaims,

> Once God was incomprehensible and inaccessible, invisible and entirely unthinkable. But now he wanted to be seen, he wanted to be understood, he wanted to be known. How was this done, you ask? God lay in a manger and lay on the Virgin's breast. He preached on a mountain, prayed through the night, and hung on a cross. He lay pale in death, was free among the dead, and was master of hell. He rose on the third day, showed the apostles the signs of victory where nails once were, and ascended before their eyes to the inner recesses of heaven. . . . When I think on any of these things, I am thinking of God, and in all these things he is now my God.[48]

The works of God genuinely do show forth the character of God. The Psalms often recount the great and mighty deeds of the Lord, repeatedly affirming the divine attributes as expressions of the one who works these wonders in our midst (Ps. 145:4–6, 10, 12, 17).[49] With these biblical emphases in mind, John Calvin would say, "Outside Christ there is nothing worth knowing, and all who by faith perceive what he is like have grasped the whole immensity of heavenly benefits. For this reason, Paul writes . . . 'I decided to know nothing precious . . . except Jesus Christ and him crucified.'"[50] They do not point to principles or maxims but to the concrete deeds of God that reveal his persona.[51]

We do well, then, to ask what the justification of the ungodly tells us about the nature of God. As Jüngel and others have reminded us, the justification of the ungodly is really a statement about the nature and ministry of Jesus. In other words, the *sola fide* is meant to help us appreciate the *solus Christus*. And, if the glory of God is revealed to us in the face of Jesus Christ, then we must press further and say that, somehow, the stunning news that God justifies the ungodly reveals the divine character to us. This ought not surprise us.

48. Bernard of Clairvaux, *Sermo in nativitate Beatae Mariae: de Aquaducto*, ed. J. Leclerq and H. Rochais, S. Bernardi Opera 5 (Rome: Cistercienses, 1968), 11.

49. Not only in the Psalms; see also Exod. 6:7; 7:5, 17; 8:10, 22; 9:14, 29–30; 10:2; 14:4, 18; 16:12; Isa. 49:23, 26; 60:16.

50. Calvin, *Institutes* 2.15.2.

51. Similar arguments have been made with compelling force by two recent Jewish theologians: Jon D. Levenson, *Sinai and Zion: An Entry into the Hebrew Bible* (New York: HarperOne, 1987), 39, 40; and Michael Wyschogrod, *The Body of Faith: God in the People Israel* (New York: HarperCollins, 1989), 113.

Paul tells the Corinthians that "in Christ God was reconciling the world to himself" (2 Cor. 5:19). This surely tells us not only that Christ was God but also that God is Christlike—reconciling, drawing others in, pulling others back, sharing and giving life and grace. But Paul presses still further, employing the language of substitution and justification: "For our sake he made him to be sin who knew no sin, so that in him we might become the righteousness of God" (2 Cor. 5:21). The precise nature of God's reconciliation in Christ takes the form of justifying the ungodly. Thus, the Christlike face of God has the texture of justifying grace and the hue of redemptive substitution. Justification runs right back to the character of God, who was in Christ.

The justifying work of the triune God, then, is not accidental or arbitrary. God does not simply happen to go this route or take this course fortuitously. God's missions express the divine processions. In other words, the course of God's economy expresses the very character of God.[52] This saving history flows from the divine will, unconditionally; therefore it shows us the very will and way of the sovereign king.

Much contemporary theology has fixed upon the historicist impulse and expressed the link between the divine economy and the divine character in a less nuanced manner. God simply is this history. In chapter 3 we will consider the work of modern-day evangelical historicists—such as Robert Jenson and Bruce McCormack—who suggest that the divine economy constitutes the triune being of God. This approach would surely affirm with us that the economy shows us who God is. This perspective, however, would deny that this God is immutable; indeed, as Jenson puts so powerfully, God's being is eschatological, attained at the end rather than held at the beginning.

But justification is a *free* expression of the loving God of the gospel. Augustine attempted to note the benefits granted by God's grace: "If you are without God, you will be less; if you are with God, God will not be greater. He is not made greater by you, but without him you are less."[53] The great theologian was not intending to deny the reality of God's gracious presence (being "with God"). No, Augustine has a rich and powerful notion of divine inhabitation, as he confesses: "You were more intimately present to me than my innermost being, and higher than the highest peak of my spirit."[54] Whether in the

---

52. See chap. 3 for one such case study. Cf. Gilles Emery, *The Trinity: An Introduction to Catholic Doctrine on the Triune God*, trans. Matthew Levering (Washington, DC: Catholic University of America Press, 2010), 159–94.

53. Augustine, *Homilies on the Gospel of John 1–40*, ed. Allan Fitzgerald, trans. Edmund Hill, Works of St. Augustine 1/12 (Hyde Park, NY: New City, 2009), 216.

54. Augustine, *Confessions*, ed. John E. Rotelle, trans. Maria Boulding, Works of St. Augustine 1/1 (Hyde Park, NY: New City, 1997), 83 (3.6.11).

incarnation of Jesus Christ, the inhabitation of the Spirit, or the presence of Christ in his church, Augustine certainly does not deny the genuine involvement of God himself in his economy. So, yes, the economy reveals God's being. But Augustine also notes that the economy does not constitute God's being. Indeed, Augustine makes much of the doctrine of divine aseity in his reading of John 5:19–30, where we are told that the Son has been granted by his Father to have "life in himself."[55] "What is the meaning of *the Father has life in himself?* He does not have his life elsewhere; he has it in himself. His being alive, in fact, is in him; it is not from outside, it is not foreign to him. He does not as it were borrow life, nor come to life as a participant, in a life which is not what he is himself; but he has life in himself, so that he is himself that life."[56] In his next homily, Augustine puts it bluntly: "Because he has the power from the Father, because he has being from the Father; for the Son, in fact, power is the same as being. That is not how it is with human beings."[57] And later: "As the Father has life in himself, so too he gave the Son the possession of life in himself, so that he does not live as one who participates, but lives without change, and is himself entirely life."[58] Augustine is not downplaying the Son's life, though he is insisting that we see its fullness and the prevenience of God's life in Christ.

In chapter 3 we will consider the doctrine of the eternal generation of the Son from the Father. Karl Barth expounds upon its importance: "God would be no less God if he had created no world and no human being. The existence of the world and our own existence are in no sense vital to God, not even as the object of his love. The eternal generation of the Son by the Father tells us first and supremely that God is not at all lonely even without the world and us. His love has its object in himself."[59] The ultimate context for understanding the doctrine of divine aseity is the trinitarian being of God: Father, Son, and Spirit sharing life and love with one another. To go the route of the evangelical historicists is to risk undercutting that triune fullness and thereby mischaracterizing the freedom and gratuity of their engagement of others, suggesting that either divine election (McCormack) or the divine economy (Jenson) constitutes

---

55. Augustine, *Homilies on the Gospel of John*, 334–56.
56. Ibid., 343.
57. Ibid., 361.
58. Ibid., 400.
59. Barth, *Church Dogmatics*, vol. 1/1, *The Doctrine of the Word of* God, ed. G. W. Bromiley and T. F. Torrance, trans. G. W. Bromiley (Edinburgh: T&T Clark, 1936), 139–40. Barth says elsewhere that "God is who He is in the act of His revelation. God seeks and creates fellowship between Himself and us, and therefore He loves us. But He is this loving God without us as Father, Son, and Holy Spirit, in the freedom of the Lord, who has His life from Himself" (*Church Dogmatics*, vol. 2/1, *The Doctrine of God*, ed. G. W. Bromiley and T. F. Torrance, trans. T. H. L. Parker [Edinburgh: T&T Clark, 1957], 257).

God's being. When God makes us, it is not to meet a divine need. When the Lord renews us, this is not a part of a self-fulfillment project.[60] Whether in creation or new creation, the divine economy is gratuitous, precisely because it manifests an already-fulfilled God sharing freely of his fullness.

Nevertheless, emphasis on the aseity and impassibility of God in no way means that we must minimize our affirmation that justification is a free *expression* of the loving God of the gospel. The economy does manifest the divine life for all to see. Perhaps a different facet of the divine economy can be used to highlight the point. Paul tells the Roman Christians that "God, desiring to show his wrath and to make known his power, has endured with much patience vessels of wrath prepared for destruction, in order to make known the riches of his glory for vessels of mercy, which he has prepared beforehand for glory" (Rom. 9:22–23). God's action—in this case his hardening of Pharaoh and his hating of Esau—"shows his wrath and makes known his power." God's patience in working out this plan—enduring "with much patience vessels of wrath"—is "in order to make known the riches of his glory for vessels of mercy." Nowhere does Paul say that God's mercy and wrath are constituted by these events, but he does emphasize that they are made known through these occurrences.[61] Similarly, then, we see not only God's judgment but also the divine justification of the ungodly as manifesting (not making) the divine character.

Indeed, the justification of the ungodly seems to be right at the heart of God's economy. It was Jesus who said that "the Son of Man came not to be served but to serve, and to give his life as a ransom for many" (Mark 10:45). The imagery of ransom speaks of a price paid in order to lawfully assume possession of another person, metaphorical language that funds our theological reflection on justification. We are rightfully God's, according to Mark 10:45, not because we have merited our release and surely not because we have led an effective slave revolt against sin and death. We are free before God and the

60. McCormack and Jenson both deny that God acts out of need. Yet their programs, I would argue, lead to such a claim, inasmuch as election or eschatology fills out God's being. For a definitive analysis of Jenson's project and an illuminating appraisal of McCormack's project thus far, see Scott R. Swain, *The God of the Gospel: Robert Jenson's Trinitarian Theology*, Strategic Initiatives in Evangelical Theology (Downers Grove, IL: IVP Academic, 2013).

61. Wrath and mercy do manifest something eternally true of God in a way not feasibly revealed apart from creation. Here we could note the scholastic language of the *logos incarnandus*, the doctrine that, though the Second Person of the Trinity was not the incarnate Word until the time of his assumption of human flesh (John 1:14), he was always the one who would become incarnate. We dare not downplay the historical manifestation of the divine traits, though we also need not overstep this affirmation of spiritual history by suggesting that it is somehow constitutive of God's very being.

very family of God precisely because a ransom was paid by another: the same Son of Man who "came to seek and to save the lost" (Luke 19:10). We dare not think about Christ apart from the justification of the ungodly, even as we dare not think of God apart from Christ. As Archbishop Michael Ramsey puts it, "God is Christlike, and there is no unChristlikeness in him."[62] This being the case, then, we should not think of the triune God apart from the justification of the ungodly.

The good news of the gospel does include this staggering truth: in Jesus Christ we find the true God revealed. So the Puritan divine Richard Sibbes says, "God's goodness is a communicative, spreading goodness. . . . If God had not a communicative, spreading goodness, he would never have created the world. The Father, Son and Holy Ghost were happy in themselves and enjoyed one another before the world was. But that God delights to communicate and spread his goodness, there had never been a creation nor a redemption. God useth his creatures not for defect of power, that he can do nothing without them, but for the spreading of his goodness. . . . God's goodness is a spreading, imparting goodness."[63] The descent of the Son shows the divine determination to be with us—indeed, it shows the generosity of the Trinity.

And the Epistle to the Romans begins with this startling statement: "For I am not ashamed of the gospel, for it is the power of God for salvation to everyone who believes, to the Jew first and also to the Greek. For in it the righteousness of God is revealed" (Rom. 1:16–17). The gospel reveals the just God. There are at least two aspects to this revelation: God's loving concern to share his life with others, even sinners; and God's holy passion to do so in a way that does not jettison his righteousness. In Romans 3 Paul will come back to this idea of God's righteousness when he addresses the sacrifice of Jesus Christ. "All have sinned and fall short of the glory of God, and are justified by his grace as a gift, through the redemption that is in Christ Jesus, whom God put forward as a propitiation by his blood, to be received by faith. This was to show God's righteousness, because in his divine forbearance he had passed over former sins. It was to show his righteousness at the present time, so that he might be just and the justifier of the one who has faith in Jesus" (Rom. 3:23–26).

The justifying work of Christ's redemption is meant to be revelatory. Twice Paul uses the phrase "this [it] was to show" to emphasize that the propitiatory sacrifice of Jesus manifests a profound truth. In both cases we are told that

62. Michael Ramsey, *God, Christ, and the World: A Study in Contemporary Theology* (London: SCM, 1969), 98.

63. Richard Sibbes, *Works of Richard Sibbes* (Edinburgh: Banner of Truth Trust, 2001), 4:113.

the sacrifice of Christ reveals the righteousness of God. But what does that mean? Surely the concluding phrase of verse 26 offers commentary: "so that he might be just and the justifier of the one who has faith in Jesus."[64] God's righteousness here involves his justice and his justification of the ungodly faithful in Christ. In other words, the atoning work of Jesus not only defines the human who is united with him but also reveals the holy God's love for the ungodly with whom he wills to share his life.

So we see here that God's wrath and mercy meet. Paul observes that God has been justifying the ungodly, "because in his divine forbearance he had passed over former sins" (Rom. 3:25). One thinks of David and Abraham, the best of the lot, and remembers that while they were justified, they were also scoundrels who were guilty of murder, mistreatment of women, and the like. Yet God genuinely redeemed them. Paul senses the incoherence and the tension laden in such claims that a holy God declared flawed men and women just. The mystery is resolved when Paul sees the justifying work of Jesus: the holy God does justify the unrighteous by identifying or uniting them to his righteous Son, whom he puts forward as a propitiation for their sins. Only now is God's holiness and justice manifest along with his grace and mercy. With Paul, John can say that the incarnate Word makes evident the "grace and truth" of God (John 1:14, 17), not merely the mercy of giving life to sinners but also the truth and justice of doing so in accordance with God's just character.

The justifying work of God does not reveal everything about God—it is not the sole ruler of Christian doctrine. For example, justification itself does not tell us that God's love of the creature flows forth from eternity past; the doctrine of divine election must be voiced to give confession to this beautiful truth.[65] But the gospel of God's justifying the ungodly does show the divine character and manifest the divine identity. Indeed, even the doctrine of divine election can be interpreted as an extension of the doctrine of justification into eternity, as Jan Rohls suggests is the case in the theology of some Reformed confessions.[66] Or we could argue the opposite: justification as the extension of

64. We read the *kai* as concessive rather than epexegetical, precisely because v. 25 presents a dilemma requiring resolution—namely, the seeming injustice of such liberal forgiveness given in the past. Further, Paul does not seem to make any suggestion that vv. 24–25 are a tradition he will oppose in v. 26. See the argument of Douglas J. Moo, *The Epistle to the Romans*, New International Commentary on the New Testament (Grand Rapids: Eerdmans, 1996), 240–42; contra Ernst Käsemann, *Commentary on Romans*, trans. Geoffrey W. Bromiley (Grand Rapids: Eerdmans, 1980), 91–100.

65. On the notion of "justification from eternity," see G. C. Berkouwer, *Faith and Justification*, trans. Lewis B. Smedes, Studies in Dogmatics (Grand Rapids: Eerdmans, 1954), 143–68.

66. Jan Rohls, *Reformed Confessions: Theology from Zurich to Barmen*, trans. John Hoffmeyer, Columbia Series in Reformed Theology (Louisville: Westminster John Knox, 1998), 148–50.

divine election, the true fount of the Protestant Reformation according to B. B. Warfield.[67] I do not wish to engage either proposal as a historiographic account of the development of Reformational or specifically Reformed theology. In any event, both divine actions flow forth from the gracious divine will and are in no way caused or impelled by a fittingness or merit in the human subject. The doctrines mutually inform one another. They are distinct, yet they are related and interconnected. Election would be quite different if it did not involve objects who were guilty sinners. And justification would look markedly odd if it were a decision of God made only in the midst of history, rather than being rooted in an eternal determination of the divine will. So we see that the justifying God performs all his works in some way that befits his gracious disposition. The Christian understanding of God's character and the works that God does would be misshapen were it not to include and be constantly in touch with his justifying word to the ungodly.

## Justification and Living on Borrowed Breath

Thus far God in the heavens. What then of men and women on the earth? Does the justification of the ungodly speak into this realm of doctrine as well? In *Ethics*, Dietrich Bonhoeffer offers a way forward: "In Jesus Christ the reality of God has entered into the reality of this world. The place where the questions about the reality of God and about the reality of the world are answered at the same time is characterized solely by the name: Jesus Christ. God and the world are enclosed in this name. . . . We cannot speak rightly of either God or the world without speaking of Jesus Christ. All concepts of reality that ignore Jesus Christ are abstractions."[68] Here Bonhoeffer reminds us that Jesus Christ not only reveals true divinity to us but also shows us what humanity— "the reality of this world"—is at its most genuine. We now want to go a step further and ask not simply what Christ shows of humanity but also what Christ's justifying the ungodly by faith alone manifests about human beings.

It helps to begin further back and then turn to the justification of the ungodly to see what connections might be drawn in the realm of anthropology. The God who gives life yet again in Jesus Christ is the same God who made the world in the beginning. Amid a world of chaos he brought order. Out of darkness light has shone. The apostle Paul explicitly links creation and new

67. B. B. Warfield, "Predestination in the Reformed Confessions," in *The Works of B. B. Warfield*, vol. 9, *Studies in Theology* (New York: Oxford University Press, 1932; repr., Grand Rapids: Baker Books, 2000), 117–18.

68. Dietrich Bonhoeffer, *Ethics* (London: SCM, 1955), 54.

creation in his Second Epistle to the Corinthians: "For what we proclaim is not ourselves, but Jesus Christ as Lord, with ourselves as your servants for Jesus' sake. For God, who said, 'Let light shine out of darkness,' has shone in our hearts to give the light of the knowledge of the glory of God in the face of Jesus Christ" (2 Cor. 4:5–6). Writing to the Romans, Paul will also remind them that the God who justified Abraham by faith is the one "who gives life to the dead and calls into existence the things that do not exist" (Rom. 4:17). Creation and new creation alike are the work of the life-giving God, who creates by his Word and Spirit.

Paul is surely not the first to see such a connection. Indeed, he merely expresses a link deeply rooted in the writings of Israel's Scriptures—namely, the tie between God's creative sovereignty and his covenantal grace. Gerhard von Rad addressed the link between the doctrine of creation and God's redemptive work in the Old Testament, noting that the former is always addressed to instill confidence in the latter.[69] Texts like Isaiah 40 reference God's creative agency as the backdrop to his restorative promise. "Have you not known? Have you not heard? The LORD is the everlasting God, the Creator of the ends of the earth. He does not faint or grow weary; his understanding is unsearchable. He gives power to the faint, and to him who has no might he increases strength" (Isa. 40:28–29).[70] The one who creates is the one who gives strength. The Old Testament prophets and psalms reiterate this time and again: that God gave life to humanity in the beginning (Gen. 2:7) means that we forevermore live on borrowed breath and can always rely confidently on God for that gift.

The doctrine of justification by faith alone only further accents this canonical account of humanity. By insisting that all our life and righteousness is in Christ—indeed, that even our faith is but a mere instrument—justification highlights yet again that we live on borrowed breath.

Dependence is not obvious. Of God it is rightly said, "He alone has of himself all that he has, while other things have nothing of themselves. And other things, having nothing of themselves, have their only reality from him."[71] For us, life—whether in the beginning or at the end—comes as gift or not at all. Humans do not make themselves, do not sustain themselves, and cannot complete themselves. Even the most basic physical activities of human

---

69. Gerhard von Rad, "The Theological Problem of the Old Testament Doctrine of Creation," in *The Problem of the Hexateuch and Other Essays*, trans. E. W. Trueman Dicken (New York: McGraw-Hill, 1966), 131–43.

70. Ibid., 134.

71. Anselm of Canterbury, "On the Fall of the Devil," I, in *Anselm of Canterbury: The Major Works*, ed. Brian Davies and G. R. Evans (New York: Oxford University Press, 2008), 194.

life—breathing, eating, and drinking—point to our need for ongoing nourishment and sustenance from the outside. The dependent shape of the middle of our history is no different from its beginning and its end. We were made by the will of God, out of nothing and for no merit of our own. We will be completed by this one in Christ, not due to our fitness or worth.

Whether in Adam or in Christ, then, we are creatures: nothing more, nothing less.

> To be a creature is to be wholly originated, owing one's being to the loving and purposive divine summons. Unlike the life of the creator, the life of creatures is not *a se* or *in se*. Creatures have being and life by virtue of the freedom and goodness of God whose will it is that their life should be life other than his own perfect life. Because this is so, the manner in which creatures "have" being and life can only be explained by extensive description of the will and work of God. Creatureliness means absolute dependence upon that will and work across the entire span of creaturely being. To be a creature, therefore, is not simply to be a self-standing product of an initial cause; it is to be and to live—without restriction—*ab extra*.[72]

Whether in the breathing of life into the dust of the ground or in the regenerating wind of the gospel summons, human life is grounded outside of itself. Our natural existence is neither initiated nor sustained by our performance, and our participation in God by grace is neither the result of our fastidious obedience nor even the reward of our belief and trust.[73] At every step, God's grace and provision uphold us: "in him we live and move and have our being" (Acts 17:28); "in him all things hold together" (Col. 1:17).

Suggesting links between creation and new creation, of course, does not imply that creation itself involves justification, or even that the relationship between God and humanity in creation is exactly the same as that between God and humanity in Christ Jesus. No, there is surely a movement from creation through fall to reconciliation and redemption. Yet we do find a consistent anthropology presented in the Bible. "One of the definitive features of Christian anthropology is that it declines to define humanity in solely human terms."[74] By the time we come to the apostolic explication of Christ's significance for humanity, we are not at all surprised to find that the just live by faith. Such a christological anthropology is entirely fitting when viewed against the biblical

---

72. John Webster, "The Dignity of Creatures," in *God without Measure*.

73. The instrumental causality of faith is confessed in the Heidelberg Catechism 61, discussed in chap. 4, n. 45.

74. Anna Williams, *The Divine Sense: The Intellect in Patristic Thought* (Cambridge: Cambridge University Press, 2007), 6.

portrayal of human life and being. "It not only belongs to the nature of the creatures, but constitutes its true honour, not merely occasionally but continuously to need and receive the assistance of God in its existence."[75]

Thus far we can see that the first article of each creed helps prepare the way for the second: creation shows the shape of human life into which our relation with Christ might fit—namely, dependence for life. Matters, however, might run the other way. Luther shapes his reflection on creation by means of his understanding of justification, as evident in his "Small Catechism."

> I believe in God the Father almighty, Creator of heaven and earth.
>
> What is this? Answer:
>
> I believe that God created me and all that exists, and that he gave me my body and soul, eyes, ears and all my members, my mind and all my abilities. And I believe that God still preserves me by richly and daily providing clothing and shoes, food and drink, house and home, spouse and children, land, cattle, and all I own, and all I need to keep my body and life. God also preserves me by defending me against all danger, guarding and protecting me from all evil. All this God does only because he is my good and merciful Father in heaven, and not because I have earned or deserved it. For all this I ought to thank and praise, to serve and obey him. This is most certainly true.[76]

Earning and deserving creation and providential care are ruled out. The beginning of life and its ongoing preservation comes "only because he is my good and merciful Father in heaven." Merit or desert need not be interpreted in a strictly legal sense; they can refer to any need or obligation that one might meet, any demand or command that might be fulfilled. In no way does the creation and sustenance of this world befit its performance. Hence Christians are committed to the doctrine of *creatio ex nihilo* precisely to signal the free work of a God who gives and does not take life.[77] All the way down goes God's grace. As Bayer says, "Creation and new creation are both categorical gift. The first Word to the human being is a gifting Word: 'You may freely eat of every tree!' (Gen. 2:16)—renewed in the gifting Word of the

75. Karl Barth, *Church Dogmatics*, vol. 3/3, *The Doctrine of Creation*, ed. G. W. Bromiley and T. F. Torrance, trans. G. W. Bromiley and R. J. Ehrlich (Edinburgh: T&T Clark, 1960), 12.

76. Martin Luther, "Small Catechism," in *The Book of Concord: The Confessions of the Evangelical Lutheran Church*, ed. Robert Kolb and Timothy J. Wengert, trans. Charles Arand (Minneapolis: Fortress, 2000), 354–55. For an insightful analysis of this link in Luther's theology, see Oswald Bayer, "Creation: Establishment and Preservation of Community," in *Martin Luther's Theology*, 95–119.

77. On the revolutionary nature of the doctrine of creation from nothing, see Janet Martin Soskice, "Athens and Jerusalem, Alexandria and Edessa: Is There a Metaphysics of Scripture?" *International Journal of Systematic Theology* 8, no. 2 (April 2006): 149–62.

Lord's Supper: 'Take and eat. This is my body, given for you!'"[78] The inverse, of course, is that human being is gift all the way down, straight through history. We began with the fruit of the garden; we end with the feast of the city to come; always we are fed by another's generous provision.

As Bonhoeffer suggests, and as we noted above, the person of Jesus Christ reveals true God and true humanity to us. By extension, we have seen that the justification of the ungodly in this same Christ speaks pointedly of God's character as merciful giver and of the shape of human life as radically dependent on life that comes from outside itself. We have been fairly brief in the case of anthropological implications, precisely because the latter chapters of part 3 tease them out more fully, showing links between justification and ethics as well as between justification and ecclesiology. In neither case have we suggested that justification is a sufficient criterion for an appropriate doctrine of God or humanity, though we have seen that it is surely a necessary aspect of both areas for theological reflection.

## Justification and the Architecture of Christian Doctrine

Having seen the interplay between the justification of the ungodly and two crucial doctrines, we are now in a position to appreciate its importance. Recent debates on justification have shown little interest in straining forward to consider the reach of the doctrine.[79] But a doctrine worth such time and effort, such care and concern, surely has much with which to inform the full span of Christian theology. It will not say everything, but it will say something absolutely pivotal to certain things and something related to everything.

In conclusion, then, we can think of justification in terms of architecture. It is surely not the only part of the house, but it does serve as the historical foundation of human fellowship with God in Christ.[80] The architect has sought

78. Bayer, "Creation: Establishment and Preservation of Community," 98–99.

79. One notable exception is Michael Gorman, *Inhabiting the Cruciform God: Kenosis, Justification, and Theosis in Paul's Narrative Soteriology* (Grand Rapids: Eerdmans, 2009), which concludes with a chapter relating these soteriological matters to the end of violence. I share Gorman's concern not only to link justification and participation but also to tease out the ethical implications of the former for Christians and Christian communities. However, I have concerns that in both relationships his account tends to confuse the two entities under discussion (justification and participation, justification and human justice). See the discussions in chapters 2 and 5.

80. Of course the eternal foundation would be the gracious will of God, and the economic foundation, ultimately, would be the election of God. With respect to the application of God's blessings in history, however, justification in Christ serves as the foundation of all other blessings. For a helpful account of this foundational role of justification in Calvin's theology, see J. Todd Billings, "John Calvin's Soteriology: On the Multifaceted 'Sum' of the Gospel," *International Journal of Systematic Theology* 11, no. 4 (2009): 428–47, esp. 446–47.

a dwelling place in his people's midst. He envisions and eventually perfects a home, wherein they can feast and delight in his presence. The banquet will surely not occur on a construction site, but in a festive setting. Yet all of this depends on a solid foundation being laid. Justification is that foundation. That God accepts us in Christ as righteous is the basis by which all other blessings can be enjoyed. It is not itself those blessings, just as the concrete foundation is not itself the banquet hall. Yet it remains constantly necessary, lest the party come to a crashing halt. Justification, then, has been and always will remain the root of all other spiritual blessings we have in Jesus.

# 2

# Justification and Participation, the Ground and Goal of the Gospel

F or many centuries the question of justification was not a primary or leading question. One can scan the writings of early Christianity—the works of Athanasius, Augustine, the Cappadocians, Hilary, and others—without encountering frequent discussions of justification. The doctrine appears from time to time, but it does not dominate the theological literature. In the time of the Reformation, however, justification in Christ alone proved to be a defining doctrine. Martin Luther heralded the truth that the "righteous shall live by faith" (Rom. 1:17). While his concerns spanned the theological deck, from sacramental practice to ecclesial authority, justification was never far from his mind or his preaching. And in this concern Luther was joined by a host of others: Zwingli, Bucer, Melanchthon, Calvin, Bullinger, Cranmer, Barnes, Vermigli, Oecolampadius, Knox, Musculus, and Ursinus, to name but a few. This focus on justification can be seen especially by looking to the rise of commentary work on Paul's Epistles to the Romans and the Galatians, both increasing rapidly during the first years of the Reformation.[1] And, of course, the literature on justification came not only from those enthused by Luther's reforms but also from those protesting his project.

1. For analysis of this commentary writing until 1556, see David C. Fink, "Divided by Faith: The Protestant Doctrine of Justification and the Confessionalization of Biblical Exegesis" (PhD diss., Duke University, 2010). Fink shows the common concern for testifying to the justification of the ungodly and the development of its understanding among the Protestant exegetes in the Lutheran and Reformed churches.

The post-Reformation writings of these churches, whether Reformational or Roman, have consistently engaged the doctrine of justification.[2] It holds an important place in the confessions of the Protestant churches as well as in the decrees of the Council of Trent.[3] It was seen as addressing a variety of questions: the question of assurance, on the one hand, and the question of ethics, on the other hand. It located the Christian's confidence as well as his or her good works, of course in different ways depending on whether one followed the Reformational or Roman pathway.

The twentieth century has seen the decline of justification's primacy in much Protestant theology. Paul Tillich has suggested that it addresses a question no longer asked by modern people: how can I, a sinner, be right with a holy God? "Indeed, it is so strange to the modern man that there is scarcely any way of making it intelligible to him. . . . We have here a breaking-down of tradition that has few parallels. And we should not imagine that it will be possible in some simple fashion to leap over this gulf and resume our connection with the Reformation again."[4] More recently, Dawn DeVries has noted that this observation still stands: "The majority of contemporary theologians do not find a reason to talk about it, not because contemporary theologians are no longer interested in sin and grace, but because the language and metaphors of the fourth century and the twelfth century and the sixteenth and seventeenth centuries do not work so well for twenty-first century men and women."[5] The gulf is there; it is deep and wide. Tillich made moves, though, to correlate this doctrine with contemporary concerns for meaning and security and therein to preserve the link between present witness and the church's heritage.[6]

How should we respond to such a genealogy? How do we assess the patristic and Reformational history? Furthermore, and more pointed for spiritual and ecclesial purposes, what must we say today about the doctrine of justification?

2. I employ the term "Reformational" with respect to the sixteenth-century context rather than any twentieth-century link to the work of Herman Dooyeweerd (as it is sometimes used).

3. Council of Trent, Session VI, Decree on Justification, esp. chap. 7, in *Enchiridion symbolorum definitionum et declarationum de rebus fidei et morum*, ed. Heinrich Denzinger and Peter Hünermann, 40th ed. (Freiburg: Herder, 2005), 1529.

4. Paul Tillich, *The Protestant Era*, abridged ed. (Chicago: University of Chicago Press, 1957), 196.

5. Dawn DeVries, "Justification," in *Oxford Handbook of Systematic Theology*, ed. John Webster, Kathryn Tanner, and Iain Torrance (New York: Oxford University Press, 2007), 209.

6. Social-scientific research seems to prove DeVries's and Tillich's point. Christian Smith and his team of researchers performed a study, the largest to date, of religion among young people in America, and the results suggested that the typical teenager believes in what Smith termed "moralistic therapeutic deism" (Christian Smith, with Melinda Lundquist Denton, *Soul Searching: The Religious and Spiritual Lives of American Teenagers* [New York: Oxford University Press, 2009]).

Is it a necessary part of the gospel? Or might we focus on other questions regarding the work of Jesus Christ? This chapter seeks to address these questions regarding the place of justification in the gospel of Jesus Christ. Paths forward have been suggested by those involved in the trenches of biblical studies as well as the fields of historical study. We will have to consider their findings, even if we find occasion to differ with some major trends in either field.

Many biblical scholars have suggested that we turn from a Lutheran or Reformational focus on justification by faith alone toward a more holistic account—namely, participation in God. In two recent books, Douglas Campbell has argued that there are essentially four approaches to Pauline theology: an antitheological approach, justification theory, salvation-history, and a participatory approach.[7] A century ago Albert Schweitzer lodged the complaint that Pauline scholars had focused too long on peripheral matters, for justification by faith was but a subsidiary crater in the wider terrain of Paul's theology.[8] Schweitzer suggested that Christ-mysticism was much more central. Ever since, Pauline scholars have debated the "center" of Paul's theology. With the work of W. D. Davies, Krister Stendahl, and E. P. Sanders in the middle of the twentieth century, the polemical target of a guilt-ridden, legalistic Judaism subsided and Paul's theology had to be refocused elsewhere.[9] Because justification is only discussed in a few Pauline texts, and inasmuch as it cannot be construed as a polemical attack on first-century legalism or Pelagianism, other matters must be more pressing in Paul's writings. In recent years, participation in Christ has proven to be the most common suggestion among those who wish to shirk the shackles of Reformational exegesis.[10] For example, Michael Gorman has argued that participation is the "focus," "central concern," "primary concern," or "integrative narrative experience" of Pauline theology, even if he prefers

7. Douglas Campbell, *The Quest for Paul's Gospel: A Suggested Strategy* (London: T&T Clark, 2005), 38–42, 56–62; and *The Deliverance of God: An Apocalyptic Rereading of Justification in Paul* (Grand Rapids: Eerdmans, 2009). Campbell specifies his approach, the fourth, as a "pneumatologically participatory martyrological eschatology."

8. Albert Schweitzer, *The Mysticism of Paul the Apostle*, trans. William Montgomery (Baltimore: Johns Hopkins University Press, 1998).

9. W. D. Davies, *Paul and Rabbinic Judaism: Some Rabbinic Elements in Pauline Theology* (London: SPCK, 1955); Krister Stendahl, "Paul and the Introspective Conscience of the West," in *Paul among Jews and Gentiles* (Philadelphia: Fortress, 1976), 78–96; and E. P. Sanders, *Paul and Palestinian Judaism: A Comparison of Patterns of Religion* (Philadelphia: Fortress, 1977).

10. The other frequently cited option has been the political or anti-imperial Paul over against the Paul supposedly focused on individual salvation. N. T. Wright has written most compellingly in this regard; see, e.g., *Paul: In Fresh Perspective* (Minneapolis: Fortress, 2009). For a brutal criticism, see John M. G. Barclay, "Why the Roman Empire Was Insignificant to Paul," in *Pauline Churches and Diaspora Jews*, Wissenschaftliche Untersuchungen zum Neuen Testament 275 (Tübingen: Mohr Siebeck, 2011), 363–88; Seyoon Kim, *Christ and Caesar: The Gospel and the Roman Empire in the Writings of Paul and Luke* (Grand Rapids: Eerdmans, 2008).

to refrain from using the terminology of a "center" per se.[11] Gorman argues in his book that participation is a more holistic portrait of the Christian life than justification, inasmuch as it speaks of moral change. For similar reasons, Richard Hays has argued that participation is a crucial replacement of justification as the center of Paul's theology.[12] Most recently, Douglas Campbell has lambasted "justification theory" as deleterious in numerous ways and has substituted a participatory approach in its stead.[13]

For many, this shift toward a supposedly more holistic account of Christ's work involves adopting, or at least sits well beside, a revisionist portrayal of the history of Protestant theology. One famed example is the Finnish account of Martin Luther's theology. Tuomo Mannermaa and his colleagues and students have offered in recent years a thoroughgoing rereading of Luther's corpus.[14] Fixing upon a line in Luther—"in faith itself Christ is really present" (in ipsa fide Christus adest)—Mannermaa and the Finnish school argue that justification is ontological and not simply forensic. Mannermaa has sought to correct the typical Lutheran focus on the imputation of Christ's righteousness, suggesting instead that Luther's description of faith and union point in another direction: Christians effectively participate in Christ. Thus, deification rather than imputation becomes the driving engine of Luther's soteriology. Mannermaa found this ecumenically fruitful, and many have adopted it for similar reasons.[15]

I would suggest that each of these trends should raise two concerns, only one of which will I address here in a sustained way. Both the shift to participationist readings of Paul and the Finnish approach to Luther's theology suffer from historical questions of grave effect. I leave these matters, however, to the experts in Paul's literature and Luther's theology.[16] For the present it suffices to point

11. Michael J. Gorman, *Inhabiting the Cruciform God: Kenosis, Justification, and Theosis in Paul's Narrative Soteriology* (Grand Rapids: Eerdmans, 2009), 171.

12. Richard Hays, "Participation in Christ as the Key to Pauline Soteriology," in *The Faith of Jesus Christ: The Narrative Substructure of Galatians 3:1–4:11*, 2nd ed. (Grand Rapids: Eerdmans, 2002), xxix–xxxiii; and "What Is 'Real Participation in Christ'? A Dialogue with E. P. Sanders on Pauline Soteriology," in *Redefining First-Century Jewish and Christian Identities: Essays in Honor of Ed Parish Sanders*, ed. Fabian E. Udoh, Susannah Heschel, Mark Chancey, and Gregory Tatum (Notre Dame: University of Notre Dame Press, 2008), 336–51.

13. Campbell, *Deliverance of God: An Apocalyptic Rereading of Justification in Paul* (Grand Rapids: Eerdmans, 2010).

14. See esp. Tuomo Mannermaa, *Christ Present in Faith: Luther's View of Justification*, ed. Kirsi Stjerna (Minneapolis: Fortress, 2005).

15. See the American responses in Carl E. Braaten and Robert W. Jenson, eds., *Union with Christ: The New Finnish Interpretation of Luther* (Grand Rapids: Eerdmans, 1998).

16. For perceptive analysis, see John M. G. Barclay, *Paul and the Gift* (Grand Rapids: Eerdmans, forthcoming). With respect to the Finnish Luther, see Carl Trueman, "Is the Finnish Line

to the second concern they raise. Both evidence a severe failure to distinguish the questions being addressed by different pieces of dogmatic or scriptural teaching. In each case, the doctrine of justification is being juxtaposed with some notion of participation or deification, as if these are at odds. The suggestion that justification and participation would be mutually exclusive is rather remarkable, at least if one reads each doctrine within its intended doctrinal matrix and in light of the questions it is (not) meant to answer. Perhaps the best one can do in engaging these controversies is to show what justification or participation is meant to do and to answer. By focusing attention on the location and function of the doctrines, one can also show what they are not meant to do. Only after doing so can we begin to ask if the notions might be mutually reinforcing rather than mutually exclusive.

In this chapter I argue that *the gospel is the glorious news that the God who has life in himself freely shares that life with us and, when we refuse that life in sin, graciously gives us life yet again in Christ. While participation in God is the goal of the gospel, justification is the ground of that sanctifying fellowship.* We will consider both the goal and the ground of this gospel, arguing that a well-ordered account of the gospel requires that consideration be given to both facets: to participation in God and to justification in Christ. We will see that justification and participation are not competitive visions of the gospel, though they describe different facets of it. We will also consider their logical relationship vis-à-vis union with Christ and how this relationship is manifested in the link between the two sacraments given to the church, baptism and the Lord's Supper. Finally, we will show that this dogmatic reflection aids good biblical exegesis by demonstrating its application to two major biblical depictions of the gospel: adoption and marriage.

## The Participatory *Telos* of the Gospel

We have seen that *the gospel is the glorious news that the God who has life in himself freely shares that life with us and, when we refuse that life in sin, graciously gives us life yet again in Christ.* Now we turn to note that *participation in God is the goal of the gospel.* We must locate the focus on participation in God biblically and work to articulate it theologically.

The biblical writings begin and end with *the God who has life in himself freely sharing that life with us.* The Bible first points to God: "In the beginning, God" (Gen. 1:1); "In the beginning was the Word" (John 1:1). Anything

a New Beginning? A Critical Assessment of the Reading of Luther Offered by the Helsinki Circle," *Westminster Theological Journal* 65 (2003): 231–44.

and everything else follows and flows from the divine reality that "all things were created through him and for him" (Col. 1:16). Theological reflection, then, must map onto this order by considering God prior to all other things in him. In chapter 1, we reflected on the divine character, the one who has life in himself and who freely shares that life. In this chapter, we turn toward its expression in the divine economy, that is, the outward works of God in relating to all other things. We do not put to the side God's self-sufficient fullness of life, but we focus on this Trinity, filled to the brim, flowing over to others in gracious and glorious activity. We consider God in action, in other words, amid a created and even cursed world.

The way the Bible depicts God's activity begins and ends with participation, the glorious gift of life with God. Eden is the symbol of such life. Having created the world and having culminated that work in the making of the man and woman, God then gave them life in Eden (Gen. 2:8, 15). The text portrays this locale like a temple. Adam is told "to work it and keep it" (v. 15), terms used elsewhere to describe the priestly activity of guarding and approaching the holy of holies, where the divine glory dwells.[17] Adam must maintain the purity of the garden because God dwells there. Indeed, the thick presence of God is portrayed by the "sound of the LORD God walking in the garden" (3:8). The Bible begins with God's presence and intimacy with his human partners.

The biblical writings conclude with this same focus: God with us. The Apocalypse of Jesus Christ, shown to John, concludes with a stunning vision of a new Jerusalem. The vision can be displayed in universal terms: "a new heaven and a new earth" (Rev. 21:1). It can be located particularly: "the holy city, new Jerusalem" (v. 2). Its reality is continuous with ours now: a city, a society, a geographic place, an architectural edifice, and so forth. Yet it is also starkly different: no tears, no death, no crying, "for the former things have passed away" (v. 4). Indeed, this dialectic is declared in the next verse, where "he who was seated on the throne said, 'Behold, I am making all things new'" (v. 5). That he makes "all things" new implies that the reality is continuous with ours. It is not a Platonic flight to the realm of the forms, nor a gnostic dismissal of the material, nor an introspective turn to the inward and individual. Jesus Christ makes *all things* new. But he does make them *new*. He leaves not a stone unturned. These few verses depict physical, emotional, relational life renewed and restored. They portray a radical disruption and change, a genuine discontinuity with our frustrating and faltering existence now.

17. See Gregory K. Beale, *The Temple and the Church's Mission: A Biblical Theology of the Dwelling Place of God*, New Studies in Biblical Theology (Downers Grove, IL: InterVarsity, 2004); and Jon R. Levenson, "The Temple and the World," *Journal of Religion* 64 (1984): 275–98.

The vision is brilliant. Yet its center is simple: "I heard a loud voice from the throne saying, 'Behold, the dwelling place of God is with man. He will dwell with them, and they will be his people, and God himself will be with them as their God'" (Rev. 21:3).[18] While the physical renewal is staggering and the emotional restoration promising, the deepest and most profound delight is the satisfaction of God's very presence with his people. Indeed, the Apocalypse is not the first biblical text to center our hopes here. For example, the prophet Ezekiel spoke of the multifaceted nature of God's restoration promises to Israel. Donald Gowan has argued that there are three crucial aspects to this hope: the transformation of the human person (Ezek. 36:25–27), the transformation of human society (vv. 24, 28, 33–36), and the transformation of nature (vv. 30, 35).[19] If we read beyond Ezekiel 36 to the next chapter, a fourth and more specific element could surely be added: the promise of the resurrection of the dead (37:12–14).[20] Remarkable promises are made that resurrection will bring restoration of all spheres of life—the personal, the social, the natural. The renewal is global. Yet Ezekiel 37 emphasizes the finale of God's faithfulness to renew his people: "I will make a covenant of peace with them. It shall be an everlasting covenant with them. And I will set them in their land and multiply them, and will set my sanctuary in their midst forevermore. My dwelling place shall be with them, and I will be their God, and they shall be my people" (vv. 26–27).

That word "dwelling" carries through the whole Bible. God dwelt in Eden. God will dwell forevermore in the new Jerusalem. In between these times, the biblical writings portray God's commitment to be present to his people even as they seek to flee his presence. That is, God, *when we refuse that life in sin, graciously gives us life yet again in Christ.* The history of Israel tells us of God's tabernacle and temple, those means whereby a holy and living God dwells amid a sinful and death-ridden people. The very word "dwell," or "dwelling," in the biblical writings points to that particular structure, the tabernacle where God was with his people in the wilderness. It becomes a symbol of God's presence to us now amid an evil age.

Indeed, the very ache of human existence is for this dwelling. The psalmist prays: "One thing have I asked of the LORD, that will I seek after: that I may dwell in the house of the LORD all the days of my life, to gaze upon the beauty of the LORD and to inquire in his temple" (Ps. 27:4). Perhaps the most famous chapter of the whole Bible celebrates this deepest of human hopes.

18. This promise has deep biblical precedent; see, e.g., Lev. 26:11–12; Isa. 52:11–12; and 1 Kings 8:10–11.

19. Donald E. Gowan, *Eschatology in the Old Testament* (London: T&T Clark, 2000).

20. See Jon R. Levenson, *Resurrection and the Restoration of Israel: The Ultimate Victory of the God of Life* (New Haven: Yale University Press, 2006), 229.

After confessing that "you prepare a table before me in the presence of my enemies; you anoint my head with oil; my cup overflows," the psalmist presses forward to say, "Surely goodness and mercy shall follow me all the days of my life, and I shall dwell in the house of the LORD forever" (Ps. 23:5–6). With statements such as these in mind, Augustine later noted that "you have made us and drawn us to yourself, and our heart is unquiet until it rests in you."[21]

The very center of the biblical narrative is the incarnation of the eternal Son of God. As the Gospel according to John portrays it, "the Word became flesh and dwelt among us, and we have seen his glory, glory as of the only Son from the Father, full of grace and truth" (John 1:14). That eternal Word—the one who was "with God" and "was God" and "was in the beginning with God" (John 1:1–2)—took fleshly form and tabernacled among us. Thus he is Immanuel, "God with us," the fulfillment of God's pledge to be with his people.

Participation is the goal of the gospel, because the end of humanity is dwelling with God. It is not merely a future hope, however, but is also experienced by the Spirit now. Paul addresses the Corinthians in strong terms morally, precisely because of an ontological truth. "Do you not know that you are God's temple and that God's Spirit dwells in you? If anyone destroys God's temple, God will destroy him. For God's temple is holy, and you are that temple" (1 Cor. 3:16–17). "Or do you not know that your body is a temple of the Holy Spirit within you, whom you have from God?" (1 Cor. 6:19). Christians are the dwelling place of God now. Indeed, the hope of glory is "Christ in you"—this temple presence of God within us is enjoyed by the Spirit.[22] This divine dwelling occurs in Christians individually as well as corporately.[23]

Some have suggested or expressed concern that Protestant theology cannot or should not affirm participation precisely because of its emphasis on the forensic reality of God's salvation of sinners. According to this take, the two necessarily contrast with each other. Perhaps the most instructive example of this can be seen in James Torrance, who argues that much post-Reformation theology in the Reformed tradition went awry in construing God's relations to humanity in contractual rather than covenantal terms.[24] He views this as theology's fall from Calvin's relational emphasis on union with Christ to Puritanism's legalistic schema.

21. Augustine, *Confessions*, ed. John E. Rotelle, trans. Maria Boulding, Works of St. Augustine 1/1 (Hyde Park, NY: New City, 1997), 39 (1.1.1).
22. See, e.g., 2 Tim. 1:14 and Rom. 8:9.
23. See, e.g., 2 Cor. 6:16–18 and Eph. 2:19–22.
24. James B. Torrance, "Covenant and Contract: A Study of the Theological Background of Worship in Seventeenth-Century Scotland," *Scottish Journal of Theology* 23 (1970): 51–76; idem, "The Covenant Concept in Scottish Theology and Politics and Its Legacy," *Scottish Journal of Theology* 34 (1981): 225–43.

We should note two approaches to a response to Torrance's claims. First, they are historically suspect, to say the least, and this from two sides. While there are shifts in theological form from the sixteenth to the seventeenth centuries, and from certain genres to the development of high scholastic literature, there is no seismic shift in terms of content. The later Calvinists, if one is to use that unfortunate description, are not so focused on legal modes of thought as to miss or elide the relational and filial emphases of Scripture. Just as important, however, is the prior mistake: Calvin and the early Reformers are not so focused on union with Christ that they fail to see its juridical and forensic connotations. Indeed, much of Calvin's famous debate with Osiander makes this point apparent, wherein Calvin defines union with Christ not in ontological terms but in moral terms, by speaking of our union with the Mediator who took human form, lived a human life on our behalf, and died a human death in our place.[25]

Reformation and post-Reformation historical theologians, from Heiko Oberman and David Steinmetz to Richard Muller and Willem van Asselt, have demonstrated the fundamental continuity between Calvin and his successors in spades.[26] While some of that work has remained bogged down in showing continuity over against discontinuity, and while historical analysis needs to move

25. On the debate between Calvin and Osiander, see the analysis of J. Todd Billings, *Calvin, Participation, and the Gift: The Activity of Believers in Union with Christ*, Changing Paradigms in Historical and Systematic Theology (New York: Oxford University Press, 2007), 53–61; contra Julie Canlis, "Calvin, Osiander, and Participation in God," *International Journal of Systematic Theology* 6, no. 2 (2004): 169–84, whose account offers some help but fails (1) to note that Calvin's view of participation maintains a strong forensic emphasis that is premised on the doctrine of imputation, and (2) to affirm, with Calvin, that we do participate in Christ's "substance." Regarding the latter flaw, note that Calvin's denial of an ontological participation does not mean that he does not employ any metaphysical terminology. As Billings shows, Calvin makes regular use of the description that we participate in the "substance" of Christ. For literature and analysis, see Billings, *Calvin, Participation, and the Gift*, 61–65. Billings notes that while the 1545 additions of "substance" language to Calvin's *Institutes* are later deleted, Calvin nonetheless continued to employ such language in late editions of his biblical commentaries. (Billings points to his comments on 1 Cor. 11:24 and Eph. 5:31, as well as his sermon on Gal. 3:26–29; these texts date from after the 1545 *Institutes*, and they remain through the 1551 and 1556 revisions.) While Calvin strongly opposed any notion of "inflowing" of substance (worries he has regarding the Lutheran doctrine of participation, as well as that of Andreas Osiander), he did affirm that there is genuine engagement with Christ's substance.

26. For key examples from a burgeoning literature over the last quarter century, see especially Richard Muller, *After Calvin: Studies in the Development of a Theological Tradition*, Oxford Studies in Historical Theology (New York: Oxford University Press, 2003); Willem van Asselt and Eef Dekker, eds., *Reformation and Scholasticism: An Ecumenical Enterprise*, Texts and Studies in Reformation and Post-Reformation Thought (Grand Rapids: Baker Academic, 2001); and Maarten Wisse, Marcel Sarot, and Willemien Otten, eds., *Scholasticism Reformed: Essays in Honour of Willem J. van Asselt* (Leiden: Brill, 2010), pts. 1–2.

on to analyze the nature of faithful development within a continuous stream of thought, nonetheless, the case argued by these and other scholars is substantial and not to be missed.[27] Indeed, one wishes that the historical analysis of thirty years ago could be ignored by this point, since it has been thoroughly debunked by the experts in its field. Yet the standard account of Torrance continues to exercise some sway outside his own field. Two examples might be mentioned. Relatively near to the world of post-Reformation studies, this Torrance reading has recently shaped Charles Partee's work on the theology of Calvin, wherein he suggests that the logical rigor of Calvin's successors led them away from Calvin's exegetical focus and that their legal categories stymied Calvin's rich theology of union with Christ.[28] But the influence of Torrance has spread much further, even to the world of Pauline studies. For example, Douglas Campbell sustains his critique of "justification theory" using the Torrance reading of Protestant history, arguing that the soteriology of the post-Reformation, especially Puritan, divines led away from the participatory and pneumatological emphasis of Paul into a legalistic, transactional, and even anthropocentric direction guilty of many things (including its failure to stop the Holocaust).[29]

27. For a recent example of thoughtful analysis that not only highlights continuity between Calvin and his heirs (the federal theologians) but also speaks of genuine development, see Aaron Denlinger, "Calvin's Understanding of Adam's Relationship to His Posterity: Recent Assertions of the Reformer's 'Federalism' Evaluated," *Calvin Theological Journal* 44, no. 2 (2009): 226–50. Cf. J. V. Fesko, *Beyond Calvin: Union with Christ and Justification in Early Modern Reformed Theology (1517–1700)*, Reformed Historical Theology 20 (Göttingen: Vandenhoeck & Ruprecht, 2012).

28. Charles Partee, *The Theology of John Calvin* (Louisville: Westminster John Knox, 2008), 19n65, 26–27, 31.

29. Campbell, *Deliverance of God*, 939n10; for the failure of "justification theory" to restrain violence against Jews, see 205–7. Campbell admits in the next footnote "that we are drawing principally on James Torrance's theological observations; his historical account of Scottish Presbyterianism does not have to be correct in all its particulars for his theological insights to hold good (although I suspect that he is reasonably accurate)" (ibid., 940n11). Given that Campbell cites no other scholar (except for Torrance's son), one is likely to place little value on the fact that he "suspects" the history to be true. His book has received praise for offering a holistic account of Paul's theology, beginning with lengthy methodological reflection on how we approach it. However, his methodological analysis (pt. 1) is largely a polemic against a historical bogeyman that does not exist as such. Furthermore, it is a polemic based entirely on a debunked reading of a historical moment (post-Reformation Protestant theology, largely in its scholastic form) that finds scholarly backing in the work of one man, James Torrance. Far from being an example of interdisciplinary cross-pollination, then, I would suggest that Campbell's book manifests the effects of sloppy engagement of a related field. We should note two examples.

First, Campbell suggests that "justification theory" renders the Trinity and the life of Christ unimportant (ibid., 210–11; cf. 987n86). Yet these Protestant theologians of the sixteenth and seventeenth centuries began their confessions and dogmatics with statements about the Trinity and viewed the entirety of their confessions as speech about the external works of the triune God. Furthermore, at the very heart of classic Protestant teaching on justification is a confession that the whole life of Christ was righteous and, thus, for our justification (witness the frequent

Nothing so obviously disproves the Torrance thesis and its extension in Campbell as the climax of Puritan divinity, the famed Westminster Confession of Faith, which combines insistent attention to matters of the application of salvation with a distinctive confessional emphasis on the filial/relational character of life with God. Whereas one can claim that it focuses largely upon individual soteriology, one can neither argue that this is divorced from a trinitarian account of the Godhead (see Westminster Confession of Faith, chap. 2) nor claim that this soteriology is not contextualized within a churchly context of the means of grace (chaps. 21, 26–31).[30]

language of the "active obedience" of Christ). This issue is addressed at length in chap. 3, where I extend Protestant discussion of the active obedience of Christ to include, primarily, his faith, and in chap. 4, where I connect the earthly life of Christ directly to the notion of imputation (so central to the Protestant doctrine of justification).

Second, Campbell regularly accuses "justification theory" of propounding a view of humanity that is not fundamentally incapacitated apart from Christ; see Campbell, "Beyond Justification in Paul: The Thesis of the Deliverance of God," *Scottish Journal of Theology* 65, no. 1 (2012): 91, where such persons are described explicitly as "a fallen but not fundamentally incapacitated humanity." Campbell believes this anthropology fits "justification theory" because Rom. 1–3 is read by these Protestants as a preface to the gospel, an account of knowing God (Rom. 1:19–20) and knowing oneself to be a sinner (Rom. 1:21–3:20); see Campbell, "Rereading Romans 1:18–3:20," in *The Quest for Paul's Gospel*, chap. 11. Unfortunately, Campbell fails to see that Protestant theology classically construed has understood the teaching of Romans here to be about divine revelation (contra the claims of *Deliverance of God*, 39–41, 74). Furthermore, the most sizable figures in the Protestant tradition (whether Luther, Bucer, Calvin, Vermigli, Ursinus, Owen, or Turretin) do not hold to a "belief voluntarism" but actually propound a radically Augustinian view of the human will (contra the claims of *Deliverance of God*, 44–45, 126). One wonders if Campbell has heard of books like Luther's *Bondage of the Will* or Calvin's *The Bondage and Liberation of the Will*, or the many works of their successors (e.g., the Westminster Confession of Faith, chaps. 6, 9, or 10, much less the Canons of the Synod of Dordt). Typically these Reformational theologians are criticized for being determinists (which is not a valid accusation, even if it is an understandable misunderstanding) rather than what Campbell suggests, which is that any emphasis on divine initiative (election) contradicts their commitment to the primacy of individual agency (see *Deliverance of God*, 44–45, 212). Of course, while these figures affirmed individual agency (see examples in Willem J. van Asselt, J. Martin Bac, and Roelf T. te Velde, eds., *Reformed Thought on Freedom: The Concept of Free Choice in Early Modern Reformed Theology*, Texts and Studies in Reformation and Post-Reformation Thought [Grand Rapids: Baker Academic, 2010]), they never claimed that it was primary: all evidence points to the contrary. While Campbell elsewhere seems to understand something of the Augustinian trend within Reformational thought, although not in Anabaptist strands of the Reformation and later "Arminian" theologies (see *Deliverance of God*, 55–61), he nowhere mentions that Augustinian anthropology as a genuine commitment and instead suggests that it winds up collapsing under the primacy of the human agent. One cannot read his tome without assessing that he has confused Rudolf Bultmann and classical Reformational theology (see esp. *Deliverance of God*, 880, 1162n126).

In sum, Campbell shows little awareness of the Reformational approach to the doctrines of the Trinity, the person and work of Christ, and the link between divine and human agency in the economy of God's works, and his historical assessments do not serve students well.

30. Note also that the Westminster Larger Catechism addresses the doctrine of the church (59–65) before considering the individual's appropriation of salvation (66–83).

The Westminster Assembly did offer precise reflection on the *ordo salutis*, specifically because they wanted to extend the perfection of God into the realm of God's interaction with his people. To that end, they not only included chapters on the covenant of God and humanity (chap. 7) and on Christ the mediator (chap. 8) but they also addressed free will (chap. 9), effectual calling (chap. 10), justification (chap. 11), sanctification (chap. 13), saving faith (chap. 14), repentance unto life (chap. 15), good works (chap. 16), the perseverance of the saints (chap. 17), and the assurance of grace and salvation (chap. 18). But the Torrance thesis cannot account for the notable attention given to another doctrine—adoption—in the Westminster Confession. For the first time in confessional history, this theme received independent treatment (chap. 14). There they confess:

> All those that are justified, God vouchsafeth, in and for His only Son Jesus Christ, to make partakers of the grace of adoption, by which they are taken into the number, and enjoy the liberties and privileges of the children of God, have His name put upon them, receive the spirit of adoption, have access to the throne of grace with boldness, are enabled to cry, Abba, Father, are pitied, protected, provided for, and chastened by Him as by a Father: yet never cast off, but sealed to the day of redemption; and inherit the promises, as heirs of everlasting salvation.[31]

Notice that justification and adoption are not equivalent, though their objects are identical (those whom God justifies, God adopts) and their cause is one and the same ("in and for His only Son Jesus Christ"). Relational "liberties and privileges" are enumerated: being named as God's own, receiving the Spirit, access to God's throne, address of God as Father, pity, protection, provision, discipline, preservation, and inheritance.

Justification is for adoption. Thus, the kind of Calvin-against-the-Calvinists thesis propounded by Torrance and Campbell cannot be maintained, as if the relational focus of Calvin was lost amid the contractual and legal apparatus of his scholastic successors. While there are no doubt stylistic, contextual, and some material differences between the second-generation Reformer (Calvin) and his heirs (who also drew inspiration from many other early precursors), the issues of union with Christ, participation, justification, and assurance, which Torrance focuses on, are not among these differences.[32] Calvin had no

---

31. Westminster Confession of Faith, in *Constitution of the Presbyterian Church (U.S.A.). Part One: Book of Confessions* (Louisville: Geneva, 1996), 188.

32. I have offered analysis of the doctrine of faith in Calvin and among the theology of Reformed orthodoxy in the next century and a half in *The Christ's Faith: A Dogmatic Account*, T&T Clark Studies in Systematic Theology 2 (London: T&T Clark, 2009), 83–94.

difficulty addressing forensic and legal issues, while the Westminster Assembly manifests a serious commitment to putting the legal in its place—that is, as a parameter for relational union with the triune God.

Second, we ought to note that participation and covenant can be, and at times have been, misconstrued. Torrance illustrates, as do Partee and Campbell, the need to articulate the precise parameters and the specific point of talking about participation as well as about justification. That analysis of our legal declaration as righteous before God would be construed as somehow contradicting or in tension with our participation in God, as Torrance, Partee, and Campbell suggest, points to a need for clarification.[33] While such a mutually exclusive way of rendering the gospel does not appear in the Protestant dogmatics of the late sixteenth and seventeenth centuries, and while it is certainly not present in their confessional texts, it is a possible misunderstanding that warrants attention.

What then can we say by way of definition? Participation is a form of fellowship, yet it is more than any kind of happenstance relation. We might define participation as transformative fellowship in God's living presence. Paul speaks of this experience as part and parcel of the Christian life now and later. "And we all, with unveiled face, beholding the glory of the Lord, are being transformed into the same image from one degree of glory to another" (2 Cor. 3:18). Second Corinthians 3 speaks of our transformation into "the same image," a christological reference and a typological reference back to Moses's experience at Sinai (Exod. 32–34). When the Israelites considered the prospect of beatific vision, they realized that sinful people could not enjoy the divine presence without dying.[34] Paul shows that things have changed. Christians now enjoy that vision "with unveiled face" because of the sacrificial work of Jesus. Thus the presence of God can be enjoyed as transformative rather than threatening. While we now enjoy our participation in God by Christ, we shall enjoy its ultimate conclusion later, upon his physical return, moving "from one degree of glory to another."

When Moses beheld God's presence, his face glowed and was transfigured. Yet we must understand transfiguration as glorification and not as

33. The other option is that justification would become redundant, as in the case of Finnish interpretation of Luther, whereby it becomes an observation of divine indwelling. See J. Todd Billings, "The Contemporary Reception of Luther and Calvin's Doctrine of Union with Christ: Mapping a Biblical, Catholic, and Reformational Motif" (paper presented at the meeting of the Calvin Studies Society and the North American Luther Forum, Luther Seminary, St. Paul, MN, April 2011).

34. Dennis Olson brings out the way in which Moses is portrayed here as a sacrifice, sure to die eventually since he had served in this mediatorial role even as a sinner. See *Deuteronomy and the Death of Moses: A Theological Reading*, Overtures to Biblical Theology (Minneapolis: Fortress, 1994).

transmutation.[35] He did not cease being physical or human, but he was glorified and changed. Here the distinction between communicable and incommunicable attributes becomes so important, pointing to those characteristics that take hold in human life lived in such close proximity to God in Christ. While humans beholding God's glory in beatific vision do become holy through and through, they do not become immense or omniscient. And even those communicable attributes are enjoyed only by way of analogy. So while participation does transform the human, so that it is fellowship among beings who share in holiness, it always remains the case that God's holiness is natural while ours is by grace or derivation from the triune fullness. John Webster has argued that the twin topics of election and reconciliation (or we might say, more specifically, justification) are materially constitutive here: our holy lives are made like unto God, but they are of his eternal election and his sacrificial work to justify us.[36] The shared reality of transformative fellowship—what we are calling "participation"—is a moral and not strictly substantial matter.[37]

Admittedly, there are ways in which participation is frequently expressed that should raise serious concern and would not be conducive to maintaining either trinitarian orthodoxy or Protestant commitments regarding grace and Christology. Three could be mentioned. First, participation might be construed so as to deny or weaken the distinction between Creator and creature. Second, participation might be taken to suggest that salvation by God is premised upon rather than a product of conformity to God's image, Jesus Christ. Third, participation might be assumed to involve a sanctifying move beyond human nature to some other shape or form.

First, the notion of participation needs to follow from thinking about God himself. Again, this is why we noted that the gospel involves *God who has life in himself freely sharing that life with us*. Participative being is thus, by definition, derivative and dependent. In early Christian reflection on the Godhead, participative being was a creaturely reality and not a divine manner of existence. Athanasius and Didymus the Blind will use precisely this distinction to argue for the divinity of the Holy Spirit: Christians participate in him, though he

35. See Kathryn Tanner, *Jesus, Humanity, and the Trinity: A Brief Systematic Theology* (Minneapolis: Fortress, 2001), 41–46; and John Webster, *Holiness* (Grand Rapids: Eerdmans, 2003), 77, 83–84.

36. John Webster, "Perfection and Participation," in *The Analogy of Being: Invention of the Antichrist or the Wisdom from God?*, ed. Thomas Joseph White (Grand Rapids: Eerdmans, 2011), 389.

37. Ibid., 393. See also similar assessment of the Pauline exegesis of Irenaeus and Cyril in Ben C. Blackwell, *Christosis: Pauline Soteriology in Light of Deification in Irenaeus and Cyril of Alexandria*, Wissenschaftliche Untersuchungen zum Neuen Testament 2/314 (Tübingen: Mohr Siebeck, 2011).

participates in none.[38] Certain Lutheran construals of participation—largely from the new Finnish school of Tuomo Mannermaa—continue to portray a notion of the two natures of Christ that offers an underdeveloped sense of the distinction between divine and human life.[39] Even more so, approaches to participation within the Radical Orthodoxy movement have oftentimes suggested a fairly global approach to participative being that fails to highlight the particular shape of different natures, especially divine nature and created natures.[40] Thus, Reformed theologians have been leery of models of participation shaped by a Lutheran Christology or by a Christian Platonism apart from a rigorous adherence to and contextualization by what Robert Sokolowski calls "the Christian distinction" and what David Bentley Hart has termed the "great discovery" of the Christian metaphysical tradition.[41] While Reformed theologians must confess with Peter that we are called to be "partakers of the *divine nature*," we would be remiss to cease emphasizing that we are called to be "*partakers* of the divine nature" (2 Pet. 1:4). Unlike God, who simply is divine eternally and unceasingly, we partake of divinity by grace; that is, we participate in its living reality only by God's mercies.

38. Athanasius, "Letters to Serapion," 1.23–24, 27, in *Works on the Spirit: Athanasius the Great and Didymus the Blind*, trans. Lewis Ayres, Mark DelCogliano, and Andrew Radde-Gallwitz, Popular Patristics (Crestwood, NY: St. Vladimir's Seminary Press, 2011), 88–90, 95; and Didymus the Blind, "On the Holy Spirit," 13, 16–20, 54–60, 265, in *Works on the Spirit*, 147–49, 160–61, 221. Jerome offers a stunningly pointed editorial comment in the midst of Didymus's text: "[Didymus] calls a substance 'capable of being participated in' (*capabilis*) when it is participated in (*capiatur*) by many and bestows on them a share in itself. But a substance is 'capable of participating' (*capax*) when it is filled through communion with another substance and participates in (*capiens*) something else, while not being participated in (*capiatur*) by another" (Didymus, "On the Holy Spirit," 55, in *Works on the Spirit*, 160).

39. See Mannermaa, *Christ Present in Faith*, 16, 21–22, where Mannermaa says: "Faith communicates the divine attributes to the human being, because Christ himself, who is a divine person, is present in faith. Therefore, the believer is given all the 'goods' (*bona*) of God in faith," 22.

40. For a paradigmatic example, see John Milbank, "Only Theology Overcomes Metaphysics," in *The Word Made Strange: Theology, Language, Culture* (Oxford: Blackwell, 1997), 36–52; and "A Christological Poetics," in *The Word Made Strange*, 123–44. Cf. Anthony Baker, *Diagonal Advance: Perfection in Christian Theology*, Veritas (Eugene, OR: Cascade, 2011), 145–46, 193, 300. For a more promising account that highlights not only the relational structure of being but also, specifically, the trinitarian distinction from other beings, thus noting that participation is intrinsically hierarchical (gesturing much more strongly toward an ongoing cognizance of the Creator-creature distinction), see Adrian Pabst, *Metaphysics: The Creation of Hierarchy*, Interventions (Grand Rapids: Eerdmans, 2012). In addition to Radical Orthodoxy, the preponderance of panentheistic approaches has only seemed to grow in recent years and to mirror the same tendencies as those of the Radical Orthodoxy movement (e.g., the work of Philip Clayton).

41. Robert Sokolowski, *The God of Faith and Reason: Foundations of Christian Theology* (Notre Dame: University of Notre Dame Press, 1982), 23; David Bentley Hart, "The Destiny of Christian Metaphysics: Reflections on the *Analogia Entis*," in White, *Analogy of Being*, 407.

Perhaps a parallel pairing clarifies matters. Partaking of the divine nature involves both union with divinity and not being divine oneself. Similarly,
Karl Barth argues that the human being is graced by God with the status
of being "taken seriously as an independent creature of God."[42] Of course,
independence, strictly speaking, is a divine trait that requires self-sufficiency
or aseity. It requires nonderivative existence and nondependent sustenance.
By definition, then, independence cannot be a creaturely trait, for creatures
are, first and foremost, created by another. They have *ek*-centric being. Yet
Barth suggests that the good news of God's determination is to give genuine
independence—relationally and ontologically—to men and women in Christ.
They do not have it in precisely the way that he has it: it is his by nature, ours
by grace. But they do have it. Similarly, 2 Peter 1:4 tells us that the impossible
is an actuality: the partaker really does enjoy the divine nature. Of course, in
partaking they show themselves to be something other than divine as such.
But they really do drink of the godly well. They are gifted with this partaking. John Webster has spoken of a "metaphysical turbulence" caused by this
kind of biblical pairing, and the term is apt. It reminds us that any doctrine of
participation must speak in such a way that the turbulent nature of its claim
is kept front and center, rather than being solved or lessened by slackening
either side of the seeming equation. "The true goal of theological inquiry is
not the resolution of theological *problems*, but the discernment of what the
*mystery* of faith is."[43] Accounts of participation that read partaking as anything
less than the startling news of a creaturely agent enjoying genuine relational
union with a fully self-realized and self-sufficient Trinity of love have tried to
whittle away a seeming problem rather than seek to discern the nature of the
mystery of the gospel and its revelation of the "differentiated union" between
God and his people in Christ.[44]

Second, participation answers a very specific question: what is the end or
greatest good (*summum bonum*) of humanity? It is the end, not the means
to that end. We encounter all manner of difficulty if we allow or ask participation to answer other questions such as, how does one get right with God?
If participation becomes the instrument and not the end, then it becomes a
burden rather than a blessing.

---

42. Karl Barth, *Church Dogmatics*, vol. 4/4, *The Doctrine of Reconciliation*, ed. G. W. Bromiley and T. F. Torrance, trans. G. W. Bromiley (Edinburgh: T&T Clark, 1969), 22.
43. Thomas Weinandy, *Does God Suffer? A Christian Theology of God and Suffering* (Notre
Dame: University of Notre Dame Press, 2000), 32.
44. The phrase "differentiated union" is employed throughout Billings, *Calvin, Participation, and the Gift*. It helpfully highlights both intimacy and the continued affirmation of the
Creator-creature distinction.

Bruce Marshall illustrates this tendency to expand participation into the realm of justification in his essay "Justification as Declaration and Deification."[45] Marshall offers a reading of the theology of Martin Luther not primarily for exegetical or historical reasons, but to suggest a possible way forward in holding together—rather than playing against one another—the forensic and participatory elements of Christian soteriology (primarily as found in the Pauline corpus of Scripture). His intent is to show that justification includes both facets. As he puts it, Luther "can freely mix forensic and transformative ideas when he talks about justification."[46] As will be seen, the terminology of "mixing" or "mixture" is particularly appropriate to describe Marshall's, if not Luther's, doctrine of justification and its relationship to the doctrine of participation.

There is much to commend in Marshall's account of Luther. Marshall is very clear that Luther does not shirk the biblical teaching on deification (e.g., 2 Pet. 1:4). Indeed, Marshall shows that Luther will even use 2 Peter 1:4 to help expound other biblical passages (for example, John 17:21 and the prayer that we might be one with another and with God in Christ). At the same time, however, Marshall points out that this notion is never meant to overwhelm the Creator-creature distinction. Indeed, Luther mentions that the union of Father and Son is enjoyed in "another, higher, inconceivable way" than our participation in the life of the triune God.[47] Marshall notes the claims of Bernhard Lohse that deification language is infrequent in Luther. While he grants the premise, Marshall rightly notes that participatory themes and judgments are present throughout the corpus (even if the specific, technical jargon of deification is rather modest).[48] All this strikes the reader as wise.

Yet there remains a sizable and insurmountable flaw in Marshall's account, indeed, in his very title "Justification as Declaration and Deification." While he powerfully demonstrates the presence of both forensic and participatory concerns in Luther's soteriology (as well as in his theology, anthropology, and sacramentology, I might add), he nowhere offers textual argument that both features constitute justification. Marshall claims, "We clearly have grounds in Luther for taking God's gift of righteousness and eternal life in Christ to involve participation in the divine nature and the deification of Christians."

---

45. Bruce D. Marshall, "Justification as Declaration and Deification," *International Journal of Systematic Theology* 4, no. 1 (2002): 3–28.

46. Ibid., 19.

47. Ibid., 6.

48. Ibid., 8; contra Bernhard Lohse, *Martin Luther's Theology: Its Historical and Systematic Development*, trans. Roy A. Harrisville (Minneapolis: Fortress, 1999), 221. Todd Billings has shown that the bulk of the most emphatic statements regarding deification are present very early in Luther's corpus (see "Contemporary Reception of Luther," 16–17).

Interestingly, however, there is no mention of righteousness in any of the Luther quotations offered prior to this point in the essay. Marshall does show a link between union with Christ and faith and, of course, between faith and justification. But the quotations he offers to this effect—linking Christ's presence, faith, and justification—occur in Luther's 1535 *Lectures on Galatians*, where he specifically clarifies that the justifying righteousness we possess is imputed, not infused. Amid the section of Luther's comments on Galatians 2, from which Marshall pulls a number of quotes regarding faith and participation in Christ, we find this statement by Luther that also brings in the notion of imputation:

> Here it is to be noted that these three things are joined together: faith, Christ, and acceptance or imputation. Faith takes hold of Christ and has Him present, enclosing Him as the ring encloses the gem. And whoever is found having this faith in the Christ who is grasped in the heart, him God accounts righteous. . . . Thus God accepts you or accounts you righteous only on account of Christ, in whom you believe. Now acceptance or imputation is extremely necessary, first, because we are not yet purely righteous, but sin is still clinging to our flesh during this life.[49]

Luther does link faith, Christ's presence, and justification. Yet there is an ordered relationship: faith puts on Christ, who both justifies and renews; but the justification and the renewal are strictly distinguished.[50] The doctrine of imputation is employed to make this distinction plain—namely, that participation is not itself involved in our justification, even though it is integrally tied to our participation in God by Christ.[51] Indeed, his wider corpus should make this evident, in that he early on makes, and nowhere denies, a distinction between passive righteousness (before God for justification) and active righteousness (before the neighbor for their service).[52]

---

49. Martin Luther, *Lectures on Galatians (1535), Chapters 1–4*, ed. Jaroslav Pelikan, Luther's Works 26 (St. Louis: Concordia, 1963), 132–33 (2:16).

50. This strict distinction is not present in the earliest Reformational writings of Luther, though by 1535 it had become a standard feature of his soteriology.

51. See also Luther, *Lectures on Galatians (1535), Chapters 1–4*, 233–34 (3:6), for further emphasis on the important function of imputation: "Therefore this is a marvelous definition of Christian righteousness: it is a divine imputation or reckoning as righteousness or to righteousness, for the sake of our faith in Christ or for the sake of Christ. . . . So far as the words are concerned, this fact is easy, namely, that righteousness is not in us in a formal sense, as Aristotle maintains, but is outside us, solely in the grace of God and in His imputation."

52. See Martin Luther, "Two Kinds of Righteousness (1519)," in *Career of the Reformer I*, ed. Harold Grimm, Luther's Works 31 (Philadelphia: Fortress, 1957), 293–306. There Luther addresses our passive and alien (justifying) righteousness that is imputed for Christ's sake (297–99) before turning to consider our active and proper (serving) righteousness that is lived for our neighbor's

Marshall has shown, as we attempt in this chapter, that both forensic categories and participatory relations are involved in God's gospel. Yet he has nowhere given evidence for construing both elements as part and parcel of justification in Luther.[53] Indeed, the very texts he cites suggest otherwise, and the wider shape of Luther's thought points against such a conflation. Much better to emphasize the sheerly forensic nature of justification and the gloriously participatory end of humanity in Christ, each as a facet of the gospel, neither as the totality of the gospel. Anything less than maintaining this distinction inevitably renders God's forensic demands less than pure and holy and/or minimizes the true glory of full participation in God's life.

Myopic focus on forensic declaration is a genuine error. Marshall keeps us from this fault. But in so doing, neither does he help our thinking about either the forensic or the participatory. Much better simply to say, not that justification is both forensic and formative, but that the gospel involves not only justification (its ground) but also sanctification's conclusion in glorious participation in God (its goal). The problem is not in the radicality of forensic justification but is whenever it becomes rootless and severed from the wider story of the gospel. Participation is an essential aspect of the gospel, but it is not meant to dial back our affirmations about the strictly forensic and imputed nature of justification.

Third, participation does not involve becoming something other than being human, though it does involve the closest imaginable union with someone not human: the triune God. In growing in holiness, however, the saint does not cease to be fully human. Didymus the Blind illustrates this notion when he identifies participation in the Spirit as "participation in the faith which comes from the Holy Spirit."[54] The Spirit does not exercise faith, yet the

---

sake (299–306). This distinction fits hand in glove with his comments—also in the 1535 *Lectures on Galatians*—that faith justifies "without love and before love," even though it does flow forth into love and service (*Lectures on Galatians [1535], Chapters 1–4*, 136–37 [2:16]). Luther is here opposing the Roman Catholic doctrine of justification by faith formed by works of love (*fides formata*). I offer further reflection in chap. 4 on the function of the distinction between the two kinds of righteousness and its relationship to the doctrine of imputation.

53. When Marshall gathers his textual evidence for this point (18n46), he references prior citations that nowhere identify participation with justification. He then offers two new texts relating to "pleasing God" and obtaining "the favor of God" not only by faith but also by "laboring to drive out sin" and dwelling "in the grace of Christ." Yet such realities need not necessarily refer to "pleasing God" in the justifying sense. There is a further reality in which believers, who are always pleasing God in Christ, at certain times please God still further with their own lived actions. Any parent can understand this: we love our children always (even when they are unlovely), yet we delight in their loveliness at certain particular times.

54. Didymus the Blind, "On the Holy Spirit," 38, quoted in *Works on the Spirit*, 155. Didymus is offering theological exegesis of 1 Cor. 12:9 here. It is apparent that Didymus has a strongly (though not necessarily an exclusively) intellectualist definition of faith (see "On the

closest possible union with the Spirit does heighten the human response in a distinctly creaturely and even humanly way. Being near the Spirit not only makes us more like the Spirit (in certain respects) but also more unlike the Spirit and more straightforwardly human (in other respects). Indeed, Didymus points to both truths: the participation in the Spirit of God brings with it diverse gifts, some of which are exercised as such by the Spirit (he mentions healing and power), others of which are not exercised as such by the Spirit (he mentions faith). While faithfulness is affirmed of the Godhead, faith is a distinctly human trait that corresponds to or images that divine faithfulness. We are transformed by the divine presence, made holy as he is holy, but we are also made perfect or complete according to our (human, creaturely, finite, dependent) kind. Job confesses: "In my flesh I shall see God," speaking of the very same skin that has been destroyed by disease and downtrodden by disappointment and yet will enjoy the deepest of all delights (Job 19:26). By participating in God through Christ and by the Spirit, we are conformed to God's image, not, strictly speaking, to being divine.[55]

This participation not only perfects our humanity (so that we are *homo*) but also involves the fulfillment of every aspect of our humanity (so that we are *vere homo*). We remember those teachings in Ezekiel 36 and especially in Revelation 21, where human life in all its brilliant fullness is engaged and renewed by Jesus Christ, who makes it all anew. The Bible and the Christian tradition, therefore, have a constant calling to point to the totalizing claims of Jesus. We are to love him with our heart, soul, and might (Deut. 6:5). We are to offer ourselves as living sacrifices (Rom. 12:1). We are not to partition some of our self for his delight. We are not to devote ourselves to him with a sliver or aspect of our being and persona. We are called to devote ourselves fully to him. More wonderfully, we are promised that he will remake us whole, top to bottom and inside out. Participation and growth in holiness due to the nearness of God do not make us less than human or something other than creaturely. As Thomas Aquinas says, "The gifts of grace are added to nature in such a way that they do not destroy it, but rather perfect it."[56]

---

Holy Spirit," 236, in *Works on the Spirit*, 216). In this regard he links "faith and trust," and he argues that by participating in the Spirit of truth, humans come to exercise faith (as a way or means of embracing that truth). This highlights the continuity and discontinuity between the one participating and the one in whom they participate: both enjoy truth, but one does so *in se* and the other only by faith.

55. See John Calvin, *The Epistle of Paul the Apostle to the Hebrews and the First and Second Epistles of St. Peter*, ed. David W. Torrance and Thomas F. Torrance, trans. William B. Johnston, Calvin's Commentaries (Grand Rapids: Eerdmans, 1963), 330–31 (2 Pet. 1:4).

56. Thomas Aquinas, *Expositio super librum Boethii De.Trinitate*, q. 2, art. 3, quoted in *Thomas Aquinas: Selected Writings*, trans. Ralph McInerny (London: Penguin, 1998), 135.

Such qualification regarding the shape and scope of participation in God is not meant, however, to suggest that God's glory comes at the expense of humanity. Karl Barth emphasizes that "God alone possesses divine glory, but alongside his glory there exists a glory which belongs to the world and to man."[57] The importance of participation in Christ is put front and center regularly in Christian worship in the practice of the Lord's Supper. Meals were regularly presented as occasions of divine grace, specifically of divine presence, throughout the scriptural writings of Israel.[58] The prophet Isaiah foretold God's restoration in terms of bread and wine provided by God: "On this mountain the LORD of hosts will make for all peoples a feast of rich food, a feast of well-aged wine, of rich food full of marrow, of aged wine well refined" (Isa. 25:6). As noted earlier, the psalmist spoke of a table being set in the presence of his enemies and of an overflowing cup (Ps. 23:5–6). Whereas other religions portrayed food as brought by servants and enjoyed by the lords, the gospel tells of a shared meal and a common feast: the wedding supper of the Lamb who was slain for our sake. The Lord provides the food; the people feast. Nothing so incisively portrays the goal of the gospel as the declaration, "The gifts of God for the people of God."

While *the gospel is the glorious news that the God who has life in himself freely shares that life with us and, when we refuse that life in sin, graciously gives us life yet again in Christ*, it takes particular form in its biblical exposition. We have seen that *participation in God is the goal of the gospel*. God's triune fullness is not an occasion for divine aloofness or transcendent separation, but is the springboard and fuel for divine engagement of humans in a transcendently gracious manner. It culminates in the great promise that Yahweh offers: "I will be your God, and you will be my people."

## The Forensic Entryway of the Gospel

To rehearse the argument thus far: *The gospel is the glorious news that the God who has life in himself freely shares that life with us and, when we refuse that life in sin, graciously gives us life yet again in Christ. While participation in God is the goal of the gospel, justification is the ground of that sanctifying fellowship.* At this point, we consider that last phrase—namely, that justification is the ground of our sanctifying fellowship with the triune God.

57. Karl Barth, *The Knowledge of God and the Service of God according to the Teaching of the Reformation: Recalling the Scottish Confession of 1560*, trans. J. L. M. Haire and Ian Henderson (Eugene, OR: Wipf & Stock, 2005), 35 (lect. 4).

58. For thoughtful reflection on this biblical imagery, see Craig Blomberg, *Contagious Holiness: Jesus' Meals with Sinners*, New Studies in Biblical Theology 19 (Downers Grove, IL: InterVarsity, 2005), esp. 63–64.

The question arose in the church regarding the way in which one might enjoy participation in God. The earliest Christians turned to the liturgical and scriptural resources of Israel, celebrating the feast of the true Passover Lamb and speaking regularly of the sacrificial work of the incarnate Son. Indeed, the most common descriptions of atonement theology in the early church came in the context of liturgy—specifically, of the Eucharist. Understanding the location of these discussions helps shed light on their very course.

God dwelt with his people, as the Scriptures of Israel testify. Indeed, God's presence was the focus of early Christian mysticism and devotion. But God's presence was not a blasé reality to be taken for granted. God was not any sort of being who might be approached in whatever way. God was a holy one and a righteous judge. The psalmist declares: "The LORD is righteous; he loves righteous deeds; the upright shall behold his face" (Ps. 11:7). The presence and the possession of a beatific vision of God's very face (the *visio Dei*) was reserved for the upright. God's character is righteous; therefore, he delights in righteous deeds done by others. The law is an expression of his being, and his judgments accord with this expressed mandate for human lives.[59] Indeed, we might say that deeds are righteous inasmuch as they accord with this God's delight. Because his character—his righteousness—is the governing reality of the economy, "the upright shall behold his face."

The problem becomes apparent immediately, however, when we consider that the Psalms identify all people as unrighteous (Pss. 14:1–3; 53:1–3; cf. Rom. 3:9–20). Thus, the sacrificial system was crucial for the continued enjoyment of God's nearness. In ancient Israel, the cultic system provided for the proximity of divine intimacy. God could dwell in the neighborhood of sinners only if atonement was made, purity was present, and the common was set apart as holy. Whether in the form of Moses or the priestly consort, an intermediary was essential to bridge the gap between God's holy presence and his unfaithful people.[60]

The question was sustained in the patristic era. Humans were made to enjoy the vision of God and yet were marred by sin and incapable of such approach on their own. The answer? John Chrysostom points to the need for an intercessor and a sacrifice.

59. "Accordingly the Eternal Law is nothing other than the exemplar of divine wisdom as directing the motions and acts of everything" (Thomas Aquinas, *Summa Theologiae*, vol. 28, *Law and Political Theory*, ed. Thomas Gilby [Cambridge: Blackfriars, 1966], 53 [1a2ae.93.1, reply]).

60. For reflection on the sacrificial and mediatorial figuration of Moses in the Pentateuch, see Dennis Olson, *Deuteronomy and the Death of Moses*, esp. 17–22. Sacrifice can vary in shape and form at different times, however, if Augustine's definition is correct: a sacrifice is "every act which is designed to unite us to God in a holy fellowship" (*Concerning the City of God against the Pagans*, trans. Henry Bettenson [New York: Penguin, 1984], 379 [10.6]).

Do we not offer the sacrifice daily? Indeed we do offer it daily, re-presenting his death. How then is it one sacrifice and not many? . . . We offer the same person, not one sheep one day and tomorrow a different one, but always the same offering. . . . There is one sacrifice and one high priest who offered the sacrifice that cleanses us. Today we offer that which was once offered, a sacrifice that is inexhaustible. This is done as a remembrance of that which was done then, for he said, "Do this in remembrance of me." We do not offer another sacrifice as the priests offered of old, but we always offer the same sacrifice. Or rather we re-present the sacrifice.[61]

The question only took developed form, however, at a time of great ecclesial trouble and deep pastoral need—namely, the late medieval era. It was Martin Luther who saw the crisis of assurance in the church of this time and who fixed upon the idiom of justification to answer this need.

Luther's focus on justification was an extension of the long-heralded reflection on the sacrifice of Jesus Christ, so it is not surprising that his initial qualms regarded sacramental practice and its relationship to sacrifice, merit, and assurance. Indeed, it is central to the argument of the apostle Paul that justification and sacrifice are joined at the hip. Perhaps no text from Paul's writings garnered as much attention by Luther and other early Protestant pastor-theologians as Romans 3:21–26.

But now the righteousness of God has been manifested apart from the law, although the Law and the Prophets bear witness to it—the righteousness of God through faith in Jesus Christ for all who believe. For there is no distinction: for all have sinned and fall short of the glory of God, and are justified by his grace as a gift, through the redemption that is in Christ Jesus, whom God put forward as a propitiation by his blood, to be received by faith. This was to show God's righteousness, because in his divine forbearance he had passed over former sins. It was to show his righteousness at the present time, so that he might be just and the justifier of the one who has faith in Jesus.

The key terms of debates old and new appear here: "righteousness of God," "apart from the law," "through faith," "justified by his grace," to name but a few. For our purposes, the crucial point to see is that "propitiation" and "redemption"—both terms tied to the sacrificial work of Christ—are identified as components of being "justified by his grace as a gift."

"Propitiation" refers to the offering of the blood upon the mercy seat in the holy of holies. The term *hilasterion* identifies the actual seat where the blood

---

61. John Chrysostom, "Homily 17," in *Nicene and Post-Nicene Fathers*, 1st ser., vol. 14, *Chrysostom: Homilies on the Gospel of Saint John and the Epistle to the Hebrews* (Peabody, MA: Hendrickson, 2004), 449 (sec. 6).

would be poured, no doubt an architectural reference meant to speak of the liturgical action performed there once a year on Yom Kippur. This sacrificial gift frees the people of Israel from the divine destroyer, who would otherwise come upon them in judgment. This notion is first expressed, of course, in the Passover account of Exodus 12:1–14. The blood of the sacrificial lamb marks out the people, redeeming them from the curse and redeeming them for freedom with God outside of Egypt. Both terms come from this conceptual world—the sacrificial ground of fellowship with God no longer experienced as slaves, but enjoyed as freed sons and daughters.

Many in our own day have suggested that propitiation and sacrifice need not—and, in many cases, should not—be a part of Christian thinking about the atonement. Kathryn Tanner has argued that "the sacrifice on the cross has nothing essentially to do with a blood sacrifice for the expiation of sin; Jesus's death is the simple consequence of the life he led on behalf of others—his soteriological mission—in a sinful world."[62] Indeed, Tanner points out that sacrifice was an arbitrary human action linked with forgiveness. It was not a mechanism with any internal efficacy. Tanner is right: the blood of bulls and goats does not atone for sin apart from God's saying so.[63] As Herman Bavinck reminds us, "The sacrificial cult of the Old Testament was incomplete. The priests themselves were sinners. The blood of bulls and goats could not take away sins. The sacrifices had to be endlessly repeated. Everything indicated that the ceremonial dispensation of the Old Testament merely had passing, symbolic, and typological significance."[64]

But Tanner fails to note that Hebrews and Romans both point to a greater sacrifice that is an intrinsically efficacious mechanism for atonement. The blood of a pure, living human is presented to God on our behalf. Tanner goes still further and argues that God's forgiveness is a statement of fiat rather than a consequence of Christ's passion.

62. Tanner, *Jesus, Humanity, and the Trinity*, 29–30. Cf. Kathryn Tanner, *Christ the Key*, Current Issues in Theology (Cambridge: Cambridge University Press, 2010), 247–73. For a helpful response to this type of objection to the theology of sacrifice (though not specifically to Tanner's project), see Robert Sherman, *King, Priest, and Prophet: A Trinitarian Theology of Atonement*, Theology for the Twenty-First Century (London: T&T Clark, 2004), 194–210. For explicit rebuttal of Tanner's claims (including her more recent arguments in *Christ the Key*), see Oliver Crisp, *Revisioning Christology: Theology in the Reformed Tradition* (Farnham: Ashgate, 2011), 129–31.

63. Augustine, *City of God*, 377–79 (10.5). Augustine observes that the psalmist "says that God does not want sacrifice, and how in the same place, he shows that God does desire sacrifice. God does not want the sacrifice of a slaughtered animal, but he desires the sacrifice of a broken heart" (377–78). But Augustine does immediately pivot to affirm the material sacrifice as a symbol of the spiritual sacrifice. His nuance is not Tanner's neglect.

64. Herman Bavinck, *Reformed Dogmatics*, vol. 3, *Sin and Salvation in Christ*, ed. John Bolt, trans. John Vriend (Grand Rapids: Baker Academic, 2006), 335.

Bruce Marshall points to the weakness in Tanner's objection, however, when he addresses the question of debt and repayment. "If God had remitted our sins by sheer forgiveness—sent them away or simply declared them nonexistent—then our sins indeed would be gone, and we no longer would be sinners. We would, however, be mere spectators to our own salvation: observers who simply noted this fact about ourselves, without any involvement of our hearts and wills. By treating our sins as a debt for which he will accept payment, God gives humanity a genuine share in its own salvation."[65] Marshall addresses the metaphor of debt and repayment (from the economic sphere) rather than impurity and purity (from the cultic sphere), but the fundamental judgment remains the same. God really does require human faithfulness to enjoy his presence; humans really have been unfaithful (Rom. 1:18–3:20); therefore, God in Christ renders genuine human faithfulness on our behalf. The gospel is not the story of God's faithfulness simply absorbing human unfaithfulness; rather, by the work of Christ and his Spirit, it speaks of "the righteousness of God [which] is revealed from faith for faith" (Rom. 1:17).[66] We are called to trust in God's faithful fulfillment of his righteousness. Romans 1:18–3:20 provides the backdrop against which this statement can be asserted; Romans 3:21–26 provides Paul's resolution, wherein God is shown to be both "just and the justifier of the one who has faith in Jesus" (v. 26). The grace of

65. Bruce D. Marshall, "Treasures in Heaven," *First Things* 199 (2010): 26. Admittedly, Marshall intends to take the matter of satisfying God in a direction that involves not only forensic elements but also a participationist or transformationist basis for them (in the sacramental and penitential direction as well as, specifically, the pathway of almsgiving). As will be noted in chapter five, while I certainly encourage charitable giving and moral transformation, there are severe problems with premising justification upon such participatory or transformative realities.

66. Contrary to the claims of many (esp. Richard Hays, "Apocalyptic Hermeneutics: Habakkuk Proclaims the 'Righteous One,'" in *The Conversion of the Imagination: Paul as Interpreter of Israel's Scripture* [Grand Rapids: Eerdmans, 2005], 119–42; and Douglas Campbell, *Deliverance of God*, 613–16), Hab. 2:4 is not referring to Christ specifically but to those who trust in God (though, of course, Christ was one of those who did trust in God [see my argument in *The Christ's Faith: A Dogmatic Account*, T&T Clark Studies in Systematic Theology 2 (London: T&T Clark, 2009)]; the exegesis of Heb. 10:37–39 ought to inform debates among Pauline scholars. Campbell acknowledges this methodological point, though he then oddly suggests that Heb. 10:37–39 may be speaking messianically (*Deliverance of God*, 614). Hays offers a more sober assessment: "Though the author of Hebrews does not think of Jesus as 'the Righteous One,' he could hardly think of a 'righteous one' without thinking of Jesus" ("Apocalyptic Hermeneutics," 134). Even Hays focuses too narrowly on Christ here, for while Heb. 11–12 portrays him as the "perfector of faith," he is not the only one in whom faith is materially present (which seems to be the implication of Hays's saying of Christ: "he is the prototype who provides its material content"). Christ is the ultimate and only perfect faithful one, but Hebrews portrays him among a great "cloud of witnesses" (Heb. 12:1). For helpful analysis of Hab. 2:4 in Paul, see Francis Watson, *Paul and the Hermeneutics of Faith* (London: T&T Clark, 2004), 43–77, where he shows that there is no evidence of a prior messianic reading of Hab. 2:4 and no compelling reason intrinsic to Rom. 1 to take it in that direction.

God that justifies really is "gift," yet this gift comes at a cost: "through the redemption that is in Christ Jesus" (v. 24).[67] The passion of the Christ "was to show God's righteousness, because in his divine forbearance he had passed over former sins" (v. 25). Indeed, this verse seems to give a direct response to the position of Tanner: forgiveness on the cheap raises questions about God's justice, and God's liberality in forgiving men and women of questionable morals throughout the Old Testament era does in fact raise such suspicions. But the work of the Son shows God to be not only gracious ("the justifier") but also holy ("just").

Here propitiation and redemption are identified with justification. In other words, the idiom of sacrifice is relocated to a new conceptual realm: the courtroom.[68] We might debate why Paul makes such a metaphorical and theological maneuver, whether this is a translation meant to address Greek or Roman thought and culture in a new way, but we cannot dismiss the explicit link of idioms. The sacrificial offering of Jesus Christ makes our enjoyment of God's presence possible. Justification names that definitive restoration of peace between God and us so that we can enjoy his triune presence. As Paul says in chapter 5, "Therefore, since we have been justified by faith, we have peace with God through our Lord Jesus Christ" (v. 1).

It is worthwhile at this point to mention another essay by Bruce Marshall, "*Beatus vir*: Aquinas, Romans 4, and the Role of 'Reckoning' in Justification." Whereas I disputed his historical argument in my comments about his essay on Luther, suggesting that he picked certain elements out of Luther's corpus without attending to their wider theological architecture, this essay on Thomas Aquinas's doctrine of justification is compelling historically. Yet it raises a problematic theological point of which Romans makes us cognizant—namely, the relationship between justification and participation.[69]

---

67. In his account of communion with the triune God, John Owen will use the phrase "purchased grace" to highlight this mystery—a debt must be paid, though it is graciously paid by the one who was owed that debt in his incarnation (see Kelly M. Kapic, *Communion with the Triune God: The Divine and the Human in the Theology of John Owen* [Grand Rapids: Baker Academic, 2007], 186–87). See also Bavinck, *Reformed Dogmatics*, 3:369–71.

68. Note that the courtroom setting has been predominant since at least Rom. 3:5. My thanks to Jonathan Linebaugh for this observation.

69. Bruce D. Marshall, "*Beatus vir*: Aquinas, Romans 4, and the Role of 'Reckoning' in Justification," in *Reading Romans with St. Thomas Aquinas*, ed. Matthew Levering and Michael Dauphinais (Washington, DC: Catholic University of America Press, 2012), 216–37. More helpful theologically is the essay by Michael Root, "Aquinas, Merit, and Reformation Theology after the *Joint Declaration on the Doctrine of Justification*," *Modern Theology* 20, no. 1 (2004): 5–22. Root shows that Thomas's account is meant to explain how glory is a fitting conclusion to the very shape of created and graced human nature. Yet he notes that Protestant sensibilities may rightly lead one to adopt a solution very different from that of Thomas (see Otto Hermann

As in his consideration of Luther, Marshall brings up the relationship of the forensic and the transformative aspects of salvation. He notes that some would suggest that the two are opposed, but he believes they cannot be so opposed. In this essay, he seeks to show that Thomas's exegesis of Romans 4—in his commentary and, by extension, in the *Summa Theologiae*—shows that the forensic aspect of justification is premised upon the participatory shape of it, even though there is a distinctly forensic moment at its inception.

> Aquinas cannot, in any case, be summoned as chief witness for a transformational theology of justification, in opposition to a dispositional and forensic one. For him the two evidently are not opposites. While justification cannot, as a whole, be purely dispositional or forensic, there must be a purely forensic moment in justification. When God declines to reckon or impute our sins to us, he does more than forgo his undoubted right to punish us for our sin and corruption rather than change us for the better, important as that is. He overlooks what is odious to him, but which he cannot change, namely, our past sinful acts themselves.[70]

Marshall does highlight the truly forensic "reckoning" mentioned in Romans 4: God does not count our sins against us. But he also notes the reason for this "reckoning," according to Thomas Aquinas: "He forgives us, it appears, not in spite of what we have done, but on account of what he will make of us."[71] The forensic moment is premised upon the participatory or transformative promise.

We should back up and consider the doctrine of justification in the theology of Thomas Aquinas. Thomas addresses the doctrine of justification in the *prima secundae* of his *Summa Theologiae*. He notes the initial and the ongoing effects of grace. God's grace given to move the human is operative grace (*gratia operans*), whereas "that effect in which our mind is both a mover and is moved" is cooperative grace (*gratia cooperans*).[72] Crucially, Thomas goes a further step and emphasizes that even in cooperative grace, human activity,

---

Pesch, "Die Lehre vom 'Verdienst' als Problem für Theologie und Verkündigung," in *Dogmatik im Fragment: Gesammelte Studien* [Mainz: Matthias Grünewald Verlag, 1987], 414–16), while he also rightly insists that Thomas's question (i.e., the question of how the new creation can nonetheless maintain an ontological and narratival identity with the first creation, or, as Root puts it, "the question [that Aquinas poses for Lutherans] of how the human self is brought to eschatological glory as self, i.e., as a self-moving and responsible agent" ["Aquinas, Merit, and Reformation Theology," 18]) is not to be overlooked and must be answered in some fashion. For further assessment of the Thomist answer to this question, see Reinhard Hütter, *Dust Bound for Heaven: Explorations in the Theology of Thomas Aquinas* (Grand Rapids: Eerdmans, 2012). In a future work on sanctification, I hope to address this question from not only a catholic but also a Reformed vantage point.

70. Marshall, *"Beatus vir,"* 237.

71. Ibid., 230–31.

72. Thomas Aquinas, *Summa Theologiae* 1a2ae.111.2, reply.

which genuinely does move, nonetheless is moved. "In this sense, that good movement of free choice itself . . . is the action of a free choice moved by God."[73] This is one example of Thomas's noncompetitive view of divine and human agency, wherein human movement ("free choice") and God's movement ("moved by God") do not negate each other, as if God had to stop acting as lord for us to move as servants.[74]

Thomas identifies five effects of grace in us: "firstly, the healing of the soul; secondly, willing the good; thirdly, the efficacious performance of the good willed; fourthly, perseverance in the good; fifthly, the attainment of glory."[75]

Grace brings growth, which then merits further grace and, eventually, "the attainment of glory." Initially, of course, the sinful human is not fit for glory. Eventually, the sanctified human is fit for glory. That movement from sinfulness to sanctification is moved by God. So Thomas says, "What is pleasing to us in someone else is presupposed to our love for him; but what is pleasing to God in man is caused by the divine love."[76] In this life, the soul participates imperfectly in the divine nature; thus, the soul is not immediately perfected; thus also, the soul does exceed its own natural capacity, for even imperfect participation in grace is higher than strictly natural existence for the human soul.[77]

Thomas seeks to unpack the significance of several New Testament texts. He regularly points to Paul's words to Timothy: "Henceforth there is laid up for me the crown of righteousness, which the Lord, the righteous judge, will award to me on that Day, and not only to me but also to all who have loved his appearing" (2 Tim. 4:8).[78] The promise of a forthcoming reward for righteousness prompts him to articulate a doctrine of "merit." To express that notion of merit, he turns to Aristotelian resources, but it is important to see that Thomas's motivation stems from his biblical exegesis and only employs Aristotelian concepts to express them.[79] He interprets justification and final judgment as of one piece: Christ's forgiveness and the merit accrued by our conformity to God's law factor into this divine judgment on our behalf.[80] Again, he follows the later Augustine in arguing that even this "merit" is God

73. Ibid., 1a2ae.112.2, reply (est actus liberi arbitrii moti a Deo).
74. See also ibid., 1a2ae.110.2, reply; 111.2, reply; 112.4, reply; 113.3, reply.
75. Ibid., 1a2ae.111.3, reply.
76. Ibid., 110.1, ad 1.
77. Ibid., 110.2, ad 2.
78. See ibid., 1a2ae.114.3, sed contra; Thomas Aquinas, Scriptum super Sententiis, vol. 2, 27.1.3, sed contra 1. Thomas also addresses the idea of merit to express promised rewards in his comments on Rom. 2 and Phil. 2:6–11.
79. See Joseph P. Wawrykow, God's Grace and Human Action: "Merit" in the Theology of Thomas Aquinas (Notre Dame: University of Notre Dame Press, 1995).
80. Karlfried Froehlich, "Justification Language and Grace: The Charge of Pelagianism in the Middle Ages," in Probing the Reformed Tradition: Historical Studies in Honor of Edward A.

crowning his own gifts: human conformity to God's law is always due to the movement of God's transforming grace.

What do we make of Thomas's doctrine of justification? It is premised upon, and not only purposed toward, participation in God. It is of course purposed toward participation in God, for the greatest end of humanity is the vision of God and the enjoyment of his presence. But it is also premised upon participation in God, wherein that sight of God's face transforms Christians and makes them fit for eternal life. Thus, Thomas interprets Romans 8:1 ("there is therefore now no condemnation for those who are in Christ Jesus") as a special revelation to Paul that could not be embraced by all Christians.[81]

But Romans suggests that participation, enjoyment of the holy of holies, is premised upon justification; justification cannot be premised upon the very participation that it makes not only possible but also actual in Christ Jesus. "Therefore, since we have been justified by faith, we have peace with God through our Lord Jesus Christ. Through him we have also obtained access by faith into this grace in which we stand, and we rejoice in hope of the glory of God" (Rom. 5:1–2). Christ brings peace with God and, therefore, the gracious presence of God now and the "hope of the glory of God" later.

As we survey the history of doctrine, we can see that the early church focused on the sacrificial imagery in her liturgy and her preaching. The practice of the Eucharist demanded sacrificial exposition: remember the Passover background to that great declaration, "let us keep the feast." The practice of confessing sin and receiving absolution called for a sacrificial basis, wherein such pardon could be offered legitimately as well as liberally.

Eventually, though, questions would arise about the precise nature of our assurance and, underneath that assurance, the specific shape of Christ's sacrifice. The apostle Paul had offered reflections along these lines, even if they were not a regular focus of the patristic writers. When he dealt with them, he plunged through the waters of baptism and then left the inner sanctum of the temple and entered the courtroom. He employed the idiom of justification to address the ability of humans to stand before God's presence in a state of blessing rather than condemnation. We saw this link drawn between sacrifice and justification in Romans 3, making the point that Jesus Christ is our life before God and, therefore, all our hope is in him.

We might add that Paul is not alone in reflecting on the basis of Christian assurance in the shape of Christ's sacrifice. The author of the Epistle to the

---

*Dowey*, ed. Elsie A. McKee and Brian G. Armstrong (Louisville: Westminster John Knox, 1989), 36; Root, "Aquinas, Merit, and Reformation Theology," 13.

81. See Charles Raith II, "Aquinas and Calvin on Romans: Theological Exegesis and Ecumenical Theology," (PhD diss., Ave Maria University, 2010), chap. 7.

Hebrews addresses just these questions. While he does not employ the idiom of justification in so doing, he nonetheless addresses the doctrine of justification in ways parallel to Paul's teaching.

A methodological point deserves highlighting.[82] The term "justification" is used differently in the realms of biblical and dogmatic theology. In the biblical writings, it specifically addresses the adjudication of our standing before God in terms of the courtroom metaphor. It is irreducibly forensic. In dogmatic literature, however, justification has ranged more widely to address not only the courtroom metaphor but any metaphor that speaks into the matter of our standing before God, whether in the temple, the marketplace, the family, or, yes, the courtroom.

Grasping the distinction in terms can be helped, I think, by looking to an argument propounded by David Yeago. In his plea for theological (and not reductively historical-critical) exegesis, Yeago argues that there is a crucial distinction between judgments and concepts.[83] Judgments are the material claims made by any given communicator, while concepts are the particular and contingent forms used to express that judgment. Importantly, judgments may be rendered by a variety of concepts, and concepts can be employed to express a number of judgments. In other words, categories and metaphors are tools. Once identified, we must still ask what theological point they are meant to render. Daniel Treier and I have applied Yeago's distinction to the doctrine of justification.

> The doctrine of justification may draw on many biblical uses of terminology insofar as they do not contradict its material import. The flip side of this claim . . . is that the presence of justification language within the biblical texts does not necessarily imply that each of these texts will bear directly upon the doctrine of justification. Equally important will be texts which bear on the doctrine without using any of the biblical terminology of justification (e.g., Eph. 2:7; 1 Cor. 15:44–45). In the process of adjudicating what texts impinge on what doctrines, the distinction between biblical and dogmatic discussion is hazy, precisely because the terminology of justification appears within both realms (unlike biblical terms like flood, womb, and tree, or theological terms like alterity, epistemology, and ontology). The doctrine of justification, precisely because this and similar terminology occurs plentifully within the Bible, requires careful analytical precision.[84]

82. Daniel Treier and I have argued this point at greater length in "Dogmatic Theology and Biblical Perspectives on Justification: A Reply to Leithart," *Westminster Theological Journal* 70, no. 1 (2008): 105–10.

83. David Yeago, "The New Testament and the Nicene Dogma: A Contribution to the Recovery of Theological Exegesis," *Pro Ecclesia* 3, no. 2 (1992): 152–64.

84. Allen and Treier, "Dogmatic Theology and Biblical Perspectives on Justification," 109.

A dogmatic account of justification, then, will draw on a variety of biblical concepts: salvation, ransom, redemption, sacrifice, and so on, as well as on the specific terminology of righteousness and justice. Furthermore, not every reference to righteousness or justice will fund our thinking on the doctrine of justification; some aspects may well speak into the realm of sanctification.

A parallel case can be found in the doctrine of sanctification. The term "sanctify" in the New Testament points to a definitive event of washing or cleansing that occurs all at once when one is made new in Christ.[85] Yet this need not force the term "sanctification" to refer only to immediate change experienced at conversion within the realm of dogmatics. And, as the history of doctrine shows, sanctification has referred typically to the ongoing process of transformation and conformity to the image of God in Christ. While there is a "definitive sanctification" that the New Testament uses the language of sanctification to describe, there is also a "progressive sanctification" that dogmatics uses the language of sanctification to attest. Confusion abounds only when one forgets the shift in discourse.[86] Many terms in the biblical writings can inform the dogmatic discussion of sanctification; at the same time, the biblical concept of being sanctified may well fund our thinking about justification better than it funds our thinking about sanctification within the realm of dogmatics. What we are teasing out here is an eschatological distinction between these two doctrines, and we might add a third as well: glorification. Biblical teaching on our new life in Christ that speaks in the past tense about what was given us once for all informs the doctrine of justification. Scriptural statements that address what is being given us presently in an ongoing manner speak into the doctrine of sanctification. Finally, the doctrine of glorification draws on texts that promise a final, definitive gift of life from God.

The Epistle to the Hebrews works explicitly with the conceptual world of the temple and the practice of sacrifice. In so doing, however, it makes claims about our standing before God in his sanctuary and as his children. It tackles the question of assurance more directly than any other biblical writing, linking God's definitive work in Christ with our enjoyment of his divine presence. Peter Martyr Vermigli argued against Pighius, a sixteenth-century contemporary and opponent of his, that Hebrews does address justification. "So then Pighius wrongly claims that in the letter to the Hebrews no mention is made of justification among the effects of faith. Although that word is not

85. David Peterson, *Possessed by God: A New Testament Theology of Sanctification and Holiness*, New Studies in Biblical Theology (Downers Grove, IL: InterVarsity, 1995).

86. See also D. A. Carson, "The Vindication of Imputation: On Fields of Discourse and Semantic Fields," in *Justification: What's at Stake in the Current Debates*, ed. Mark Husbands and Daniel Treier (Downers Grove, IL: InterVarsity, 2004), 46–78 (esp. 47–50).

found there, still it is necessarily and plainly derived from those things that are written there."[87] With Vermigli, we consider it in our study of justification and participation.

Hebrews describes the life of the incarnate Son. God has spoken in many and various ways, but now he has done so in a Son (Heb. 1:1–2). This Son assumed genuine human form. "Therefore he had to be made like his brothers in every respect, so that he might become a merciful and faithful high priest in the service of God, to make propitiation for the sins of the people" (2:17). Not only a sacrifice but also glory is given: "For it was fitting that he, for whom and by whom all things exist, should make the founder of their salvation perfect through suffering" (2:10). Athanasius highlights the double purpose of the incarnation: "The Word became flesh in order both to offer this sacrifice and that we, participating in His Spirit, might be deified."[88]

Hebrews fixes upon the death of Jesus. As it compares Jesus and the priests who came before, in the Old Testament era, it informs us that "the point in what we are saying is this: we have such a high priest, one who is seated at the right hand of the throne of the Majesty in heaven, a minister in the holy places" (Heb. 8:1–2). Like other priests, this one offers gifts and sacrifices. In this case, "he offered himself without blemish to God" (9:14; see also 8:3; 9:12–14). Indeed, we are told that this occurred once and for all. "When Christ had offered for all time a single sacrifice for sins, he sat down at the right hand of God. . . . For by a single offering he has perfected for all time those who are being sanctified" (10:12, 14).

Hebrews focuses more than any other text on the exalted life of Christ. David Moffitt has presented the shape of Hebrews' atonement theology in a fresh and compelling way. Whereas most have focused on the death of Christ as making sacrifice, Moffitt reminds us that the Yom Kippur ritual fixed on not only the death of the animal but also the offering of its blood upon the mercy seat.[89] Commentators have long noted parallels between this ritual and Hebrews, but Moffitt suggests that the second aspect—the sacrificial offering—has remained underdeveloped in exegesis of Hebrews. Here in Hebrews 10, it reminds us that Christ made not only a "single sacrifice" (v. 12) but also a "single offering" (v. 14). In so doing he has opened a "new and living way . . . through the curtain" (v. 20).

87. Peter Martyr Vermigli, *Predestination and Justification: Two Theological Loci*, trans. and ed. Frank A. James III, The Peter Martyr Library 8, Sixteenth Century Essays and Studies 68 (Kirksville, MO: Truman State University Press, 2003), 182–83.

88. Athanasius, *De decritus* 14, quoted in J. N. D. Kelly, *Early Christian Doctrines*, rev. ed. (Peabody, MA: Prince, 2004), 277n2.

89. David M. Moffitt, *Atonement and the Logic of Resurrection in the Epistle to the Hebrews*, Supplements to Novum Testamentum 141 (Leiden: Brill, 2011), 256–77.

In all these ways, the Epistle to the Hebrews sketches the shape of Christ's sacrificial offering. In his incarnate life, his substitutionary death, and his atoning offering before God—upon the *hilasterion*—he offers himself not only as the great high priest but also as the final sacrifice. Thus, the people of God can have solid assurance that they, united to him by faith, will be kept by him. "Therefore, brothers, since we have confidence to enter the holy places by the blood of Jesus, by the new and living way that he opened for us through the curtain, that is, through his flesh, and since we have a great priest over the house of God, let us draw near with a true heart in full assurance of faith, with our hearts sprinkled clean from an evil conscience and our bodies washed with pure water. Let us hold fast the confession of our hope without wavering, for he who promised is faithful" (Heb. 10:19–23). Indeed, faith can be identified as "the assurance of things hoped for, the conviction of things not seen," precisely because this God who promises has already made *the* sacrifice (11:1). And Hebrews can conclude with that glorious benediction: "Now may the God of peace who brought again from the dead our Lord Jesus, the great shepherd of the sheep, by the blood of the eternal covenant, equip you with everything good that you may do his will, working in us that which is pleasing in his sight, through Jesus Christ, to whom be glory forever and ever. Amen" (13:20–21).

Hebrews promises participation in God—enjoyment of his presence in what is portrayed spatially as the holy of holies—but it is premised upon the sacrificial and priestly work of Jesus on the cross and before the mercy seat, his dying and then offering his very blood before the Father. But this is accomplished. Hebrews 9 expands on this idea that Christ has offered the greater sacrifice and been the greater high priest in two ways. First, he really deals with sin: "not by means of the blood of goats and calves but by means of his own blood, thus securing an eternal redemption" (v. 12). Redemption is offered, but (as Rom. 3 tells us) it must be secured at a cost, in this case, "by means of his own blood." Second, he really takes his people into the presence of God: "through the greater and more perfect tent (not made with hands, that is, not of this creation) he entered once for all into the holy places" (vv. 11–12). So we now have "confidence to enter the holy places by the blood of Jesus" (10:19).

As Hebrews unpacks this participation and its premise in chapters 8–10, it has offered an exegesis of the new covenant promised in Jeremiah 31:31–34.

> Behold, the days are coming, declares the Lord,
>> when I will establish a new covenant with the house of Israel
>> and with the house of Judah,

not like the covenant that I made with their fathers
  on the day when I took them by the hand to bring them out of the
    land of Egypt.
For they did not continue in my covenant,
  and so I showed no concern for them, declares the Lord.
For this is the covenant that I will make with the house of Israel
  after those days, declares the Lord:
I will put my laws into their minds,
  and write them on their hearts,
and I will be their God,
  and they shall be my people.
And they shall not teach, each one his neighbor
  and each one his brother, saying, "Know the Lord,"
for they shall all know me,
  from the least of them to the greatest.
For I will be merciful toward their iniquities,
  and I will remember their sins no more. (Heb. 8:8–12; cf. 10:16–17)

Notice that the final verse (Heb. 8:12, citing Jer. 31:34) offers the basis for the rest: God's pledge that "I will be merciful toward their iniquities, and I will remember their sins no more" undergirds his promise that "I will be their God, and they shall be my people," and there will thus be genuine obedience (with the law written on the hearts of God's people). Indeed, when these verses are cited again in Hebrews 10, this is drawn out more explicitly. After citing Jeremiah 31:34 in verse 17, the text of verse 18 then expounds: "Where there is forgiveness of these, there is no longer any offering for sin." A definitive dealing with sin occurs as pathway and ground of participatory and transformative enjoyment of the Trinity in the Spirit.

The precise idiom employed by the biblical authors is not the main point. Paul explicitly mentions justification, especially in Galatians and Romans (albeit drawing on sacrificial and redemption language in both Gal. 3 and Rom. 4), whereas Hebrews makes do with sacrificial imagery. Both authors are addressing the basis of human fellowship with God, however, and are seeking to explain the ground of Christian assurance. In the history of doctrine, this has led to the dogmatic conceptuality of justification in Christ as the baseline for enjoyment of God's presence or, as we have called it, participation in God by Christ.

Our focus on both the goal and the ground of the gospel can be illustrated by considering two famous questions from the most widely used Protestant catechisms. The Westminster Shorter Catechism asks in its first question, "What is the chief end of man?" and answers, "To glorify God and enjoy him forever." The Heidelberg Catechism begins elsewhere, asking, "What is your only comfort in life and in death?" and answers,

That I am not my own, but belong—body and soul, in life and in death—to my faithful Savior, Jesus Christ. He has fully paid for all my sins with his precious blood, and has set me free from the tyranny of the devil. He also watches over me in such a way that not a hair can fall from my head without the will of my Father in heaven; in fact, all things must work together for my salvation. Because I belong to him, Christ, by his Holy Spirit, assures me of eternal life and makes me wholeheartedly willing and ready from now on to live for him.[90]

Sometimes one will hear members of Reformed churches espouse preference for one question or the other. Comparison, however, is beside the point. Each question addresses a different point. The Westminster Shorter Catechism begins with a panoramic view, asking what the goal of the gospel is—namely, the glorification of God and the delight of the redeemed in him. The Heidelberg Catechism fixes more particularly upon the ground of the gospel, inquiring about comfort and assurance and locating it firmly in the work of "my faithful Savior, Jesus Christ."

Perhaps the relationship between justification and participation can best be viewed by way of a parallel: sacramental practice. In the Christian church, there are two sacraments that are practiced by all. As we have seen, the practice of the Lord's Supper symbolizes and truly communicates the very presence of God in Christ. It reminds us and reorients us, precisely because it makes real to us the very presence of God in Christ through these practices.[91]

Christian baptism initiates the Christian life in a public sense. While regeneration and faith may precede baptism, of course, one is not a visible and full communing member until one has been baptized in the name of the triune God. In baptism, one is no longer identified with Adam—sin, death, and devil—but with the new Adam and the people of God. Whether an adult convert or a child of believers, the baptized Christian is identified as God's own. The sacrament is not an inviolable pledge that they will manifest genuine faith and be eternally redeemed, yet it is a sure pledge that God has stamped them as his own and treats them as members of the people of God. Baptism marks that new identity in public.

90. Heidelberg Catechism 1, in *Reformed Confessions of the Sixteenth Century*, ed. Arthur C. Cochrane (Louisville: Westminster John Knox, 2003), 305.

91. It is far outside the bounds of this discussion to address the nature of the presence of Christ in the Eucharist. Suffice it to say that a full account would have to argue for the reality of his presence as well as the link between that presence and the practice (rather than directly to the elements as such).

The celebration of the Eucharist expresses ongoing communion with the triune God. This sacramental practice is to be maintained until the Lord returns, as an expression—a sign and seal—of his communion with us. His name is proclaimed, his work remembered, his presence invoked. In the eucharistic meal, the saints come to keep the feast and to feed on the gifts of God for the people of God. Only those in Jesus can enjoy the life with God, for he alone is the way, the truth, and the life. That sinners who so long satiated themselves on the wares of the sinful world now find satisfaction in Christ testifies to their new identity in him. Holy Communion sustains that new identity in public.

Christians affirm a necessary order, even as they also see a particular teleology. Baptism and Eucharist must come together, and this must happen just so. Robert Louis Wilken says of the early church, "The Eucharist was the central act of Christian worship, and its communal celebration each Sunday set the rhythm of Christian life. In the early church there was no Christianity without an altar. But there was also no Christianity without a bath, without passing through the waters of baptism."[92] Only the baptized eat, but the baptized are killed and raised anew, cleansed again precisely for that celebratory feast.[93] Similarly, we can say that we are made for life with God in this world, renewed and perfected by his glory. But we must also say that we will only be perfected for this renewed fellowship with God in a new heaven and new earth if, with Christ, we are killed and raised anew, inviolable and glorious.

Considering debates between Roman Catholic and Reformed theologians, George Hunsinger observes: "The statement that 'grace does not destroy but perfects nature' is at best a half-truth. From a Reformation theological standpoint, at least, grace perfects nature precisely by destroying it."[94] Hunsinger's

92. Robert Louis Wilken, *The Spirit of Early Christian Thought: Seeking the Face of God* (New Haven: Yale University Press, 2003), 36.

93. This classical position involves opposition to recent suggestions (especially in the Episcopal Church, where some parishes have opposed the teaching that "no unbaptized person shall be eligible to receive Holy Communion in this Church," according to the *Constitution and Canons of the Episcopal Church*, 1.17.7) to move toward so-called open Communion or an open table, where unbaptized persons are invited to partake of the Lord's Supper, with the idea that it might serve as a converting ordinance. For such argumentation, see Kathryn Tanner, "In Praise of Open Communion: A Rejoinder to James Farwell," *Anglican Theological Review* 86, no. 3 (2004): 473–85; and Stephen Edmondson, "Opening the Table: The Body of Christ and God's Prodigal Grace," *Anglican Theological Review* 91, no. 2 (2009): 213–34. James Farwell has offered replies to the open table movement in the Episcopal Church, including "Baptism, Eucharist, and the Hospitality of Jesus: On the Practice of 'Open Communion,'" *Anglican Theological Review* 86, no. 2 (2004): 215–38; and "A Brief Reflection on Kathryn Tanner's Response to 'Baptism, Eucharist, and the Hospitality of Jesus,'" *Anglican Theological Review* 87, no. 2 (2005): 303–10.

94. George Hunsinger, "Baptized into Christ's Death: Karl Barth and the Future of Roman Catholic Theology," in *Disruptive Grace: Studies in the Theology of Karl Barth* (Grand Rapids: Eerdmans, 2000), 269–70.

statement reminds us of two important questions for theological work. First, what is the end of the gospel? (What does it work? What is its result?) Second, what is the manner of the gospel? (How does it work? What is its means of getting to its result?) Hunsinger reminds us that while the gospel results in nothing other than nature perfected, it weaves its way to that end precisely through the course of destroying nature. We are called to eat with God, but we must be cleansed in Christ if we are to keep the feast.

The sacramental vision proves illustrative. In ancient days catechumens would be baptized on the eve of Easter in a vigil. By identifying with the body of Christ in that time—the span of his death and the shock of his resurrection—they were then readied for participation in the celebration of the risen Lord's Communion on Easter morning. The journey is necessary, and it must be wholly in Christ. The feast is the goal, and it too finds its focus solely in the risen Lord.

## Reading Aids: Understanding Adoption and Marriage in the Bible

Dogmatic theology is meant to flow from and to serve biblical exegesis. Doctrinal concepts ought to help the theologian affirm the full breadth, the emphases, and the coherence of the biblical material, or else these concepts are simply a distraction from the subject matter and the revelatory substance of the Christian faith. Our dogmatic reflection on the relationship of justification and participation as ground and goal of the gospel can end nowhere more fitting than by turning to its function in helping exegesis along in a more faithful manner.

God's gospel is often portrayed as the adoption of orphans into the divine family. What is Christ's by nature—genuine sonship—becomes ours by grace. The life of Israel with God is regularly described in adoptive terminology, and the New Testament does not hesitate to extend that imagery to describe all believers, whether Jew or Greek. At other times the gospel is portrayed as the marriage of God and his people, Christ and his church. The Song of Songs celebrates this truth most gloriously, though it is surely not alone in trumpeting the marriage supper of the Lamb.[95]

In both cases, the dogmatic schematic of justification and participation helps us to go back and read the texts better. It provides useful second-order categories for understanding the first-order language of the biblical texts

95. According to the Jewish theologian Michael Wyschogrod, "In speaking of God's love for Israel, one finds oneself alternating between the language of man-woman love and parent-child love" (*The Body of Faith: God in the People Israel* [New York: Rowman & Littlefield, 1983], 12).

themselves. The marriage precedes the married life, while the adoptive declaration founded the familial ties. But the marriage is for the sake of a life together, and the adoption proceedings aim solely at genuine commitment to daily household existence. It would be foolish to suggest that life together makes one married or that household proximity equates with adoption per se. Such relational closeness can mimic these states, but apart from a genuine declaration of marriage or adoption, one is always in a tenuous state.

# PART 2

# CHRIST FOR US

# 3

# "From the Time He Took On the Form of a Servant"

## *The Christ's Pilgrimage of Faith*

The gospel recounts the gracious history of God's work on behalf of his people, of his bringing them into loving fellowship with himself by redeeming them from sin and death. As such, the gospel centers on the course of Jesus's human history. "He is before all things, and in him all things hold together. . . . For in him all the fullness of God was pleased to dwell, and through him to reconcile to himself all things" (Col. 1:17, 19–20). This history is recounted in the creeds and confessions of the church, and it spans the full course of his human journey: conception and birth, life and ministry, suffering and death, resurrection and ascent. "From the time he took on the form of a servant," Calvin says, "he began to pay the price of liberation in order to redeem us."[1] An orderly theology of the gospel, then, must take into account the life and faith of the incarnate Son, or else it risks narrowing and throwing off balance the salvation wrought by the Messiah. Dogmatic theology attempts to reflect synthetically on the full breadth of the gospel revelation,

1. John Calvin, *Institutes of the Christian Religion*, ed. John T. McNeill, trans. Ford Lewis Battles, Library of Christian Classics (Philadelphia: Westminster, 1960), 2.16.5.

taking in the "multifaceted 'sum' of the gospel."[2] "The church has a mission: to see to the speaking of the gospel, whether to the world as message of salvation or to God as appeal and praise. Theology is the reflection internal to the church's labor on this assignment."[3] Along the way it reflects on issues of coherence and implication. In all things, it seeks "to comprehend with all the saints what is the breadth and length and height and depth" of the love of God in Christ (Eph. 3:18).

This chapter reflects on one moment in that story—the earthly journey of Jesus as a pilgrimage of faith—as a constituent aspect of the gospel. Note that this moment has been identified as an aspect rather than a part of the gospel.[4] As it will be explicated, the earthly fidelity of Jesus is a distributed doctrine inasmuch as it manifests itself in every part of his earthly sojourn: the willingness of the eternal Son to assume human nature, the virgin birth, the patient apprenticeship of a Son being brought to perfection, the ministry, and, finally, the passion and bruising at the behest of his neighbors. Faithful in eternity, this one proved faithful to the end.

Dogmatics listens to the Word of God. It is a positive and not a *poietic* science; it does not make but receives its object from outside itself. Thus the exegetical stance of dogmatics permeates its method and its style. This chapter is prompted to further dogmatic analysis by discussions arising among interpreters of some key biblical passages. In particular, a recent debate within the realm of Pauline studies provides the prompt for our analysis. In the past three decades, scholars have argued at great length about the meaning of the recurring phrase *pistis Christou* ("the faith of Christ"). The phrase occurs in some crucial contexts regarding salvation and the gospel (Rom. 3:22, 26; Gal. 2:16 [twice], 20; 3:22; Eph. 3:12; Phil. 3:9), and it can be rendered in at least two major ways: as a reference to Christian faith in Jesus ("faith in Christ") or as pointing to the faith exercised by Jesus himself ("the Christ's faith").[5] The discussion had been preceded by reflections offered decades earlier by some

2. J. Todd Billings, "John Calvin's Soteriology: On the Multifaceted 'Sum' of the Gospel," *International Journal of Systematic Theology* 11, no. 4 (2009): 428–47.

3. Robert W. Jenson, *Systematic Theology*, vol. 1, *The Triune God* (New York: Oxford University Press, 1997), 11.

4. Karl Barth helps process the distinction between "part" and "aspect," in terms of the work of Christ, in *Church Dogmatics*, vol. 4/2, *The Doctrine of Reconciliation*, ed. G. W. Bromiley and T. F. Torrance, trans. G. W. Bromiley (Edinburgh: T&T Clark, 1958), 503.

5. The debate fundamentally addresses the translation of the genitive "of Christ" in either an objective or a subjective manner. In Greek a genitive construction connotes some notion of logical relationship between the genitive term and a nominative term (in this case, between "Christ" and the nominal term "faith"). There are many such logical connections, though they can be abbreviated into two major clusters: faith directed toward Christ by us (with Christ as object of faith) or faith expressed by Christ (with Christ as subject of faith).

notable figures, most especially by Karl Barth and Thomas Torrance. But it was Richard Hays's influential book *The Faith of Jesus Christ* that brought the debate to a wider audience in the early 1980s.[6] Hays argues forcefully for the subjective genitive construal of the phrase ("the Christ's faith") throughout Galatians, and he argues that the two translations actually represent two fundamentally different approaches to Paul's theology as a whole. He calls them the "christological approach" and the "anthropological approach."[7] I will address this distinction in the next chapter, where the relationship between the work of Christ and our faith is considered. In this chapter, I want to pull back and consider some more fundamental christological issues. Indeed, Hays charges that "the greatest weakness of the traditional post-Reformation understanding of 'faith' and 'justification' is, as Gerhard Ebeling rightly observed, that it offers no coherent account of the relation between the doctrine of justification and Christology."[8] The person and work of the incarnate Son merits our attention as we consider his mediatorial work of justification.

A number of figures have opposed the arguments of Hays and other advocates of the subjective renderings, not for exegetical reasons alone, but for directly theological reasons. In considering the proposals of Hays, for example, Douglas Moo observes that these scholars "must interpret Jesus more as the 'pattern' for our faith than as the object of our faith. . . . This interpretation not only misreads key parts of Paul's letters but places too much emphasis on Christ as example in the atonement."[9] Further, Moo suggests that some christological issues render the Christ's faith untenable: "It is necessary to introduce some very dubious theology in order to speak meaningfully about 'the faith exercised by Jesus Christ.'"[10] Christological and soteriological suspicion is evident here.

Morna Hooker has noted two major concerns mentioned time and again by those who express dissatisfaction with the subjective rendering.[11] First, there is a worry that this rendering makes little sense within the christological categories afforded by the creedal terminology of Nicaea and Chalcedon. In

6. Richard B. Hays, *The Faith of Jesus Christ: The Narrative Substructure of Galatians 3:1–4:11*, 2nd ed., Biblical Resource Series (Grand Rapids: Eerdmans, 2001).

7. Richard Hays, "ΠΙΣΤΙΣ and Pauline Christology: What Is at Stake?," in *Pauline Theology*, vol. 4, *Looking Back, Pressing On*, ed. David Hay and Elizabeth Johnson, Society of Biblical Literature Supplement Series 4 (Atlanta: Scholars Press, 1997), 35–60; cf. Hays, *Faith of Jesus Christ*, 293.

8. Hays, *Faith of Jesus Christ*, 203 (see also his prefatory material on p. lii).

9. Douglas J. Moo, *The Epistle to the Romans*, New International Commentary on the New Testament (Grand Rapids: Eerdmans, 1996), 225n29.

10. Ibid., 225.

11. Morna D. Hooker, "ΠΙΣΤΙΣ ΧΡΙΣΤΟΥ," *New Testament Studies* 35, no. 3 (1989): 322–23.

other words, some suggest that it is incoherent for the incarnate Son to express faith.[12] Second, others focus on a soteriological, as opposed to a metaphysical or christological, concern—namely, the possibility that the subjective rendering runs against the grain of a classic Protestant reading of Pauline texts like Galatians 2–3, Philippians 3, and Romans 1–5. Here the bother is fixed upon the seeming realignment away from Christian faith and toward the Christ's own faith; dangers of legalism or nominalism might well loom large if the call for faith and the call for faith alone are minimized in any way, or it may even be the case that Jesus becomes more an example of faith than a substitute for sin. In any event, the exegetical possibility of this Pauline phrase referring to faith exercised by Jesus is viewed by many—for various reasons—as an interpretive nonstarter.

This chapter addresses this debate by relocating it. Grammarians and exegetes have battered each other for well over two decades with little sign of progress. As Hooker notes, some underlying doctrinal concerns seem to shape the exegetical flexibility of many involved, whether rightly or wrongly.

I have elsewhere addressed this issue in book-length form in a study titled *The Christ's Faith: A Dogmatic Account*.[13] I maintain the argument of that volume here and in the next chapter, but I also want to extend it somewhat. That book focuses on the recent exegetical debates and seeks to provide two doctrinal suggestions: that the Christ's faith is coherent within a Christology in the Nicene and Chalcedonian tradition and that the Christ's faith is necessary for those espousing a Protestant soteriology, in particular for those who affirm the hallmark of Lutheran and Reformed soteriology—the notion of justification by faith alone by means of double imputation. As reviewers have noted, that book shows that the Christ's faith is a coherent and necessary aspect of the gospel. I stand by those christological and soteriological arguments and in this chapter will also consider the two arguments of coherence and necessity. In doing so, however, this chapter will begin earlier by taking them in reverse order and by arguing for the necessity of the Christ's faith not only as a constituent element of the work of Christ but also as a manifestation of the eternal relationship between the Father, Son, and Holy Spirit. In other words, I will root my soteriology in Christology and will show that the

12. Thomas Aquinas, *Summa Theologiae* 3a.7.3; cf. Thomas Aquinas, *Commentary on the Epistle to the Hebrews*, trans. Chrysostom Baer (South Bend, IN: St. Augustine's, 2006), chap. 2, lecture 3, 66, where Thomas affirms the need for trust (though not faith) in Christ.

13. R. Michael Allen, *The Christ's Faith: A Dogmatic Account*, T&T Clark Studies in Systematic Theology 2 (London: T&T Clark, 2009). The closest parallel is David L. Stubbs, "The Shape of Soteriology and the *pistis Christou* Debate," *Scottish Journal of Theology* 61, no. 2 (2008): 137–57, although there are some serious differences exegetically, historically, and dogmatically between his approach and mine.

christological account flows forth from the eternal relations of the Trinity. The chapter will conclude by considering two implications for contemporary theology and exegesis.

The chapter will unpack the thesis that *in the eternal life of the perfect God, the divine Son pleases the Father in the Spirit and, therefore, the divine Son trusts the Father by the Spirit's power during his earthly pilgrimage, constituting himself perfect and pleasing to his heavenly Father.*

## Obedience Is Part of His Nature

Soteriology follows from the doctrine of God. The gospel itself is shaped by the God of the gospel, for it is the good pleasure of his eternal will and the manifestation of his faithful commitment to do his people good. Indeed, it is crucial to maintain vigilantly the two topics in dogmatics: God and the works of God. Both considerations follow biblical imperatives. Creatures are to profess the glory of their creator and savior: "Hear, O Israel: The LORD our God, the LORD is one" (Deut. 6:4). Further, his covenant partners are to dwell upon his works: "Come and see what God has done: he is awesome in his deeds toward the children of man" (Ps. 66:5). Such dwelling turns to declaration as a key component of grateful receptivity: "I will give thanks to the LORD with my whole heart; I will recount all your wonderful deeds" (Ps. 9:1).

Much contemporary theology moves briskly past any reflection on the eternal depth of salvation, fixing its sights much more emphatically on the earthly career of Jesus, the constitutive practices of the church, or the political repercussions of the kingdom of God's inception. Indeed, in various ways, the immanent and the historical dominate the theological approach of much Protestant and Roman Catholic soteriology. There is a sound impulse present here: the gospel does climax a long history of promise and fulfillment, the church does attain a real visibility in its hearing and feasting upon the Word, the reconciliation wrought by Christ will unsettle the foundations of bourgeois communities. Yet the very force and faithfulness of such movements—the source of their generating power—is derived not from their empirical specification or their pragmatic technique but from their roots in the perfect life of the eternally triune God. Because God really is the God of the gospel—now and throughout the ages—the earthly career of Jesus can be described as the doing of God's will, and the cross can be the predetermined purpose of God: we do not speak of Pilate's determination when with the prophet we confess that "it was the will of the LORD to crush him" (Isa. 53:10).

In reflecting upon the necessity of the Christ's faith, then, we begin with the doctrine of the Trinity, because all Christian theology begins with the doctrine of God himself. Classic Protestant divinity, like medieval theology before it, honored this principle: first God, then the works of God by extension (*sub specie divinitatis*).[14] We will reflect upon the triune fellowship, of which the external works of the triune God are but a manifestation. We will then consider the wider economy of God's works, noting the way that the faith of the incarnate Son during his earthly pilgrimage is "fitting" given the wider canonical and creedal structure of the gospel. As noted above, we affirm that *in the eternal life of the perfect God, the divine Son pleases the Father in the Spirit and, therefore, the divine Son trusts the Father by the Spirit's power during his earthly pilgrimage.*

First, *in the eternal life of the perfect God, the divine Son pleases the Father in the Spirit.* The triune life is ordered such that equality does not require sameness. This formal statement can be specified in material fashion by noting that there are true personal distinctions between the Father, the Son, and the Spirit. The differences are not merely varieties of capacity or of interest; they are lived differences. If God is pure act—ever and always in motion (whether internally or also externally)—then personal distinctions play out in personal interrelations.[15] Speaking of the faith of the incarnate Son brings us into the heart of the mystery of the Trinity, the wellspring of all Christian doctrine and the center of the gospel *kerygma*.

The baptism of Jesus manifests the eternal relations of the Trinity in their unified yet diverse personal forms: "And when Jesus was baptized, immediately he went up from the water, and behold, the heavens were opened to him, and he saw the Spirit of God descending like a dove and coming to rest on him; and behold, a voice from heaven said, 'This is my beloved Son, with whom I am well pleased'" (Matt. 3:16–17). The Father speaks. The Son goes into and out of the water. The Spirit descends upon and anoints the Son at the Father's behest. The entire event brings about one action: the public anointing and announcement of the Son in whom the Father is well pleased and upon whom the Spirit remains. The trinitarian principle that the external works of the Trinity are undivided

---

14. See, e.g., Thomas Aquinas, *Summa Theologiae*, vol. 1: *Christian Theology*, trans. Thomas Gilby (Oxford: Blackfriars, 1964), 1a.1.7, reply; Calvin, *Institutes* 1.1.1; as well as the structure of Karl Barth's *Church Dogmatics*. Early creedal summaries of the faith included "two elements" that "remain constant": the identity of God and the exposition of the works of God (in particular, the gospel narrative), according to Jaroslav Pelikan, *The Christian Tradition: A History of the Development of Doctrine*, vol. 1, *The Emergence of the Catholic Tradition (100–600)* (Chicago: University of Chicago Press, 1971), 117.

15. See Heinrich Bullinger, *Decades*, ed. Thomas Hardin (Cambridge: Cambridge University Press, 1851), 4.3.

is quite apparent here: Father, Son, and Spirit are all participating in this same action. At the same time, however, it is plain that each person has specific ways of involvement in that common action. As the Angelic Doctor says, "Just as the entire Trinity was operative in making both the dove and the human nature assumed by Christ, so likewise it was operative in forming the voice; yet by the voice the Father alone is manifested as speaking, just as the Son alone assumed human nature and the Holy Spirit alone is manifested in the dove."[16]

By extension, we might address the common question of whether any and every member of the Trinity could have become incarnate.[17] Every person in the Trinity is involved in the incarnation—the Father wills this plan, the Son assumes this flesh, the Spirit enables this conception and birth. And yet each person engages in this harmonious action in their own distinct manner. As Thomas says, "Assumption holds two notes, the act itself and its term. The act comes from the divine power, common to the three persons; but the term is a person. . . . Therefore, what belongs to the act of assuming is common to the three persons; what belongs to its meaning as a term belongs to one person in such a way that it does not belong to another."[18] Thomas does not go further to note that there is something character-specific to the Son such that it will necessarily be the Son to be made flesh and not the Spirit or Father. In fact, Thomas rejects this statement outright, based on his concern to uphold the equal divine power of the three persons. Even though Thomas does affirm that "their personal properties are distinctive," he does not relate this to the kind of attributes that would lead one—free from outside coercion and free from any external necessity, yet from internal necessity and freely from one's own character—to become incarnate.[19] A full response and a thorough expansion of a christological approach to the divine perfections and, more specifically, to the personal properties of each triune person is beyond the scope of our study here; suffice it to say that Thomas needs a bit of Karl Barth to help in this regard.[20]

16. Thomas Aquinas, *Summa Theologiae* 3a.39.8, *ad* 2; cf. Augustine, *Quaestiones evangeliorum. Quaestiones XVI in Matthaeum*, ed. A. Mutzenbecher, Corpus Christianorum: Series Latina 44B (Turnhout: Brepols, 1980), 2, 6.

17. Thomas Aquinas, *Summa Theologiae* 3a.3.5, 3a.3.8.

18. Ibid., 3a.3.4, reply. Protestant theologians (e.g., Amandus Polanus, Herman Witsius) would maintain this distinction between the "inchoative" inception of the incarnation (common to the three persons as an *opus commune*) and then the "terminative" completion of the incarnation (specific to the Son as his *opus proprium*); see Richard A. Muller, *Post-Reformation Reformed Dogmatics*, vol. 4, *The Triunity of God* (Grand Rapids: Baker Academic, 2003), 272.

19. Thomas Aquinas, *Summa Theologiae* 3a.3.5, reply.

20. For some helpful thoughts along these lines, see the "post-Barthian Thomism" of Kevin J. Vanhoozer, *Remythologizing Theology: Divine Action, Passion, and Authorship*, Cambridge Studies in Christian Doctrine (Cambridge: Cambridge University Press, 2010), esp. pt. 2.

The baptism shows the manner in which triune action undergirds the whole incarnational economy. Indeed, it is paired with the transfiguration as a narrative occurrence that peels back the curtain, so that one can see a new layer of agency and metaphysical depth beyond the full recital of the gospel history (Matt. 17:1–8). In the transfiguration, the Son stands atop a mountain with his disciples, the Father declares his pleasure from the heavens, and the Spirit illumines forth the glory of the Lord. The name "Immanuel" is proclaimed audibly and visibly atop that edifice. Thomas argues that the glorious light represents the luminosity of the Son's divinity pouring through his temporarily porous flesh, even as he says that the "bright cloud . . . signifies the glory of the Holy Spirit or the power of the Father."[21] Even if we disagree with the particulars, based on our reading of the recalibration of the tabernacle tradition, we can concur with his broader judgment: "Just as at the time of his baptism, . . . the operation of the entire Trinity was manifested, because the Incarnate Son was present there, the Holy Spirit appeared in the form of a dove, and the Father proclaimed his presence there in a voice; so also at the time of the transfiguration, . . . the entire Trinity appears—the Father in the voice, the Son in the man, the Holy Spirit in the bright cloud."[22] Both baptism and transfiguration manifest the relations internal to the triune life: the Son delighting the Father by the Holy Spirit; in other words, the Son depending on the Father by the power of his Spirit. The *opera Dei ad extra* pour forth real light upon the *opera Dei ad intra*.

Yet the momentum of so much contemporary theology moves firmly against efforts to speak in this way. Few theologians spend serious time giving attention to the immanent life of God prior to the external works of the Trinity. We will consider two accounts that have gained a certain prestige in recent years: the trinitarian theology of the Lutheran Robert Jenson and the Presbyterian Bruce McCormack. Though working within an evangelical catholic and a Barthian context, respectively, they both propose a historicist manner of construing the divine identity. Both express great worry that any account of the immanent divine life—the works of God *ad intra*—will smuggle in alien theological presuppositions and give the store away to a natural theology undisciplined by theology's christological concentration. Jenson and McCormack construe the divine life as not merely manifested but also constituted by the events of the gospel story. The gospel presents the actuality of our being with God—in spite of hell and all else—even as, for historicists, it also presents the actuality of God's being with us and with himself. The gospel, then, is a recital of

---

21. Thomas Aquinas, *Summa Theologiae* 3a.45.3, *ad* 3.
22. Ibid., 3a.45.5, *ad* 2.

God's self-determination, nay, of the Trinity's self-constitution and eschato-logical actualization. This approach avoids deistic portraits of God not only by surveying the gospel story before considering the divine attributes and divine existence but also by constituting the divine attributes and existence upon that very gospel story.

In evangelical historicism, however, there is a fundamental loss of the eter-nal roots of the gospel and the free nature of God's kind determination to be involved in *this* way (as opposed to merely actions internal to the godhead) with *these* persons (as opposed to simply intratrinitarian relations). Indeed, without an operative account of divine perfection and aseity, God becomes a historical agent to be feared. Indeed, the remarkable presupposition of assur-ance is lost. Consider the conclusion of Romans 8, where the apostle declares, "If God is for us, who can be against us? He who did not spare his own Son but gave him up for us all, how will he not also with him graciously give us all things?" (vv. 31–32). The text here assumes that the same God who bruised his Son in the gospel account continues to minister grace to his people years later. The argument falls apart if the person of the Father is not perfect in and of himself. Indeed, this is why the argument so quickly turns to address-ing the obvious objection: it seems that God has turned against or failed to provide for his elect people, the children of Abraham (cf. Rom. 9–11). Paul qualifies but defends God's earlier determination, his present advocacy, and his future reliability. All Paul's reflections eventually circle around to praise, in which the apostle confesses, "For who has known the mind of the Lord, or who has been his counselor? Or who has given a gift to him that he might be repaid?" (Rom. 11:34–35). The Lord plans and prosecutes the economy out of self-sufficient perfection—life in himself—not out of weakness and a desire for self-fulfillment or divine maturation or even personal self-constitution. No, the economy manifests the eternal fullness of God's own triune being. Herman Bavinck reflects on this notion: "The covenant of grace revealed in time does not hang in air but rests on an eternal, unchanging foundation. It is firmly grounded in the counsel of the triune God and is the application and execution of it that infallibly follows."[23]

There is an evangelical impetus behind this historicism, and it should not go unnoticed. Jenson and McCormack respond to intellectual approaches that develop lengthy and detailed accounts of the inner life of God apart from revelation. Indeed, there is a sense in which they are furthering the antispecu-lative tendency seemingly advanced in key moments by Martin Luther and

23. Herman Bavinck, *Reformed Dogmatics*, vol. 3, *Sin and Salvation in Christ*, ed. John Bolt, trans. John Vriend (Grand Rapids: Baker Academic, 2006), 215.

Philipp Melanchthon, if not also by John Calvin himself.[24] No doubt Calvin is the most precise in his concern, hoping to avoid any utterance about God not traceable back to the apostolic witness formalized in Holy Scripture. Calvin's approach did not stem the tide of modern natural theology; while Jenson and McCormack are astute enough to avoid blasting the very development of scholastic terminology and concepts in the post-Reformation era, they do tend to make much of material errors that modify the course of Lutheran and Reformed theology in the seventeenth and eighteenth centuries. A "theology of glory" develops with little or no influence from the economy of the gospel. God becomes identified with philosophical tenets demonstrated by verbose and detailed a priori reasoning.[25]

So the historicist tendency rightly wishes to avoid this rabid speculation. As a corrective, it moves to identify theology and economy.[26] It focuses on the way in which Jesus Christ makes God the Trinity known (John 1:18)—this particular man is "full of grace and truth" (John 1:14). This focus on Christ as the epistemological revelation of the triune character has a long pedigree.

> Once God was incomprehensible and inaccessible, invisible and entirely unthinkable. But now he wanted to be seen, he wanted to be understood, he wanted to be known. How was this done, you ask? God lay in a manger and lay on the Virgin's breast. He preached on a mountain, prayed through the night, and hung on a cross. He lay pale in death, was free among the dead, and was master of hell. He rose on the third day, showed the apostles the signs of victory where nails once were, and ascended before their eyes to the inner recesses of heaven. . . . When I think on any of these things, I am thinking of God, and in all these things he is now my God.[27]

24. In addition to Luther's famous "Disputation against Scholastic Theology," see Martin Luther, *Lectures on Genesis, Chapters 1–5,* ed. Jaroslav Pelikan, trans. George Schick, Luther's Works 1 (St. Louis: Concordia, 1958), 11, 13–14 (1:2); and Philipp Melanchthon, "Loci Communes Theologici," in *Melanchthon and Bucer,* ed. Wilhelm Pauck, Library of Christian Classics (Louisville: Westminster John Knox, 1969), 20–22. On Calvin's antispeculative tendency, see David Steinmetz, "Calvin among the Thomists," in *Biblical Hermeneutics in Historical Perspective,* ed. M. S. Burrows and P. Rorem (Grand Rapids: Eerdmans, 1991), 198–214.

25. See the historical analysis offered by Michael J. Buckley, *At the Origins of Modern Atheism* (New Haven: Yale University Press, 1987); and Amos Funkenstein, *Theology and the Scientific Imagination: From the Middle Ages to the Seventeenth Century* (Princeton: Princeton University Press, 1989).

26. For astute analysis of the approach of modern trinitarian theology, see Matthew Levering, *Scripture and Metaphysics: Aquinas and the Renewal of Trinitarian Theology,* Challenges in Contemporary Theology (Oxford: Blackwell, 2003), esp. chap. 6, "Biblical Exegesis and Sapiential Naming of the Divine Persons."

27. Bernard of Clairvaux, *Sermo in nativitate Beatae Mariae: de Aquaducto,* ed. J. Leclerq and H. Rochais, S. Bernardi Opera 5 (Rome: Edition Cistercienses, 1968), 11.

The revelatory identification of theology and economy for Bernard becomes the ontological identification of theology and economy in Jenson and McCormack. In Jenson's case, this involves the claim that involvement in history, far from being a weakness, is actually a sign of divine strength. The persons of the Trinity are "*dramatis dei personae*, 'characters in the drama of God,'" and can be identified with his fellowship with creatures.[28] "Presumably God could have been himself on different terms, established in his identity without reference to us or the time he makes for us. . . . As it is, God's story is committed as a story with creatures. And so he too, as it is, can have no identity except as he meets the temporal end toward which creatures live."[29] The preexistence of the Son, then, can be identified only as a narrative existence in the form of Israel. The immanent life of the Son within the eternal Trinity has been entirely reduced to the economic foreshadowings of his earthly imprint.[30] In McCormack's argument, the very triunity of God is identified with his external works—he determines to be triune by willing to be with us and not apart from us in Jesus.[31] Both accounts regularly suggest that the classical divine attributes are in many if not all cases terribly misdirecting judgments about the nature of the gospel's God. McCormack has expressed his vote of approval for a "Reformed kenoticism" that pairs a strong Spirit-Christology with a thoroughgoing reconsideration of the divinity of the Son propelled by the historical travail of the gospel.[32]

The error of Charybdis is no less dangerous than the failure of Scylla. Speculation and historicism are two sides of the same coin, and this coin must be tossed aside. Theology really is manifest in the economy; theology really

28. Jenson, *Systematic Theology*, 1:59, 75.

29. Ibid., 1:65.

30. For analysis of Jenson's modification to the Son's preexistence, see Oliver D. Crisp, "The Pre-existence of Christ," in *God Incarnate: Explorations in Christology* (London: T&T Clark, 2009), 56–76; and Simon Gathercole, "Pre-existence and the Freedom of the Son in Creation and Redemption: An Exposition in Dialogue with Robert Jenson," *International Journal of Systematic Theology* 7, no. 1 (2005): 36–49. It should be noted that Jenson offers an equally radical reconfiguration of the postexistence of Jesus: "the church is the risen Christ's Ego" (*Systematic Theology*, vol. 2, *The Works of God* [New York: Oxford University Press, 1997], 215).

31. Bruce L. McCormack, "Election and the Trinity: Theses in Response to George Hunsinger," in *Trinity and Election in Contemporary Theology*, ed. Michael T. Dempsey (Grand Rapids: Eerdmans, 2011), 115–37. Cf. McCormack, "Divine Impassibility or Simply Divine Constancy? Implications of Karl Barth's Later Christology for Debates over Impassibility," in *Divine Impassibility and the Mystery of Human Suffering*, ed. James F. Keating and Thomas Joseph White (Grand Rapids: Eerdmans, 2009), 150–86, esp. 179.

32. Bruce L. McCormack, "'With Loud Cries and Tears': The Humanity of the Son in the Epistle to the Hebrews," in *The Epistle to the Hebrews and Christian Theology*, ed. Richard Bauckham (Grand Rapids: Eerdmans, 2009), 37–68; and "Karl Barth's Christology as a Resource for a Reformed Version of Kenoticism," *International Journal of Systematic Theology* 8, no. 3 (2006): 243–51.

does precede the economy. Thus, the historical shape of God's fellowship with creatures speaks not only of creaturely nature but also of the character of God. As that great nineteenth-century theologian Isaak Dorner said, "The economic Trinity . . . leads back to immanent distinctions in God himself, all the more so because in the world of revelation we have to do not merely with a teaching of truths, but with the true *being* of God in the world, with God's actions, indeed with his self-communication."[33] As I have argued elsewhere, the Christ's faith is the "economic echo of eternal filiation which marks the Son in relation to his Father."[34] So we must briefly consider the eternal relations that are echoed in this aspect of the economy.

"Obedience is part of his nature"—so argues Gregory of Nyssa, not about the divine nature, but about the personal nature and properties of the Son.[35] The Son freely wills to repose in his Father's decree. Polanus reflects:

> The Son, indeed, is incarnate because he wills voluntarily to be made our sponsor, voluntarily subjecting himself to the Father not according to nature, but according to the voluntary arrangement (*oeconomia*) or dispensation: a natural subjection is, surely, distinct from an economic or dispensatory subjection: he is made freely obedient to the Father, not according to the divine nature in itself (*in se*), but according to will: obedience, indeed, is not the natural act of a nature (*actus naturalis naturae*), but of the will or free accord of the person of Christ (*voluntarius personae Christi*).[36]

Here a divine distinguishes between that which is consequent upon the divine nature itself (*in se*) and that which depends fundamentally upon the will of a particular divine person. Obedience is a part of the Son's personal nature, not the common divine nature. To put it in other words, it is a personal property and not a collective property. The distinction is revealed throughout the economy, and it is highlighted by the discourse between Father and Son. The economy of the Son shows not only his praise and glory (as God in himself with the Father and Spirit) but also his trust and obedience (as the person ever flowing forth from the Father's life).

33. Isaak Dorner, *A System of Christian Doctrine*, trans. A. Cave (Edinburgh: T&T Clark, 1883), 2:370.

34. Allen, *Christ's Faith*, 180.

35. Gregory of Nyssa, "Against Eunomius," in *Nicene and Post-Nicene Fathers*, 2nd ser., vol. 5, ed. Philip Schaff and Henry Wace, trans. H. C. Ogle (Peabody, MA: Hendrickson, 1994), 122 (bk. 2, sec. 11). Cf. Barth, *Church Dogmatics*, vol. 4/1, *The Doctrine of Reconciliation*, ed. G. W. Bromiley and T. F. Torrance, trans. G. W. Bromiley (Edinburgh: T&T Clark, 1956), 177–80, 199–201; and Thomas Aquinas, *Summa Theologiae* 1a.39.1.

36. Polanus, *Syntagma theologiae christianae*, 6.13, quoted in Muller, *Post-Reformation Reformed Dogmatics*, 4:267.

T. F. Torrance has expressed this concern more recently: "What Jesus is toward us he is antecedently and eternally in himself, in God." Indeed, he expands upon the claim helpfully.

> Were that not so, the revelation we are given in Christ would not have eternal validity or ultimate reality. That is why the fourth Gospel begins with the wonderful prologue of the eternity of the Word in God, for it is from the eternal God that the Word proceeded, and all that follows in the Gospel—all that Jesus said and was in his dependence as the incarnate Son upon the Father—goes back to and is grounded in that eternal relation of Word to God within God. Similarly, the epistle to the Hebrews begins its exposition of the high priestly work of Christ by teaching that the Son came forth from the Godhead, the Son by whose word all things were created. It is that Son who came and manifested himself, and now in the incarnation stands forth as the divine servant Son to fulfill his work of atonement in entire solidarity with man, eternal Son of God though he was. But all that Jesus did has reality and validity just because it rests upon that eternal relation of the Son with the Father, and therefore reaches out through and beyond the span of years in his earthly ministry into God. Again, what Christ is in all his life and action, in his love and compassion, he is antecedently and eternally in himself as the eternal Son of the Father.[37]

The shape of the earthly economy is suspended from the divine determination of trinitarian life. The assurance enjoyed by those "in Christ" follows from the ontological link between theology and economy. As John Webster puts it, "Salvation is secure because the works of the redeemer and the sanctifier can be traced to the inner life of God, behind which there lies nothing."[38]

The economy is not vacated or vitiated. Indeed, history is exalted rather than expunged of meaning, inasmuch as history is located in the eternal will of God. Again Webster points to the biblical roots of this link, as well as its synthetic shape.

> The rescue of lost creatures is secured by the acts and sufferings in time of God's Son and servant, supremely in his passion. His being led away like a lamb to the slaughter, his being taken away by oppression and judgment, his grave made with the wicked—all this does not take place in some time other than that in which Adam's children live out their days under a curse, but precisely in their creaturely, bodily history. But what kind of creaturely, bodily history is this if it is indeed

---

37. T. F. Torrance, *Incarnation: The Person and Life of Christ*, ed. Robert T. Walker (Downers Grove, IL: InterVarsity, 2008), 176–77.

38. John Webster, "'It Was the Will of the Lord to Bruise Him': Soteriology and the Doctrine of God," in *God without Measure: Essays in Christian Doctrine* (London: T&T Clark, forthcoming).

for our salvation? It is history which "realizes" God's "eternal purpose" (Eph. 3:11), history which saves "not in virtue of our own works but in virtue of his own purpose and the grace which he gave us in Christ Jesus ages ago" (2 Tim. 1:9). It is history "suspended" from the divine purpose; and that purpose itself extends from the perfection of God's own life.[39]

He did make peace "by the blood of his cross" (Col. 1:20), employing the contingencies and social happenstances of the history of Adam's descendants to enact cosmic reconciliation. Yet that very cross held the "foundation of the world in the book of life of the Lamb who was slain" (Rev. 13:8).

Two terms have been employed to highlight the filial and dependent character of the Son over against the Father: the idea of procession and the concept of eternal generation. A host of other theological terms and images have been employed along these same lines—for example, the Nicene language of "God of God, light of light, true God of true God"—but we will focus only on these two concepts.

First, Western trinitarian theology has spoken of the procession of the Son from the Father. The basic methodological principle behind such reflection is that economic sending points to theological procession; the ontological principle runs in the opposite direction: the theological procession eventuates in the economic sending.[40]

The notion of procession is expanded, even if not entirely clarified, by the idea of eternal generation. The doctrine remains mysterious, inasmuch as it employs creaturely language of generation in a way that manifests a strong concern to distance it from everyday occurrence. In place of language of "making," the Son is "generated" or "begotten." Whereas most sons begin to exist at a certain point in time, this Son is generated eternally—that is, constantly—yesterday, today, and forever (Heb. 13:8).[41] These two modifications to regular language about fathers and sons point, no doubt, to the serious danger that the relationship of Father and Son might be misconstrued. "For all its unsuitability, for all the ineffability of its object, generation retains the personal character of the Father-Son relation, and thereby ensures that

39. Ibid.
40. Gilles Emery, *The Trinity: An Introduction to Catholic Doctrine on the Triune God*, trans. Matthew Levering, Thomistic Ressourcement 1 (Washington, DC: Catholic University of America Press, 2011), 142–43. For analysis of ways in which this classical tenet of Christian divinity relates to modern debates about the immanent and economic Trinity, see Bruce D. Marshall, "Trinity," in *Blackwell Companion to Modern Theology*, ed. Gareth Jones (Oxford: Blackwell, 2004), 183–203, esp. 193–97.
41. Language about generation (or, with respect to the Holy Spirit, spiration) is not meant to imply passivity on the part of the Son (see Thomas Aquinas, *Summa Theologiae* 1a.41.1, *ad* 3).

conceptual articulation of the faith echoes the scriptural economy of revelation in the evangelists."[42]

It has been suggested by some that eternal generation and eternal subordination are sub-Nicene conceptualities. The typical historical analysis along these lines highlights the term "subordinationist" in anti-Origenist theology and identifies any hint of eternal subordination with this Origenist error. But this is to miss the thrust of Athanasius's distinction between production and procession. The Son is not generated after some interval of solitary existence enjoyed only by the Father; no, the Son proceeds eternally and spontaneously from the Father.[43] Thus Karl Barth wonders, "Does subordination in God necessarily involve an inferiority and therefore a deprivation, a lack? Why not rather a particular being in the glory of the one equal Godhead. . . . Why should not our way of finding a lesser dignity and significance in what takes the second and subordinate place (the wife to her husband) need to be corrected in the light of the shared essence (*homoousios*) of the modes of divine being?"[44] It is to bring a priori judgments about natures and persons to the table of theological reflection if one judges such a scheme implausible simply on principle. But dogmatic theology will think in an a posteriori manner, following hard after the gospel with as much intellectual faithfulness as can be mustered. Metaphysical relations between persons and natures can only be offered after depicting or expositing the manner of triune interaction. The biblical materials force us to say that the three are equal, even as they also pressure us to speak of the three as distinct and, further, of the Son and the Spirit as being sent personally by the Father.[45] Anyone reading the patristic evidence will see that they sustain such concern to pattern metaphysical language—persons and nature—around the judgments of Scripture. Furthermore, it is obvious that virtually every character in the patristic debates employed language of "subordination" without thereby teaching what might be called "subordinationism" (of which Arianism would be the most infamous form). It is worth reflecting briefly on why this feature, so easily misleading

42. John Webster, "The Eternal Begetting of the Son," in *God without Measure*. On the "ineffability" of eternal generation, see Thomas Aquinas, *On Boethius' De Trinitate*, q. 2, a. 1, *ad* 4.

43. Athanasius, *Against the Arians*, in *Nicene and Post-Nicene Fathers*, 2nd ser., vol. 4, trans. John Henry Newman and A. Robertson (Peabody, MA: Hendrickson, 2004), 323–24 (disc. 1 sec. 29); Bullinger, *Decades* 4.3; Jerome Zanchi, *De tribus Elohim, aeterno Patre, Filio. Et Spiritu Sancto* (Neustadii Palatinorum, 1597), pt. 2, 5.6.8; Zacharius Ursinus, *Commentary on the Heidelberg Catechism*, trans. G. W. Williard (Phillipsburg, NJ: P&R, 1985), 138.

44. Barth, *Church Dogmatics*, 4/1, 202. Cf. William Perkins, *A Golden Chaine*, in *Workes of Mr. William Perkins* (Cambridge: John Legatt, 1612), 1:14 (sec. 5).

45. The Bible also impels us to speak of the Spirit being sent by the Son with the Father (again, this would be a single work jointly done by both Father and Son, sending forth the Spirit, each in their own way), but I do not have the time and space to address the *filioque* debate here.

in the face of the Arian controversy, continued to linger in patristic trinitarian theology.

The Son's filiation is not driven primarily by phenomenological analogy, that is, by some account of how sons or children relate to fathers or parents. The analogy is there, to be sure, or else the language would be entirely arbitrary. But the analogy does not drive the doctrinal analysis. Rather, exegesis of biblical texts forces us to say something about the Son's immanent receptivity on the Father by the Spirit. Our limited reflections along these lines are motivated by an intellectual concern to give an account not of what it means to be a juvenile but of what it means to listen to Jesus. He repeatedly states that he does the will of another—that he is sent.[46] Dogmatics is faithless if it fails to honor this biblical emphasis—more pointedly, this christological emphasis—regarding the proper way to understand the mission of the Son, that is, as one sent by the Father.

"For as the Father has life in himself, so he has granted the Son also to have life in himself" (John 5:26). Both Father and Son have life in and of themselves; they are equally divine, sharing the one divine essence and all its properties. But they are equally distinct, existing as particular persons with all their own properties. John 5:26 requires us to speak of each person in both ways. The Second Person of the Trinity has "life in himself" according to his divine nature, even while this life is "granted the Son," according to his personal properties, by his eternal Father. William Perkins says that he is "not Son in himself, but God in himself."[47] Thomas Aquinas observes that "since life pertains to the nature, if the Son has life in himself as does the Father, it is clear that he has in himself, by his very origin, a nature indivisible from and equal to that of the Father."[48] The Son is God, fully alive and entirely fulfilled. This is teased out most fully in Calvin's insistence that the Son is *autotheos*.[49] Yet the Son

---

46. John 3:34; 4:34; 5:23, 30, 36–38; 6:38–39, 44, 57; 7:16, 18, 28–29, 33; 8:16, 18, 26, 29, 42; 9:4; 10:36; 11:42; 12:44–45, 49; 13:16, 20; 14:24; 15:21; 16:5; 17:3, 8, 18, 21, 23, 25; 20:21.

47. William Perkins, *Exposition of the Creed* (London, 1616), 171 (rendering "*non autohuios tamen autotheos*").

48. Thomas Aquinas, *Commentary on the Gospel of John*, vol. 1, *Chapters 1–5*, trans. Fabian Larcher and James Weisheipl (Washington, DC: Catholic University of America Press, 2010), 288 (no. 783).

49. Note that Calvin affirms both the eternal generation of the Son and his being God in himself (*autotheos* and *a se*). He makes the distinction between language about the Son's personal properties and the Son's common divinity: "Therefore we say that deity in an absolute sense exists of itself; whence likewise we confess that the Son since he is God, exists of himself, but not in respect of his Person; indeed, since he is the Son, we say that he exists from the Father. Thus his essence is without beginning; while the beginning of his Person is God himself" (*Institutes* 1.13.25). A number of interpreters have suggested that the latter was proposed as an alternative to the former, but this fails to honor the breadth and context of Calvin's teaching on the

receives this "life in himself" from his Father, "for they are distinct, because the Father gives, and the Son receives . . . because in the Son there is nothing that exists prior to reception."[50] This didactic reflection given by Jesus is narratively bookended by events at the beginning and end of his life. He hands himself over to the Father's design in becoming incarnate, and he then delivers himself to the Father's will that he be crushed (Luke 22:42).

One final note on eternal generation: the eternality of the Son's procession or generation is not a statement about its antiquity. Rather, the Son's procession is consistent and ongoing; the Son receives from the Father his personal properties at every step of the journey. We may say that this procession of the Son is a continual reality that is personally constitutive (of Son qua Son) and essentially manifesting (of Son qua God); with Turretin, we distinguish as we say that "the Son is God from himself although not the Son from himself."[51] The one God is eternal, and the triune relations are both primal and immutable. The eternal generation of the Son, then, speaks of the Son's personal receptivity from his eternal Father, an event that is eternal because of the Son's eternal essence as God in himself. This eternal generation—this intratrinitarian dependence of the Son on the Father for his personal properties—flows externally in lived dependence in the economy. As Andreas Köstenberger and Scott Swain describe, the Gospel of John presents Jesus as one who "depends upon the Father for his life (5:16), power (5:19), knowledge (8:16), message (7:16), mission (7:28), instruction (14:31), authority (17:2), glory (17:24), and love (10:17)."[52] He is God, light, and true God—but he is "God of God, light of light, true God of true God, begotten" of the Father. Even the depth of his humiliation, his willing embrace of the cup of judgment, bodies forth the eternal repose of the Son in the Father.[53]

---

matter. For a fuller account, see Michael Allen, "The Perfect Priest: Calvin on the Christology of Hebrews," in *Christology and Hermeneutics: Hebrews as an Interdisciplinary Case Study*, ed. Jon Laansma and Daniel Treier, Library of New Testament Studies 423 (London: T&T Clark, 2012), 120–34.

50. Thomas Aquinas, *Commentary on the Gospel of John*, 288 (no. 782).

51. Francis Turretin, *Institutes of Elenctic Theology*, ed. James T. Dennison Jr., trans. George Musgrave Giger (Phillipsburg, NJ: P&R, 1997), 292 (3.28.40). The dogmatic tradition—from the patristic period onward—links eternal generation and filiation with the spiration of the Spirit by the Father with the Son. The Son's capacity with the Father to spirate the Spirit is itself a gift from the Father (see Augustine, *The Trinity* 15.17.29; and Thomas Aquinas, *Commentary on the Sentences*, bk. 1, dist. 12, q. 1, a. 2, *ad* 3).

52. Andreas Köstenberger and Scott Swain, *Father, Son, and Spirit: The Trinity and John's Gospel*, New Studies in Biblical Theology 24 (Downers Grove, IL: InterVarsity, 2008), 118.

53. "The perfect human life of Jesus in all his words and acts reposes entirely upon the mutual relation of the Son to the Father and the Father to the Son. . . . The act of Jesus in laying down his life is grounded upon the entire solidarity and mutuality between the Father and the Son, so that all that he does in his human life is identical with the act of God himself, but also so that

A brief word about the Spirit's relation to the Son can conclude our consideration of the eternal relations of the triune persons. The Spirit is sent on his mission by the Father with the Son. This was the dogmatic concern of the controversial *filioque* clause, and it must be maintained as a good piece of exegetical reasoning. There is nothing in the economy that suggests that the Spirit resolves an eternal or even economic antinomy between the other two persons, nor that the Son proceeds from or in the Spirit in any way. Quite to the contrary, the Spirit shows forth the mutual agreement of the other two, in that he is sent by the Father (John 14:26) and by the Son (John 15:26).[54] The Spirit always goes forth and brings back glory to the Son—in the economy and throughout eternity.

Second, because the eternal fellowship of the Trinity occurs in the manner described, *therefore, the divine Son trusts the Father by the Spirit's power during his earthly pilgrimage.* Economy follows theology; the external works of the Trinity manifest the internal movement of the triune fellowship. As Gilles Emery has said, the economic works of God are an "embassy of the eternal, bringing a part of its home country into our history."[55] There is an earthly chronicle of the Son's fidelity in the face of oppressive isolation and demonic temptation. The plot of the Son's earthly span manifests a long-growing momentum flowing forth from the centuries of divine promise amid Israel. The economy of the Son's faith, then, is one of anticipation and actualization, a season of expectation as well as an entrance to consummation. As one surveys the long history of God's works *ad extra*—how "long ago, at many times and in many ways, God spoke to our fathers" (Heb. 1:1)—it becomes quite obvious that there is a soteriological necessity for the incarnate Son to exercise faith perfectly in his Father's promise.

"Out of Israel, God in due time raised up Jesus. His faith and obedience were the promise of the perfect child of God."[56] The earthly career of this Nazarene, and his filial loyalty, are interpreted within the matrix of Israel's

nothing is done in his human life except what issues out of the love of the Father for the Son and the Son for the Father" (Torrance, *Incarnation*, 127).

54. Jenson suggests that the Spirit is a necessary third, who eschatologically mediates the tension between the Father and Son (*Systematic Theology*, 1:155–56). For analysis and critique, see Scott R. Swain, *God according to the Gospel: Robert Jenson's Trinitarian Theology*, Strategic Initiatives in Evangelical Theology (Downers Grove, IL: InterVarsity, 2013), chap. 7. On the proposal that the Son proceeds in the Spirit, while the Spirit also proceeds from the Son, see Thomas G. Weinandy, *The Father's Spirit of Sonship: Reconceiving the Trinity* (Edinburgh: T&T Clark, 1995).

55. Gilles Emery, *The Trinitarian Theology of St. Thomas Aquinas* (New York: Oxford University Press, 2007), 368.

56. "Confession of 1967," 1B, in *Constitution of the Presbyterian Church (U.S.A.)*, Part One: *Book of Confessions* (Louisville: Geneva, 1996), 324.

covenant life. Indeed, this confessional text offers a helpful phrasing inasmuch as it identifies God's righteous action—manifest in Jesus's righteous disposition and acts—"out of Israel." The economy of the Son's redemptive work cannot be severed from the story of Israel, and yet the fulfillment of that story in Jesus is a sign of movement beyond ("out of") Israel. This one is "the promise" fulfilled in our very midst.

The identification of Jesus as the true Israelite and the faithful son of Adam suggests that his soteriological work can best be discerned in categories manifest in the law and the prophets. If the Son is the *hypothesis* of the Old Testament, then the Old Testament lays out the scope and shape of the Son's history. The shape of the covenant with Israel focuses itself on structures—people, places, and practices—that manifest human dependence on divine help. The Sabbath points to human dependence for sustenance, not just that day, but every day. The Levites remind the people that not only this one tribe but all tribes fundamentally look to God for their provision. The tithe reminds the Israelites that not only a small portion but the entirety of their material possessions are given by the Father of Lights. So the Psalm says: "And those who know your name put their trust in you, for you, O LORD, have not forsaken those who seek you" (Ps. 9:10).

Jesus fulfills the priesthood and the law. Jesus brings real Sabbath rest. Jesus not only wanders without earthly possessions but is also personally dispossessed and selflessly offers himself as a ransom for others. This Jesus declares, "I will put my trust in him" (Heb. 2:13). Indeed, Jesus recapitulates the entirety of Psalm 18: calling upon the Lord in his distress (v. 6), being entangled in the cords of Sheol and confronted with the snares of death (v. 5), hearing the reeling and rocking of the earth and the shaking of the cosmos's very foundations (v. 7). This one was bruised and beaten, judged and condemned. He was alone, exalted only in isolation as the accursed one. He drank from the Lord's cup, not the wine of the feast but the full wrath of God to the very dregs of hell. Amid that *passio*, he cried out, "My God, my God, why have you forsaken me?" (Mark 15:34).[57] The descent was real and brutal. Yet he marked his endurance by his final words: "Father, into your hands I commit my spirit" (Luke 23:46). Silence had not turned him from his Father. It had focused his vision of God into the sight of faith, the vantage point of hope rising from just beyond the hellish horizon.

57. See Kelly M. Kapic, "Psalm 22: Forsakenness and the God Who Sings," in *Theological Commentary: Evangelical Essays*, ed. Michael Allen (London: T&T Clark, 2011), 41–56. Reflecting on the words of Psalm 22 screamed from the cross by the dying Lord, Kapic states, "Whereas the Psalmist trusts God to deliver him *from* death, Jesus trusts the Father to deliver him *through* death" (53).

There is no Jesus untethered from the cords of the divine will and unsuspended from the determination of eternity. Similarly, there is no Jesus separate from or discernible apart from the shape of Israel's life with God. As Irenaeus notes, "There is thus only one God, the Father, as we have shown, and one Jesus Christ our Lord, who came according to the economy and who recapitulated all things in himself."[58] The concept of recapitulation stresses the continuity and the progression of the Son's ministry with respect to the Old Testament economy. Indeed, the progression only makes sense within the continuous narrative arc.

The Epistle to the Hebrews grants soteriological prestige to the perfection of the priesthood in the person of the incarnate Son. The argument constantly moves from the good to the great, with the symbols of the old covenant as but touchstones for the trajectory culminating in the new covenant, dawning with the first advent of the Messiah. This trajectory involves his life as well as his sacrifice. Indeed, his life is constitutive of his sacrifice for sin and thanksgiving. He assumes human form in its fullness, "for it was fitting that he, for whom and by whom all things exist, in bringing many sons to glory, should make the founder of their salvation perfect through suffering" (Heb. 2:10). The incarnate one shared in our "flesh and blood. . . . For surely it is not angels that he helps, but he helps the offspring of Abraham" (2:14, 16). The mediator must be human—creaturely, dependent, attuned to the Lord's provision, in fellowship with the eternal Father—if humans are to be redeemed. "Therefore he had to be made like his brothers in every respect, so that he might become a merciful and faithful high priest in the service of God" (2:17).[59] And he "was faithful to him who appointed him"—indeed, he was more so than even Moses (3:2, 3), because he was "faithful over God's house as a son" and not as a servant (3:6).

Faithfulness takes time. "In the days of his flesh, Jesus offered up prayers and supplications, with loud cries and tears, to him who was able to save him from death, and he was heard because of his reverence. Although he was a son, he learned obedience through what he suffered. And being made perfect, he became the source of eternal salvation to all who obey him, being designated by God a high priest after the order of Melchizedek" (Heb. 5:7–10). The Son's journey into the killing fields led him to offer up "prayers and supplications," to plead "with loud cries and tears," to encounter death and suffering. His march into this sinful madness—and his willingness to endure such hostility

---

58. Irenaeus, *Against Heresies* 3.16.6, in *The Ante-Nicene Fathers,* ed. Alexander Roberts and James Donaldson, 10 vols. (Repr., Peabody, MA: Hendrickson, 2004), 1:442–43.
59. Parallels with 1 Sam. 2:35 are crucial here.

"in the days of his flesh"—constitutes him "perfect" as a mediator. Note that he prayed "to him who was able to save him from death," even though Jesus very well could have removed the pangs of death with his own power; he trustingly turned his future over to the Father's command. Of this moment he declared: "Behold, I have come to do your will, O God, as it is written of me in the scroll of the book" (Heb. 10:7; cf. v. 9).

Eventually, the anonymous writer considers the economy in its breadth, spanning the entirety of the canon from Abel to the Anointed One (Heb. 11:4–12:3). The recurring phrase "by faith" marks the continuity of this long line of witnesses: each hallmark of God's salvation is a life opened up in self-conscious dependence on divine generosity. Journeys and battles, childbirths and boat rides: all are enacted because of fundamental trust in God's being and God's commitment to bless others: "for whoever would draw near to God must believe that he exists and that he rewards those who seek him" (Heb. 11:6). The pinnacle of this recital of faith is the "author and perfecter of faith" (my translation)—Jesus, "who for the joy that was set before him endured the cross, despising the shame, and is seated at the right hand of the throne of God" (Heb. 12:2).[60] Jesus pleases God. This should not be surprising, given that he is the beloved Son in whom the Father takes delight, and, as Hebrews makes plain, "without faith it is impossible to please him" (Heb. 11:6).

The Epistle to the Hebrews does not initiate this emphasis, though it does articulate it more clearly than any other New Testament text. In a provocative monograph, Walter Moberly has considered the typological relationship between the call to obedient faithfulness in suffering, as given to Abraham in Genesis 22, and the divine sonship that Matthew's Gospel claims for Jesus.[61] After noting the tie between testing and faith in the *akedah* account (Gen. 22), Moberly claims that such testing is inherent in the very relationship of divine Father and Son as evidenced during the Son's journey into the wilderness of creaturely life.[62] He then explicitly talks of Jesus as believer: "Jesus's sonship means unqualified trust in God" or "faithfulness when tested."[63] This faith is later given some definition: "For Jesus to be Son means living in constant trust and obedience towards God as his Father. . . . One fundamental issue within this is Jesus's need to remain receptive to God giving that dominion

60. Note that the key phrase is not a reference to Jesus's stance vis-à-vis "our" faith (as all translations have, even though the word "our" is not found in the Greek text) but vis-à-vis faith itself: "author and perfecter of faith."

61. R. W. L. Moberly, *The Bible, Theology, and Faith: A Study of Abraham and Jesus*, Cambridge Studies in Christian Doctrine (Cambridge: Cambridge University Press, 2000). The remainder of this paragraph previously appears in Allen, *Christ's Faith*, 23.

62. Moberly, *Bible, Theology, and Faith*, 196.

63. Ibid., 207; cf. 203.

which it would be natural to strive to take."[64] Moberly notes the parallel between Matthew's account of divine sonship as enduring faithfulness and the
christological narrative found in Philippians 2:5–11.[65] He finds this to have
anthropological importance in that Christ demonstrates what it means to be
creaturely—enduring, receptive, faithful, self-emptying.[66] If Jesus does fulfill
this economy that runs from the time of Abraham and Abel, then he must be
the "author and perfecter of faith" (my translation), the one who *trusts the
Father . . . during his earthly pilgrimage.*

The problem throughout the old covenant was the one-sided fulfillment of
the covenant fellowship between God and his people. "I will be your God":
God showed himself capable and committed to this task. "You will be my
people": in spite of some impressive beginnings and the occasional hiccup of
loyalty, Israel recanted this calling. Indeed, the prophet identifies the flaw named
by God, who is lamenting "my covenant that they broke, though I was their
husband" (Jer. 31:32; cf. Heb. 8:9). The one who is called into a fellowship of
faith needs life—yet Israel proves to be a valley of dry bones. New hope must
be stirred. The Spirit must brood over the depths and bring newness.

Unsurprisingly, then, as in a theology of the internal life of God, so the
economy shows forth the relations of Father and Son with Spirit. Indeed,
there is a double reference in this respect. The Son sends the Spirit with the
Father on his mission; Pentecost represents this moment in the recital of God's
works. But there is a reflex: the Spirit is sent by the Son to perfect humans and
to conform them to the human image of Christ Jesus. First, though, the Spirit
conforms the Son's own humanity to that of the Word himself. The Spirit
empowers the incarnate Son, according to his human nature, throughout his
earthly journey.[67] His conception to the virgin (Matt. 1:20), his development
as a child before his neighbors and his God (Luke 2:40, 52), his baptism (Matt.
3:16), his preaching (Luke 4:17–21; cf. Isa. 61:1), his miracles (Matt. 12:28),
and his resurrection (Rom. 1:4) are all attributed to the operative power of the
Holy Spirit. From birth to new birth, the grace of the Spirit bookends the life
of the Christ. Specific to the concerns of this chapter, the Spirit sends him out
to the wilderness to be tempted and ministers grace upon grace to him, such
that he resists the tyrannies of the tempter (Matt. 4:1; Luke 4:14).[68] The most

64. Ibid., 223.
65. Ibid., 220–23.
66. Ibid., 224.
67. See Allen, *Christ's Faith*, 135–42; McCormack, "With Loud Cries and Tears," 38–46; Alan
Spence, *Incarnation and Inspiration: John Owen and the Coherence of Christology* (London:
T&T Clark, 2007).
68. One could go further and observe the sacramental shape of the Spirit's grace upon the
incarnate Son, as in Herman Witsius, *The Economy of the Covenants between God and Man:*

lavish display of the Spirit's power, however, comes in his sustaining grace to enable the human Jesus to submit to the Father's will and offer himself a willing sacrifice for sin: Christ, "who through the eternal Spirit offered himself without blemish to God" (Heb. 9:14). The Spirit is not a replacement for the divine nature, as if the Son's divinity were merely an ascription of inspiration or of moral achievement. Against such adoptionistic schemes, the Christian tradition has insisted that the Son is "God of God, light of light, true God of true God." But the Son takes human form only as one "conceived by the Holy Spirit." That form is conformed to the shape of the divine life only by the wind of the Spirit. The Spirit is the vitality of the Father and Son's love in the internal life of God; folded over into salvific history, the Spirit is the font of human life, in Christ and for those included within him.[69] So the faithful journey of the Son occurs *by the Spirit's power.*

"Jesus steps into the actual situation where we are summoned to have faith in God, to believe and trust in him, and he acts in our place and in our stead . . . and provides us freely with a faithfulness in which we may share."[70] The earlier stages of the economy of God's works *ad extra* have prepared the way for a fitting conclusion, the advent of a Son who manifests perfect faith and enduring trust—a "beloved Son," in whom God might be well pleased. There is a soteriological necessity, then, for the faith of the incarnate Son. The Word has descended to assume flesh. He faithfully must descend and endure hell itself before he may be resurrected and may ascend to glory.[71]

In these two ways, we see the necessity of the Son's faith—this is the kind of God and the kind of gospel revealed in the divine works and recounted in the divine Word given to us. It is something demonstrated not by means of a priori speculation but by means of analytic reflection on the way in which God reveals himself and his works.

Yet questions likely remain regarding the fittingness of such a claim, particularly with regard to the christological orthodoxy made public by the creedal language of Nicaea and Chalcedon. Elsewhere some analytical questions would need to be engaged—questions regarding the definition of faith, its exercise by the incarnate Son, and the relationship between his person and his two natures inasmuch as that metaphysical construal relates to the claim

*Comprehending a Complete Body of Divinity*, trans. William Crookshank (London: R. Baynes, 1822; repr., Kingsburg, CA: den Dulk, 1990), 1:276–77.

69. See Irenaeus, *Against Heresies* 3.9.3.

70. T. F. Torrance, *The Mediation of Christ* (Colorado Springs, CO: Helmers & Howard, 1992), 92.

71. See Eph. 4:7–8, as well as the descent/ascent pattern in John's Gospel, on which see Köstenberger and Swain, *Father, Son, and Spirit*, 127.

that he trusted his Father.[72] Thomas Weinandy reminds us that "the true goal of theological inquiry is not the resolution of theological *problems*, but the discernment of what the *mystery* of faith is."[73] Theological analysis is not an attempt to remove all mystery, but it is a concerted effort to think through the breadth and coherence of the mysteries of salvation as revealed by God. Questions of fittingness and synthesis, then, are quite appropriate, so long as they are pursued in a posteriori and not a priori fashion.

Surely much more can be said—indeed, I have argued elsewhere that much more should be said (at least a book's worth)—yet the preceding argument should make plain that the Christ's faith cannot be written off as a theological dead end or an element of belief unbefitting the wider exposition of the gospel.[74] It, like the gospel as a whole, remains baffling and mystifying, indeed incomprehensible, yet it is discernible and reasonable, truly apprehensible.

## On Dogmatics and Exegesis

The whole life of the Son constitutes the work of Christ and the guarantee of redemption. We have moved from theology to economy, that is, from the inner life of God to the external works of that triune God. In both cases, we see the necessity of the Son's faith in the Father by the Spirit. If the arguments of this chapter are convincing, then there are at least two implications for contemporary theology and exegesis.

First, Protestant dogmatics must maintain its concern to focus on the substitutionary work of Jesus Christ—the gospel news that he has fulfilled the human vocation perfectly and suffered our punishment comprehensively—while avoiding any juxtaposition of the forensic and the filial, the legal and the loving.[75] Calvin notes a common question: "Now someone asks, 'How has Christ abolished sin, banished the separation between us and God, and acquired righteousness to render God favorable and kindly toward us?'" He offers a programmatic response in reflection on Romans 5: "he has achieved this for us by the whole course of his obedience."[76] Thus, we must care about the scope of the gospel, avoiding any fixation that might lead us to narrow its breadth and width.

72. See Allen, *Christ's Faith*, chaps. 2–4.

73. Thomas Weinandy, *Does God Suffer? A Christian Theology of God and Suffering* (Notre Dame: University of Notre Dame Press, 2000), 32 (emphasis added).

74. See Allen, *Christ's Faith*.

75. I have addressed suggestions regarding the effects of this doctrine within Roman Catholic dogmatics in ibid., 144–53. Cf. Gerald O'Collins and Daniel Kendall, "The Faith of Jesus," *Theological Studies* 53, no. 3 (1992): 403–23.

76. Calvin, *Institutes* 2.16.5.

But we must also consider the shape of the gospel, not merely its scope. In Christ this filial relation is ours. Indeed, the first word of Christ's model for Christian prayer addresses sonship: "At the very beginning of our prayer Christ wants to kindle in us what is basic to our prayer—the childlike awe and trust that God through Christ has become our Father."[77]

Reflection on a key aspect of the gospel's scope helps accent a crucial tenet of its shape. The lifelong fidelity of the Son manifests the covenantal fellowship enjoyed by the incarnate one with his heavenly Father by the Spirit. The luminosity of divine love comes to expression in the transfiguration. The determined kindness of the Father is displayed in the daybreak of new creation. Any reflection on the legal character of their relationship must be put in such a way that it does not depersonalize or instrumentalize their personal interactions; indeed, the law and love are not at odds.

The Son and Father relate in a willed and covenantal manner: the Father expresses his will, and the Son submits to that determination; the Father outlines the expectations of the covenant, and the Son fulfills those conditions. Such ordered relations can be described legally and forensically. Indeed, the apostles consistently employ legal language to describe the salvific work of Jesus. They learn this emphasis from the incarnate Son himself, who describes his mission as offering himself "as a ransom for many" (Mark 10:45). The repetition of and rumination on ransom and redemption language by Jesus and the apostles makes concrete reference to the slave market, a financial and legal context of the most formal order.

But it is the Son's devotion that compels him to obey the commandments and satisfy the divine will. There is a danger that reflection on his obedience and law-keeping may make it into a transactional and not fully covenantal tenet. Highlighting his faith may go a long way in alleviating this possible distortion. Liam Walsh, in his editorial comments on Thomas Aquinas's *Summa Theologiae*, states that "it has never been seriously suggested in the Christian tradition that Christ lived by faith."[78] If we are to honor the full breadth of the gospel, we cannot overlook its scope and we must consider its filial shape. So a more concerted focus on the covenantal relationship of the incarnate Son to his heavenly Father—in particular, the Son's faith in the Father's promise—may well help avoid potential malformations in Christian dogmatics.

Second, biblical exegesis must be freed of dogmatic overdetermination and reoriented in its approach to the *pistis Christou* debate. Dogmatics is meant

---

77. Heidelberg Catechism 120, in *Reformed Confessions of the Sixteenth Century*, ed. Arthur C. Cochrane (Louisville: Westminster John Knox, 2003), 329.

78. Thomas Aquinas, *Summa Theologiae*, vol. 49, *The Grace of Christ*, ed. and trans. Liam G. Walsh (London: Blackfriars, 1974), 15 note b.

to enable exegetes to run, to free readers for the bold venture of following its divine course. Some may think that dogmatics is rationalist and restrictive, or that it forecloses freedom and creativity and short-circuits the need for exegetical faithfulness. May it never be. Dogmatics is the fruit of exegetical wisdom attuned to the scope and shape of the canon, intended for the development and sustenance of saints formed by the divine Word. Zacharias Ursinus points to the "highest" goal of church doctrine as preparation "for the reading, understanding, and exposition of the holy Scriptures. For as the doctrine of the catechism and Common Places are taken out of the Scriptures, and are directed by them as their rule, so they again lead us, as it were, by the hand to the Scriptures."[79]

The *pistis Christou* debate has suffered from some overdetermined dogmatic presuppositions. Texts should be read and engaged on their own merits, without any unwarranted fear of overturning Nicene orthodoxy or Reformation soteriology.

This chapter has reflected on the importance of Christology for justification—namely, the need to follow the logic of the gospel in its every aspect if we are to appreciate how Jesus Christ is righteousness from God (1 Cor. 1:30). In so doing, I hope that this analysis has provided a large-scale paradigm, with which exegetes can engage with eyes wide open the interpretive debates circling around the *pistis Christou* texts. I have sought to show that there is a need for the doctrine of the Christ's faith in Christian dogmatics, because of fundamental theological and soteriological beliefs. Furthermore, I have claimed that some concerns about this doctrine, concerns that might have prima facie decisiveness, are in fact beside the point and not valid reasons for its dismissal.

Karl Barth may well be exemplary here, even if not to be followed in every particular. In his second commentary on Romans, he writes, "The faithfulness of God and Jesus the Christ confirm one another. The faithfulness of God is established when we meet the Christ in Jesus."[80] Barth understands *pistis Christou* to be the Christ's faith directed to God in the midst of a sinful world. Though Jesus is no hero, no magician, and no sage, he renders to God perfect obedience, willful submission, and the self-negating prayer that fittingly encapsulates creaturely existence.[81] It is noteworthy, however, that Barth does

79. Zacharias Ursinus, *Commentary on the Heidelberg Catechism*, trans. G. W. Williard (Phillipsburg, NJ: P&R, n.d.), 13.
80. Karl Barth, *The Epistle to the Romans*, trans. Edwyn C. Hoskyns, 6th ed. (London: Oxford University Press, 1968), 96.
81. Ibid., 97. For similar reflections in a noncommentarial writing, see Karl Barth, "Gospel and Law," in *Community, State, and Church: Three Essays*, trans. G. Ronald Howe (Garden City, NY: Anchor, 1960), 74.

not always interpret *pistis Christou* phrases subjectively, even if he certainly finds the Christ's faith to be an essential element of Pauline theology.[82]

Those opposing the subjective genitive interpretation should marshal exegetical and contextual reasons. Again, there are helpful examples. Whereas John Murray quickly dismisses the notion that *pistis Christou* refers to the Christ's own faith, he notes that it "would not be contrary to the analogy of Scripture in general, yet there is not good warrant for this interpretation."[83] More recently, James D. G. Dunn has been an ardent opponent of the subjective genitive interpretation, although he has mentioned consistently that he is not an opponent of the doctrine that Jesus believed, an idea that he believes is surely found explicitly in the Epistle to the Hebrews. His arguments are grammatical, syntactical—that is, they are exegetical by nature.

Nevertheless, a pointed question remains: how do we relate the Christ's faith to the call for Christian faith? I will address that soteriological relationship in the next chapter.

82. See his objective interpretation of Phil. 3:9 in Karl Barth, *The Epistle to the Philippians: 40th Anniversary Edition*, trans. James W. Leitch (Louisville: Westminster John Knox, 2002), 99–103.

83. John Murray, *The Epistle to the Romans: The English Text with Introduction, Exposition, and Notes*, vol. 1, *Chapters 1–8*, New International Commentary on the New Testament (Grand Rapids: Eerdmans, 1959), 111.

# 4

# "It Is No Longer I Who Live"

## *Christ's Faith and Christian Faith*

Two recent debates in Pauline studies prompt my reflections. First, the *pistis Christou* debate has proceeded in a way that has led some to assert that the very shape of the debate determines whether one takes a christological or an anthropological approach to Paul's theology. Richard Hays starkly suggests that there is a "christological approach" and an "anthropological approach," and they can be paired with one's reading of certain Greek genitives.[1] If these texts are about human faith in Jesus, then surely Paul's overriding interest is anthropological. But if they are about the faith(fulness) of Jesus of Nazareth, then they can point to a story beyond our own: salvation in the Messiah's life, death, and resurrection.

1. Richard Hays, "ΠΙΣΤΙΣ and Pauline Christology: What Is at Stake?," in *Pauline Theology*, vol. 4, *Looking Back, Pressing On*, ed. David M. Hay and E. Elizabeth Johnson, Society of Biblical Literature Symposium Series (Atlanta: Scholars Press, 1997), 39. Mark Reasoner makes the point clearly: "Why does it matter whether we read *pistis Christou* as objective (faith in Jesus) or subjective (Jesus's faith)? First, the degree to which we emphasize faith in the human affects how we present the gospel. Proponents of the subjective genitive, who hold that Christ's faith is what saves, will not call for a distinct, conversion-constituting act of placing one's faith in Jesus. They will rather call people to join the church that lives out in a concentric pattern the faith that Jesus displayed. Second, we will begin to read Paul's gospel not as primarily based around the dichotomy of works and faith, which both have a human subject, but rather as a dichotomy between law and Christ" (*Romans in Full Circle: A History of Interpretation* [Louisville: Westminster John Knox, 2005], 39–40).

Second, the recent debate about the nature of Paul's gospel or the supposed "center" of his theology has focused on the relationships of participation in Christ and justification by faith, apocalyptic and salvation-history. The work of Louis Martyn exemplifies the most trenchant and thoroughgoing attack on human religion at the hands of God's apocalyptic invasion of the cosmos. His work is fundamentally a reorientation of Paul's proclamation in Galatians regarding God's action in making the world right, not sociological organization and inclusion of gentiles within the people of God.[2] Whereas so much recent work on Galatians had focused on Greco-Roman backgrounds and sociopolitical reorganization, Martyn puts God and divine action back on the scholarly map.[3] The reception of Martyn's work by Douglas Campbell and others continues to employ and even extend these categories as seeming opposites: christological and anthropological become "christocentric" and "anthropocentric" in Campbell's *The Deliverance of God*.[4] In so doing, Campbell has proposed that one approach to Paul's theology (what he calls "pneumatologically participatory martyrological eschatology") upholds the christocentric emphasis of Paul, whereas others ("justification theory," in particular) fold into anthropocentric emphases.

These two debates suggest that scholars working in Pauline studies have a difficult time making coherent sense of the relationship between divine and human action. Any scheme that divides interpretation between "christological" and "anthropological" approaches renders the confession of the name "Immanuel" difficult, inasmuch as such confession involves the full-throated affirmation that *God* is with us, indeed that God is with *us*. Karl Barth reflects on this double affirmation in his ruminations on the common vocation and the differences among the early leaders of the Reformation.

> The turning of *God* to *humankind* is . . . a double reality: the turning of *God* to humankind, and the turning of God to *humankind*; and according to the degree of sharpness and one-sidedness with which either the one or the other

2. J. Louis Martyn, "The Abrahamic Covenant, Christ, and the Church," in *Theological Issues in the Letters of Paul* (Edinburgh: T&T Clark, 1997), 170. Cf. idem, *Galatians: A New Translation with Introduction and Commentary*, Anchor Bible 33a (New Haven: Yale University Press, 1997).

3. For an example of the trends to which Martyn responds, see Hans Dieter Betz, *Galatians*, Hermeneia (Minneapolis: Fortress, 1989).

4. Campbell combines the participationist emphasis (over against what he calls "justification theory") with a Hays-like rhetoric regarding the "christocentric" approach to the *pistis Christou* debate (over against the "anthropocentric," modern approach of "justification theory"). See *The Deliverance of God: An Apocalyptic Rereading of Justification in Paul* (Grand Rapids: Eerdmans, 2010), e.g., 1, 200, 879, 930, 932, and esp. 1162n126 (where it is clear that Bultmann's combination of neo-Kantian moral anthropology and the Lutheran language of justification by faith alone forms Campbell's real polemical target).

is emphasized, the "and," which binds both definitions to each other, can come to sound like an "or." By means of the categories of our consciousness we are able to make clear what the one and the other mean; in the one case, we would speak principally of *God's* activity, of his good will towards us, of the mercy and power with which he takes up our cause, though not without the most powerful recollection that bound up with this action of God there is, of course, a new human activity; in the second case, however, we would speak principally of *human* activity, of our appointment to life as human beings for the glory of God, of the duty of obedience, though not without the most powerful recollection of the activity of God which is, of course, presupposed in this human action of which it alone is really the ground.[5]

Divine and human action—like divine and human being—are intrinsic to the story of the gospel and must be accounted for in any theological construct meant to serve as expository elucidation of the biblical text. Resources exist deep within the Protestant tradition to help in such an endeavor. Unfortunately, however, most New Testament scholars exemplify little or no engagement of the classical tradition of Protestant divinity. *Ressourcement* for the sake of contemporary exegetical reasoning is much needed.

In pursuing such work, one Pauline text frames my reflections: "I have been crucified with Christ. It is no longer I who live, but Christ who lives in me. And the life I now live in the flesh I live by faith in the Son of God, who loved me and gave himself for me" (Gal. 2:20). I seek to offer a dogmatic expansion on this verse and to do so in three parts. First, I will argue that Christ lives for us. Second, by faith we really do live in Christ. Third, there is an order and sequence to these two statements, and they require a theological framework within which they can be related. To that end, I point to two ways in which the common Reformational teaching on imputation was teased out in Luther's definition of Christian freedom and the Reformed tradition of distinguishing between the covenant of works and the covenant of grace. These are not the only possible constructions that could maintain this order and sequence, but they have great historical prominence and a greater than commonly appreciated viability.[6] My hope is that analytic expansion will show these dogmatic constructs to be exegetical extensions and thus foreclose the kind of quick and easy dismissal so often rendered them by contemporary New Testament studies.

---

5. Karl Barth, *Die Theologie Zwinglis, 1922/1923. Vorlesung Göttingen Wintersemester 1922/1923* (Zurich: Theologischer Verlag, 2004), 62–63.

6. A more recent proposal is the "Chalcedonian Pattern" suggested by George Hunsinger—focusing on the integrity, intimacy, and fundamental asymmetry of divine and human action—though his proposal has thus far gained no confessional articulation. See *How to Read Karl Barth: The Shape of His Theology* (New York: Oxford University Press, 1991), 185–88.

## "It Is No Longer I Who Live, but Christ Who Lives in Me"

The apostle Paul makes plain that Christ lives. Indeed, this is the primal truth of the Christian. The verse negates one basis for self-definition: "it is no longer I who live." The autonomous soul is nonexistent. And the sinful shape is no longer self-determining. Augustine declares this glorious news: "For where I am not I, I am more happily I."[7] Paul then turns to another basis for self-constitution: "but Christ who lives in me."

John Calvin notes two ways to understand "Christ living in me." He says: "Christ lives in us in two ways. The one consists in his governing us by his Spirit and directing all our actions. The other is what he grants us by participation in his righteousness, that, since we can do nothing of ourselves, we are accepted in him by God. The first relates to regeneration, the second to the free acceptance of righteousness, and this is how I take the passage."[8]

Is Calvin right in reading "Christ living in me" in this participatory way? The first exegetical conundrum is the prepositional phrase *en emoi* ("in me"). Some would suggest that this speaks of a mystical presence of Christ within the believer, thus rendering the preposition locatively, literally "within me." But the wider context pushes away from just such an intrinsic reading. The self is being crucified (Gal. 2:19–20); the law is not bringing righteousness by personal fulfillment (v. 21). Some have suggested that the great contrast Paul makes in Galatians is between "works of the law" and "faith," but this is to miss the fact that faith points beyond itself to its object: the Christ, who fulfills the Abrahamic promise. The contrast is between "works of the law" and Christ himself. Thus, it is much more likely that *en emoi* refers to Christ's life "with respect to me." In other words, Christ lives outside of me, yet for me (*pro me*).

A few words ought to be said about the recent debate regarding Paul's repeated phrase *pistis Christou*. I have argued elsewhere at length that the idea of the Christ's faith not only is coherent with Christian doctrine but is also a necessary aspect of it.[9] The Epistle to the Hebrews is most explicit in this regard. Jesus not only claims that "I will put my trust in him" (Heb. 2:13) but also that he must "be made like his brothers in every respect" (v. 17); not only does he learn "obedience through what he suffered" (5:7–8) but he is also the "author and perfecter of faith" (12:2, my translation). And Paul does come

7. Augustine, *On Continence*, Patrologiae Latina 44, ed. J. P. Migne (Paris: Garnier, n.d.), 865–66 (29).

8. John Calvin, *Commentary on the Epistles of Paul the Apostle to the Galatians, Ephesians, Philippians, and Colossians*, trans. T. H. L. Parker (Grand Rapids: Eerdmans, 1965), 43.

9. R. Michael Allen, *The Christ's Faith: A Dogmatic Account*, T&T Clark Studies in Systematic Theology 2 (London: T&T Clark, 2009).

close at times, in Romans 5:12–21 and Philippians 2:6–11, to describing the incarnate Son's dependence upon his heavenly Father. More widely, however, we know that the Son must trust the Father, for it is impossible to please God without faith (Rom. 14:23; Heb. 11:6), and the Son is his beloved Son with whom he is well pleased (Mark 1:11). All roads seem to point forcefully to the Christ's faith.

Yet that does not mean that the phrase *pistis Christou* refers to the Christ's faith. In Galatians, even if it is not a reference to "the faith of Christ" that tells us of Christ's living on our behalf before our heavenly Father, the christological emphasis is still present. "It is no longer I who live, but Christ who lives in me": this generates a doctrine of the Son's life and faith. This verse does not specify the full extent or the precise nature of the Son's life, but it affirms and celebrates its centrality.

And what might we say of his life? Jesus is the faithful Adam, the great high priest, the mediator of fellowship. He resists temptation, triumphs over evil, frees the captives. His character is holy, resolute, and obedient. His story moves from apprenticeship to baptism, from the wilderness to the public eye, from Gethsemane to the cross of Golgotha. In all this, he is the one of whom the Father says: "You are my beloved Son; with you I am well pleased" (Mark 1:11). Jesus pleases God. More specifically, a man, who is born in Bethlehem and who dies outside Jerusalem, pleases God. If the doctrine of Nicaea and Chalcedon is not mere addition to the biblical witness, then our reflections on Jesus must appreciate the way that he pleased his Father as a human being and, more particularly, as a human son.

The Reformers employed the language of imputation here to note that Christ lives with respect to me, but that this occurs outside my own immediate course of existence.[10] In other words, imputation renders the two clauses

10. Imputation describes the manner of union. Primarily, we are united to Christ. Yet our union is not mainly moral, but personal and relational. For this reason, many in the Reformed tradition refer to it as a covenantal union. We are wed to Christ. Imputation is not simply an exchange of property, as some crass critics portray it. Quite the contrary, it was Martin Luther who said, "If Christ is a bridegroom, he must take upon himself the things which are his bride's and bestow upon her the things that are his. If he gives her his body and very self, how shall he not give her all that is his? And if he takes the body of the bride, how shall he not take all that is hers?" ("The Freedom of a Christian [1520]," in *Career of the Reformer I*, ed. Harold Grimm, Luther's Works 31 [Philadelphia: Fortress, 1957], 351). Notice that the primary act is a marriage; joint custody of property is real, yet secondary. By analogy, then, Christians are united with Christ primarily, and they enjoy his every spiritual blessing and his full inheritance in the heavenly places only secondarily. For further reflection on the relationship of union with Christ and imputation in Calvin's theology (especially as articulated in debates with Andreas Osiander), see J. Todd Billings, "John Calvin's Soteriology: On the Multifaceted 'Sum' of the Gospel," *International Journal of Systematic Theology* 11, no. 4 (2009): 428–47; and Michael S.

of this sentence coherent: "It is no longer I who live, *but* Christ who lives with respect to me." Imputation honors the "but" placed there by the apostle Paul. It is a contrast meant to highlight our need for grace from the outside, indeed, for life from beyond our own death.[11] W. H. Auden tells us, "Nothing that is possible can save us; we who must die demand a miracle."[12] We can confess with Karl Barth (in his exegesis of Gal. 2:20), "The fact that I live in the faith of the Son of God, in my faith in Him, has its basis in the fact that He Himself, the Son of God, first believed for me, and so believed that all that remains for me to do is to let my eyes rest on Him, which really means to let my eyes follow Him. This following is my faith. But the great work of faith has already been done by the One whom I follow even in my faith."[13]

### "And the Life I Now Live in the Flesh I Live by Faith in the Son of God"

The apostle is not satisfied to speak only of a Christ who lives, but he presses on to speak of how this risen Lord shares that life with others. He does not share Dorothee Sölle's suspicion that notions of substitution or imputation render personal identity moot and relational authenticity impossible.[14] Paul will put it pneumatologically later: "If we live by the Spirit, let us also keep in step with the Spirit" (Gal. 5:25). One not only exists but also acts out his or her Spirit-wrought life. In Galatians, this gift of the Spirit is the most frequently discussed result of the Son's work and the fulfillment of the Abrahamic promise. Here,

---

Horton, "Calvin's Theology of Union with Christ and the Double Grace: Modern Reception and Contemporary Possibilities," in *Calvin's Theology and Its Reception*, ed. J. Todd Billings and I. John Hesselink (Louisville: Westminster John Knox, 2012).

11. As we need grace from the outside in creation, so it is not at all surprising that new creation must also come from outside. For connections between justification and creation, see Oswald Bayer, "The Doctrine of Justification and Ontology," *Neue Zeitschrift für Systematische Theologie und Religionsphilosophie* 43, no. 1 (2001): 44–53; Eberhard Jüngel, "On Becoming Truly Human: The Significance of the Reformation Distinction between Person and Works for the Self-Understanding of Modern Humanity," in *Theological Essays II*, ed. John Webster, trans. Arnold Neufeldt-Fast and John Webster (Edinburgh: T&T Clark, 1995), 216–40; and David Kelsey, *Eccentric Existence: A Theological Anthropology* (Louisville: Westminster John Knox, 2009), pt. 1.

12. W. H. Auden, "For the Time Being," in *Collected Poems*, ed. Edward Mendelson, Modern Library (New York: Modern Library, 1976), 353.

13. Karl Barth, *Church Dogmatics*, vol. 2/2, *The Doctrine of God*, ed. G. W. Bromiley and T. F. Torrance, trans. G. W. Bromiley (Edinburgh: T&T Clark, 1957), 559.

14. Dorothee Sölle, *Stellvertretung: Ein Kapitel Theologie nach dem "Tode Gottes"* (Stuttgart: Kreuz, 1982). Sölle fundamentally distinguishes between a "substitute" (*Ersatz*) and a "representative" (*Stellvertreter*), suggesting that only the latter relational term allows for genuine relational reciprocity—yet her argument runs aground on the close textual link between Gal. 2:20 and 3:10–12.

however, Paul speaks with reference to the Son and not the Spirit. Paul does live a life.[15] Though Christ is his life, he nonetheless lives in the wake of Christ. We do well to remember Karl Barth's observation: "As in general so here in particular, God's omnicausality must not be construed as God's sole causality. . . . [Thus] the faithfulness to which we are summoned is not an emanation of God's faithfulness. It is really our own faithfulness, decision and act."[16]

There is a Christian life, and here it is depicted in three ways: its contemporaneity, its fleshly nature, and its manner of proceeding "by faith in the Son of God."

*Paul lives "now."* The Judaizers are not met with an eschatological denial of present agency. Their call for participation in certain religious rites is not matched by a polar opposite: death or divestment. Rather, Paul says that he does live "now."

*Paul lives "in the flesh."* The Judaizers are not met with an ascetic denial of embodied existence or even denigration of its metaphysical and moral importance. Their call for the fulfillment of the "works of the law" is not matched by an abstract push toward the forms or ideas of the mind. Rather, Paul says that he lives "in the flesh." Erasmus Sarcerius pointed out in the Reformation era that "Paul makes a distinction here between life according to the flesh and life in the flesh."[17]

*Most important, though, Paul lives "by faith in the Son of God."* Paul does not merge faith and obedience. In his vision, terms like "faithfulness," "fidelity," "faith," "obedience," and the like do not function merely as synonyms. Karl Barth is much more attuned to Paul's point: "Faith is not obedience, but as obedience is not obedience without faith, faith is not faith without obedience. They belong together, as do thunder and lightning in a thunderstorm."[18] Galatians 5:6 necessitates such a claim—faith does work itself out *in love* (they belong together), but faith does *work itself out* in love (faith is not obedience, nor obedience faith).

Over against the tendency to conflate faith with fidelity, Martyn and others have suggested that Paul's apocalyptic teaching "does not speak of two

15. The christological angle remains primary in Galatians, signaled by its emphasis here in 2:20 as well as later in 5:1, where we read, "For freedom Christ has set us free; stand firm therefore, and do not submit again to a yoke of slavery."

16. Karl Barth, *Church Dogmatics*, vol. 4/4, *The Doctrine of Reconciliation*, ed. G. W. Bromiley and T. F. Torrance, trans. G. W. Bromiley (Edinburgh: T&T Clark, 1969), 22.

17. Erasmus Sarcerius, *Annotations on Galatians*, Gal. 2:20 (cited in *Galatians Ephesians*, ed. Gerald Bray, Reformation Commentary on Scripture 10 [Downers Grove, IL: InterVarsity, 2011], 80).

18. Karl Barth, *Church Dogmatics*, vol. 4/2, *The Doctrine of Reconciliation*, ed. G. W. Bromiley and T. F. Torrance, trans. G. W. Bromiley (Edinburgh: T&T Clark, 1958), 438.

alternatives or two possibilities between which we choose [i.e., faith and works of the law], but of two worlds that are in conflict with one another."[19] But this confuses levels of argument. That there are two ages and two worlds is without dispute: faith has come and invaded (Gal. 3:26). Yet the polarity of Galatians 2 is precisely between human actions: faith and "works of the law." There is no point in denying the necessity of human agency of one sort or another. Much debate has focused on the latter phrase, trying to narrow its historical reference point. Francis Watson's suggestion is measured: "'Works of the law' really does refer to a Jewish praxis centered upon a text—and not, for example, to morality in general or to questionable ecclesial practices."[20] Of course, if even these text-centered actions (originally taught by God himself) were extraneous to justification and to be condemned with the strongest of anathemas (Gal. 1), then, by extension, morality in general and questionable ecclesial practices would be even more ardently critiqued.

Luther makes precisely this argument from greater to lesser: he notes that the Judaizers require the best of all possible additions to faith (law observance that was at one time required by God), yet they are still rebuked as gospel repudiators; Luther sees the medieval Romans of his day as far worse, requiring not divinely mandated obedience, but that rendered toward their own human traditions.[21] He is most straightforward in his commentary on Galatians 3:10, where he states: "Paul might have said, by a general proposition, whatsoever is without faith, is under the curse. He saith not so, but he taketh that which, besides faith, is the best, the greatest, and most excellent among all corporal blessings of the world; to wit, the law of God. . . . Now if the law of God do bring men under the curse, much more may the same be said of inferior laws and blessings."[22] Here and elsewhere in his later lectures on Galatians, Luther plainly shows his awareness of contingent differences between the Judaizers in Galatia and the flaws he perceived in late medieval Roman Catholic piety. It will not do for New Testament scholars to continue suggesting that Luther simply read the Pharisees or the Judaizers as ancient appearances of his own opponents. Clearly, he did not.

Yet Luther does show that engagement with the Judaizers can connect with battles in his own day by extension. Here another problem arises in the

19. Nancy J. Duff, "The Significance of Pauline Apocalyptic for Theological Ethics," in *Apocalyptic in the New Testament: Essays in Honor of J. Louis Martyn*, ed. Joel Marcus and Marion L. Soards, Journal for the Study of the New Testament Supplement Series 24 (Sheffield: Sheffield University Press, 1989), 279–96, quote on 280.

20. Francis Watson, *Paul and the Hermeneutics of Faith* (London: T&T Clark, 2004), 29n61.

21. Martin Luther, *Lectures on Galatians (1535)*, trans. Erasmus Middleton (Grand Rapids: Kregel, 1979), 23 (1:7), 34 (1:14), 36–37 (1:15–17), 42–43 (2:1), 46 (2:3), 144–45 (3:10), 285 (4:27), 289 (4:27).

22. Luther, *Lectures on Galatians (1535)*, trans. Middleton, 144–45 (3:10).

way that many contemporary New Testament scholars seek to chastise the Reformer. N. T. Wright has reflected on the groundbreaking historical work of E. P. Sanders and suggested that prior to the appearance of Sanders's book *Paul and Palestinian Judaism*, "most Protestant exegetes had read Paul and Judaism as if Judaism was a form of the old heresy Pelagianism, according to which humans must pull themselves up by their moral bootstraps and thereby earn justification, righteousness, and salvation. No, said Sanders. Keeping the law within Judaism always functioned within a covenantal scheme."[23] Wright has won widespread popular acclaim, especially in America, even if scholars continue to poke holes in his claims, especially in Germany and Britain. If we reflect on his argument here and elsewhere, Wright surely claims too much and too little.

First, it simply will not do to suggest that the Reformers read the Judaizers in light of their own opponents—namely, so-called Pelagians. The flaws here are numerous. The Reformers did not oppose Pelagians, inasmuch as the Roman Catholic Church had officially renounced such teaching long before (in its reflections on baptism and original sin). The Reformers sometimes referred to their opponents as semi-Pelagians, but that is an altogether different grouping.

Second, it cannot be sustained that "Judaism" was uniformly committed to a theology of grace in the sense that the New Testament defines it. Jewish life and thought in the first century was diverse. To the extent that Sanders has shown diversity and, indeed, the place of grace in much of Jewish thought, he has surely helped remove some caricatures, for example, of the behavior and motivations of the Pharisees. Yet texts like Wisdom of Solomon continued to exercise some sway, speaking of grace but defining it in a manner radically contrary to the gospel. For Wisdom, grace means fittingness or just desert. A gift given in grace is a gift given to one who will make best use of it; they may not have already deserved it, but they will do so.[24] Other Jewish texts suggest

23. N. T. Wright, *What Saint Paul Really Said: Was Paul of Tarsus the Real Founder of Christianity?* (Grand Rapids: Eerdmans, 1997), 19. Sanders argues that first-century Judaism fit a pattern that he calls "covenantal nomism," which involves the following tenets: "(1) God has chosen Israel and (2) given the law. The law implies both (3) God's promise to maintain the election and (4) the requirement to obey. (5) God rewards obedience and punishes transgression. (6) The law provides for means of atonement, and atonement results in (7) maintenance or re-establishment of the covenantal relationship. (8) All those who are maintained in the covenant by obedience, atonement and God's mercy belong to the group which will be saved" (*Paul and Palestinian Judaism: A Comparison of Patterns of Religion* [Minneapolis: Fortress, 1977], 420).

24. On Wisdom of Solomon, see Jonathan Linebaugh, "God, Grace, and Righteousness: Wisdom of Solomon and Paul's Letter to the Romans in Conversation" (PhD diss., University of Durham, 2011). For wider comparative analysis of grace and gift, see John M. G. Barclay, *Paul and the Gift* (Grand Rapids: Eerdmans, forthcoming).

that Sanders has not provided a completely fair portrayal of Judaism.[25] The term "grace" appears frequently, but the New Testament notion of grace is not always in place and is frequently directly opposed.

Third, and most important, Luther and the other Protestant Reformers did not suspect the Roman Catholic Church of denying grace or faith or even God's initiative. Given Rome's practice of infant baptism, it would be very difficult to charge her with Pelagianism—and Luther never did. But Luther did believe that Rome required "faith formed by love" for justification with God. In addition to the grace of God given in Christ, the human transformation and the gratitude of the redeemed factors into their acceptance before God.[26] Luther summarizes Rome in this way: "We must believe in Christ, and that faith is the foundation of our salvation, but it justifieth not, except it be furnished with charity."[27] Comparison with Thomas Aquinas's commentary on Galatians shows that he is not skewing the data: "For no one is made just before God by works but by the habit of faith, not acquired but infused . . . by the habit of faith vivified by charity."[28] "This is what he means when he says, the just man lives by faith. Furthermore, this is to be understood of faith acting through love."[29] For Luther, faith's value is entirely in its instrumental function: it unites one to Christ. To state that faith must be formed by some other human activity, then, is to minimize the Christ-centered basis of justification.

The rhetorical practice of denigrating Reformational exegesis and dogmatics cannot pass muster. The Reformational figures may make exegetical mistakes and may synthesize poorly in their dogmatic work, but they must be engaged as sensitive exegetes and dogmaticians cognizant of their work in moving from Paul's horizon to their own.

The Reformers employed the terminology of impartation here to speak of grace's taking hold within our very lives. Grace flowers over into faith and all its fruits—eventually into love (Gal. 5:6) and the fruit of the Spirit (5:16–24).[30] These concrete actions of the Christian flow fundamentally, though, from the work of Christ—from his grace given by his Spirit through his Word. So Augustine says,

25. A. Andrew Das, "Paul and Works of Obedience in Second-Temple Judaism: Romans 4:4–5 as 'New Perspective' Case Study," *Catholic Biblical Quarterly* 71, no. 4 (2009): 795–812.

26. For a recent articulation, see Robert Louis Wilken, "Faith Formed by Love," *Nova et Vetera* 9, no. 4 (2011): 1089–1100.

27. Luther, *Lectures on Galatians (1535)*, trans. Middleton, 47 (2:4–5).

28. Thomas Aquinas, *Commentary on Saint Paul's Epistle to the Galatians*, trans. Fabian Larcher, Aquinas Scripture Commentaries 1 (Albany, NY: Magi, 1966), 80 (chap. 3, lect. 4).

29. Ibid., 83.

30. See, e.g., Luther, *Lectures on Galatians (1535)*, trans. Middleton, 315 (5:6).

This is to preach Christ: to say not only what one must believe about Christ but also how one must live who wishes to be joined to the body of Christ; to say, in fact, everything that one must believe about Christ . . . , but also what kind of members, of whom He is the head, He desires, He forms, loves, sets free, and leads to eternal life and glory. When all this is said, whether at times more fully or profusely, or at times more briefly and concisely, then is Christ preached, and still in all, nothing is left out.[31]

Christ lives for us, and Christ lives in us—Galatians prompts us to speak of both realities, each with their own integrity and reality.

## Order and Sequence: Two Reformational Approaches

"The church has a mission: to see to the speaking of the gospel, whether to the world as message of salvation or to God as appeal and praise. Theology is the reflection internal to the church's labor on this assignment."[32] Theology aids worship and witness by reflecting carefully on what is heard and what is to be said. As such, the gospel centers on the course of Jesus's human history. "He is before all things, and in him all things hold together. . . . For in him all the fullness of God was pleased to dwell, and through him to reconcile to himself all things" (Col. 1:17, 19–20). This history is recounted in the creeds and confessions of the church, and it spans the full course of his human journey: conception and birth, life and ministry, suffering and death, resurrection and ascent. "From the time he took on the form of a servant," Calvin says, "he began to pay the price of liberation in order to redeem us."[33] An orderly theology of the gospel, then, must take into account the life and faith of the incarnate Son, or else it risks narrowing and throwing off balance the salvation wrought by the Messiah. But a confession of the gospel must also take into account the effects of Jesus's work: his faithfulness does elicit faith, his session does supply grace, his reign does register sway in the spiritual devotion of his people. And so a theology of the gospel must also move to speak of Jesus as the one who not only believes but also demands and elicits faith in others.

The mediator does exercise faith on our behalf, but this does not absolve the believer of the responsibility to believe. It elicits such belief. Even so, we must be vigilant to avoid placing undue burdens upon the believer's faith, or else its

31. Augustine, *On Faith and Works*, Ancient Christian Writers 48, trans. Gregory Lombardo (New York: Newman, 1988), 20 (9.9).
32. Robert Jenson, *Systematic Theology*, vol. 1, *The Triune God* (New York: Oxford University Press, 1997), 11.
33. John Calvin, *Institutes of the Christian Religion*, ed. John T. McNeill, trans. Ford Lewis Battles, Library of Christian Classics (Philadelphia: Westminster, 1960), 2.16.5.

anthropological emphasis will overwhelm its christological focus. Indeed, the modern era saw a number of liberal Protestant theologians sever the doctrine of faith from an operative doctrine of Christ, thereby giving faith an autonomous value that it never warranted in traditional Protestant dogmatics. Friedrich Schleiermacher and Albrecht Ritschl are indicative of this trend, inasmuch as faith ceases functioning as an instrument uniting one to Christ and serves more as a cipher for human self-divestment or a sense of absolute dependence.

Paul Tillich, commenting on the danger of separating faith from an operative doctrine of grace in Christ, says,

> A word must be said about the expression "Justification by grace through faith." It is often used in the abbreviated form of "Justification through faith." But this is extremely misleading, for it gives the impression that faith is an act of man by which he merits Justification. This is a total and disastrous distortion of the doctrine of Justification. The cause is God alone (by grace), but the faith that one is accepted is the channel through which grace is mediated to man (through faith). The *articulus stantis et cadentis ecclesiae* must be kept clear, even in the formulation of Justification by grace through faith.[34]

Tillich highlights a thorny problem—namely, that faith itself might be viewed as the ground of justification. He responds to this rendering by requiring the adjoining phrase "by grace" to be paired with the phrase "through faith," lest faith be taken as a replacement for grace in Christ. Indeed, he articulates the same concern espoused by the Westminster Larger Catechism.

> Q. How doth faith justify a sinner in the sight of God?

> A. Faith justifies a sinner in the sight of God, not because of those other graces which do always accompany it, or of good works that are the fruits of it; nor as if the grace of faith, or any act thereof, were imputed to him for justification; but only as it is an instrument, by which he receiveth and applieth Christ and his righteousness.[35]

Faith points beyond itself to something far more interesting: the very righteousness of the Messiah, which is only received through its instrument, faith.

Julie Canlis argues that John Calvin understood the instrumental nature of faith in a way not true of Martin Luther. "In Luther's *Praefatio* to his Latin

34. Paul Tillich, *Systematic Theology*, vol. 2, *Existence and the Christ* (Chicago: University of Chicago Press, 1957), 179.

35. Westminster Larger Catechism 73, in *Constitution of the Presbyterian Church (U.S.A.)*, Part One: *Book of Confessions* (Louisville: Geneva, 1996), 259.

works (1545) he describes his exegetical breakthrough as realizing that God's righteousness is to be grasped *by faith*. Calvin contradicts this, noting that Luther's emphasis on the responsive faith of the believer *to Christ* should instead be construed as the "'active' faithfulness *of God* as the stable foundation of salvation.'"[36] Canlis is surely right that Calvin appreciates that the steadiness of faith is not in itself but in its object. Calvin speaks of faith only within the context of a broader discussion regarding the manner in which the person and benefits of Christ are enjoyed by others in union with him (book 3 of the *Institutes*, e.g., 3.2.10). However, I suspect that Canlis's account does not give enough credit to Martin Luther, who does frequently use the shorthand term "faith" to speak of what saves, but who often clarifies by saying that faith saves instrumentally by uniting one to Jesus, who is salvation in his person and work. One does not have to follow the Finnish school of Tuomo Mannermaa to see such christological focus in Luther; one simply has to read his more nuanced account (as in his 1535 Galatians lectures).[37] For Luther, faith has tremendous value and plays a nonnegotiable role—it is the "chiefest worship, the chiefest duty, the chiefest obedience, the chiefest sacrifice"—yet this need not imply that an existential narrative is specifically prescribed.[38]

Indeed, it is arguable that even Philipp Melanchthon, who supposedly reduces Christ to his benefits, does not fit the common caricature. T. F. Torrance has argued,

> But to return to the words of Melanchthon, "This is to know Christ, to know his benefits." His famous words are part of a wider sentence that reads, "to know Christ means to know his benefits, and not as they [the scholastics] teach, to reflect upon his natures and the modes of his incarnation." It is clear from the context here that Melanchthon was not focusing simply on what Christ does in us, as though it was what he did in us that was important and not also what he was in himself, but was rather contrasting scholastic arguments as to the nature of the incarnation with living knowledge of the saving Christ. Melanchthon thus meant the words not as Ritschl and others interpreted them, for whereas what they made central was the fact that Christ acts upon us, and so reveals himself

36. Julie Canlis, *Calvin's Ladder: A Spiritual Theology of Ascent and Ascension* (Grand Rapids: Eerdmans, 2010), 130, referencing Calvin's exegesis of Ps. 7:17 and Ps. 22:31 (emphasis original).

37. For a remarkably fruitful account of Luther's exegesis of Galatians and its christocentric shape, see Stephen Chester, "It Is No Longer I Who Live: Justification by Faith and Participation in Christ in Martin Luther's Exegesis of Galatians," *New Testament Studies* 55, no. 3 (2009): 315–37. For Luther's dogmatic connection between justification and Christ, see Oswald Bayer, *Martin Luther's Theology: A Contemporary Introduction*, trans. Thomas H. Trapp (Grand Rapids: Eerdmans, 2008), 42–43, 63–64.

38. Luther, *Lectures on Galatians (1535)*, trans. Middleton, 125 (3:6).

to us in giving us his benefits; Melanchthon's primary emphasis is the other way round, on the glory of God. It is not because Christ brings us benefits that he is the Son of God, but the reverse. He is the Son, and it is because he is the Son who reveals God to us and of himself that he heals us, gives us his benefits, and we know ourselves to be sheltered and healed in him. Melanchthon's emphasis is on the living Christ and on what it is to know Christ. For him faith is a living knowledge of a living and saving Christ.[39]

Much later—in the Enlightenment era—Lutheran views on justification fix upon existential categories with little or no controlling work done by trinitarian realism and the economy of salvation.[40] Indeed, the Reformed theologian Schleiermacher severs faith from Christ and imputation entirely.

If we are to express ourselves with any accuracy we cannot say, either, that Christ fulfilled the divine will *in our place* or *for our advantage*. That is to say, He cannot have done so *in our place* in the sense that we are thereby relieved from the necessity of fulfilling it. No Christian mind could possibly desire this, nor has sound doctrine ever asserted it. Indeed, Christ's highest achievement consists in this, that He so animates us that we ourselves are led to an ever more perfect fulfillment of the divine will. . . . Neither can He have fulfilled the divine will in any way *for our advantage*, as if by the obedience of Christ, considered in and for itself, anything were achieved for us or changed in relation to us.[41]

But Schleiermacher, Ritschl, and the modern liberal project are not to be equated with Luther and Melanchthon.

Indeed, Luther was insistent that faith itself is not our fundamental righteousness before God. Thomas Aquinas had lauded the intrinsic value of faith (seated in the faculty of the mind).

Therefore in all things it must be said that God is the first principle in justice and that whosoever gives to God, namely, the greatest thing that lies in him by submitting the mind to Him, such a one is fully just: "Whosoever are led by the Spirit of God, they are the sons of God" (Rom. 8:14). And hence he says, Abraham believed God, i.e., submitted his mind to God in faith: "Believe God,

39. T. F. Torrance, "Introduction to Christology," in *Incarnation: The Person and Life of Christ*, ed. Robert T. Walker (Downers Grove, IL: IVP Academic, 2008), 35. Quotations from Melanchthon are from "Loci Communes, 1521," in *Melanchthon and Bucer*, ed. Wilhelm Pauck, Library of Christian Classics 19 (Philadelphia: Westminster, 1969), 21–22.

40. See, e.g., Albrecht Ritschl, *The Christian Doctrine of Justification and Reconciliation: The Positive Development of the Doctrine*, trans. H. R. Mackintosh and A. B. Macaulay (Edinburgh: T&T Clark, 1900), 121, 155, 180–83.

41. Friedrich Schleiermacher, *The Christian Faith*, ed. H. R. Mackintosh and J. S. Stewart (Philadelphia: Fortress, 1976), 456.

and he will recover thee: and direct thy way, and trust in him" (Ecclus. 2:6); and further on (2:8): "Ye that fear the Lord believe him," and it was reputed to him unto justice, i.e., the act of faith and faith itself were for him, as for everyone else, the sufficient cause of justice.[42]

Luther presents the matter quite differently: "These three things, faith, Christ, acceptation, or imputation, must be joined together. Faith taketh hold of Christ, and hath Him present, and holdeth Him enclosed, as the ring doth the precious stone. And whosoever shall be found having this confidence in Christ apprehended in the heart, him will God accept for righteous."[43] Indeed, Luther will identify "faith" with the "presence of Christ," inasmuch as faith's soteriological value is entirely instrumental: thus, it can be identified by relation with its object. Notice his way of putting faith and Christ together: "Faith therefore must be purely taught: namely, that thou art so entirely joined unto Christ that He and thou art made as it were one person: so that thou mayest boldly say, I am now one with Christ, that is to say, Christ's righteousness, victory, and life are mine. And again, Christ may say, I am that sinner, that is, his sins and his death are Mine, because he is united and joined unto Me, and I unto him."[44]

The dogmatic terminology Luther employed to maintain his point was reference to faith as an instrument (*instrumentum*). Instrumentality language is not existential or psychological language; in other words, calling faith instrumental does not mean that it is somehow not really experienced or psychologically less potent.[45] Far from it. Instrumentality language simply locates faith on the metaphysical plane—it is not ultimate. As noted above, the Westminster Larger Catechism illustrates this terminological usage well.

42. Thomas Aquinas, *Commentary on Galatians*, chap. 3, lect. 3, 76.

43. Luther, *Lectures on Galatians (1535)*, trans. Middleton, 71 (2:15–16).

44. Ibid., 90 (2:20); cf. 128–29 (3:6), 133 (3:6–7). Indeed, Luther's strong insistence that faith is only an instrumental condition to justification, rather than a material condition, undergirds his and later Lutheran critiques of Augustine's theology of justification (which was less focused on imputation). See, e.g., Steven D. Paulson, "The Augustinian Imperfection: Faith, Christ, and Imputation and Its Role in the Ecumenical Discussion of Justification," in *The Gospel of Justification in Christ: Where Does the Church Stand Today?*, ed. Wayne C. Stumme (Grand Rapids: Eerdmans, 2006), 104–24; and Heiko Oberman, *The Dawn of the Reformation* (Edinburgh: T&T Clark, 1986), 119–20. However, Mark Ellingsen has recently argued (drawing on certain texts like Augustine's *Enchiridion on Faith, Hope, and Love*) that Luther's criticisms of Augustine are not entirely accurate; see "Augustinian Origins of the Reformation Reconsidered," *Scottish Journal of Theology* 64, no. 1 (2011): 13–28, esp. 26–27.

45. In a similar vein, Luther identifies the life of faith as a passive life (*vita passiva*). This is not a statement of existential vacuousness or the loss of the ego in a psychological sense; it is a statement of humanity's metaphysical contingency and trustful dependence (see Bayer, *Martin Luther's Theology*, 42–43).

Q. How doth faith justify a sinner in the sight of God?

A. Faith justifies a sinner in the sight of God, not because of those other graces which do always accompany it, or of good works that are the fruits of it; nor as if the grace of faith, or any act thereof, were imputed to him for justification; but only as it is an instrument, by which he receiveth and applieth Christ and his righteousness.[46]

Faith is not efficacious in itself nor for its accompanying graces, but only inasmuch as it is an instrument for the reception and application of Christ's person and righteousness.

The need for such righteousness to enjoy life with God is not merely a proposition by Paul—it is a preoccupation throughout the canon. We see it in the biblical finale, the final chapter of John's Apocalypse, where we read, "Blessed are those who wash their robes, so that they may have the right to the tree of life and that they may enter the city by the gates" (Rev. 22:14). It seems to speak of the need for moral cleansing; in fact, those kept out are identified by their iniquity: "Outside are the dogs and sorcerers and the sexually immoral and murderers and idolaters, and everyone who loves and practices falsehood" (Rev. 22:15). Yet the chapter goes on, and it is made very clear that moral achievement is not the ground for entry. While moral transformation is necessary, entry is not bought by newness. Rather, we then read, "The Spirit and the Bride say, 'Come.' And let the one who hears say, 'Come.' And let the one who is thirsty come; let the one who desires take the water of life without price" (Rev. 22:17). Somehow the washing of the robes and concomitant moral transformation, real though they are, can nonetheless be characterized as acceptance "without price." Human agency matters for the saving of sinful creatures, even if those sinners' merit matters not at all. This juxtaposition of material—here in Revelation and elsewhere in the canon—must reshape our expectations about divine and human agency.

With such expectations in mind, faith is the fitting moral directive. The expectations involve the requirement of washing one's robes prior to entrance

---

46. Westminster Larger Catechism 73. The Westminster Confession also refers to faith as the "alone instrument" and reiterates in several ways that faith's value, soteriologically speaking, is not in itself but in the Christ to whom it unites one (see Westminster Confession of Faith 13.2). Similar statements are found in the Heidelberg Catechism (61): "Q. Why do you say that you are righteous by faith alone? A. Not because I please God by virtue of the worthiness of my faith, but because the satisfaction, righteousness, and holiness of Christ alone are my righteousness before God, and because I can accept it and make it mine in no other way than by faith alone" (in *Reformed Confessions of the Sixteenth Century*, ed. Arthur C. Cochrane [Louisville: Westminster John Knox, 2003], 315).

into the city and eating from the tree of life. Yet the expectations are clearly not requiring moral achievement or advancement, inasmuch as they are also identified as the simple hunger, thirst, and desire of those who acknowledge their deep need. Theologically speaking, such biblical language points to the requirement that Christians live by faith, for it is faith that points away from one's self to one's sustenance in another.

The apostle Paul addresses the relation of divine and human agency in a wide range of ways and in a variety of texts. He unpacks the shape of human life before God by reflecting on the way grace takes hold in our lives. John Barclay has surveyed a host of Pauline texts that relate divine and human agency, and he has shown that "the relationship between divine grace and human actors can be expressed by a variety of prepositions: grace may be described as 'toward me' (eis eme, 1 Cor. 15:10; 2 Cor. 9:8), 'with me' (sun emoi, 1 Cor. 15:10), 'through me' (di emou, Rom. 15:18), and 'in me' (en emoi, Gal. 2:20; Phil. 2:13)."[47] Each phrase speaks of an external source entering into a personal relation. This is Paul's emphasis: salvation invades from without, our identity is defined outside us, in Christ; yet it is in fact defined and then lived out.[48] To show how the two tenets can sit together, they must be placed in a wider context. The key is to see that imputation precedes and grounds, but really does generate and sustain, impartation. That connection has proven difficult to maintain over the years, with the danger of veering toward one end or another. So churches have developed traditions of ways to make sense of this connection. I wish to mention two possibilities for further use by exegetes and dogmaticians today.

## Luther on Two Kinds of Righteousness

In the Lutheran context, Martin Luther's famous definition of the two kinds of righteousness organizes these categories in a well-known sermon from 1519.[49] Luther's sermon is premised on another crucial Pauline text, the Christ hymn of Philippians 2. He expounds: "There are two kinds of righteousness, just as man's sin is of two kinds."[50] The first is an alien righteousness. "This righ-

47. John Barclay, "Grace and the Transformation of Agency in Christ," in Re-Defining First Century Jewish and Christian Identities: Essays in Honor of Ed Parish Sanders, ed. Fabian Udoh (Notre Dame: University of Notre Dame Press, 2008), 383.

48. Here is Martyn's great strength, of course, in noting the invasion of the cosmos and the self by Christ; see Martyn, Theological Issues in the Letters of Paul, pt. 2.

49. Luther, "Two Kinds of Righteousness (1519)," in Career of the Reformer I, ed. Harold Grimm, Luther's Works 31 (Philadelphia: Fortress, 1957), 293–306.

50. Ibid., 297.

teousness is primary; it is the basis, the cause, the source of all our own actual righteousness."[51] "Therefore this alien righteousness, instilled in us without our works by grace alone—while the Father, to be sure, inwardly draws us to Christ—is set opposite original sin, likewise alien, which we acquire without our works by birth alone."[52] Christ is this alien, external righteousness. Yet Christ is not our only righteousness, for there is a proper righteousness that follows in the wake of this alien, justifying righteousness. "The second kind of righteousness is our proper righteousness, not because we alone work it, but because we work with that first and alien righteousness."[53] "This righteousness is the product of the righteousness of the first type, actually its fruit and consequence, for we read in Galatians 5[:22]: 'But the fruit of the Spirit [i.e., of a spiritual man, whose very existence depends on faith in Christ] is . . .'"[54] "This righteousness follows the example of Christ in this respect [1 Pet. 2:21] and is transformed into his likeness [2 Cor. 3:18]. It is precisely this that Christ requires. Just as he himself did all things for us, not seeking his own good but ours only—and in this he was the most obedient to God the Father—so he desires that we also should set the same example for our neighbors."[55]

The link between the two kinds of righteousness can be elucidated by considering Luther's definition of Christian freedom (from 1520): "A Christian is a perfectly free lord of all, subject to none. A Christian is a perfectly free servant of all, subject to all."[56] In Christ, the self is lord and perfectly free; in one's own living, the self is servant to all and perfectly subjected. Reinhard Hütter says there are three ways to misread this thesis: first, forgetting "perfect freedom"; second, forgetting "perfect subjection"; third, total separation of the two claims—not appreciating that freedom sustains service.[57] And, of course, Luther's thoughts expand on the logic of Galatians itself. In Christ you have been set free (Gal. 5:1). "You were called to *freedom*. . . . Through love *serve* one another" (5:13).[58] Christ frees the Christian with his perfect life and death; then the Christian is freed to trust God and serve his or her neighbor. There is an active righteousness, but it is based on the passive righteousness received

---

51. Ibid., 298.
52. Ibid., 299.
53. Ibid.
54. Ibid., 300.
55. Ibid.
56. Luther, "Freedom of a Christian [1520]," 344.
57. Reinhard Hütter, "Freedom and Commandment: The Twofold Center of Christian Ethics," in *Bound to Be Free: Evangelical Catholic Engagements in Ecclesiology, Ethics, and Ecumenism* (Grand Rapids: Eerdmans, 2005), 154.
58. For helpful comments on the relationship of Gal. 5:1 and 5:13, see Todd A. Wilson, "Wilderness Apostasy and Paul's Portrayal of the Crisis in Galatians," *New Testament Studies* 50, no. 4 (2004): 550–71, esp. 565–70.

fully in Christ. Why this focus on the distinction yet link between these two claims? Robert Kolb points to their pastoral and exegetical utility.

> Luther's distinction between two kinds of righteousness takes seriously the whole of the person but also differentiates the identity that constitutes our being from the performance that flows from that identity and being. Because of that, this definition of our humanity speaks to those many in contemporary societies who encounter crisis in their failure either to find satisfaction in their identity or to create contentment through their performance. . . . This path to the rightness or true humanness of a person's core identity casts a different light upon the questions of success or failure at performances of what God, self and others expect. The highest worth and worthiness fall to us by pure mercy and only as gift, and they are free for the trusting. Secondary meaning and worth in life remain important but not matters of our core identity when Christ comes to justify and thus place himself as the loving Lord of human lives.[59]

Defined in Christ, Christians are dispersed to serve as those freed from the terrible burden of actively attaining righteousness. Having a passive righteousness in Christ, their activity can be turned toward their neighbor in love and their God in cheerful obedience.

Luther explicitly expounds this distinction between freedom before God and bondage to one's neighbor in his *Lectures on Galatians (1535)* when he comes to 5:13, and he explicitly addresses those same verses in the earlier essay "The Freedom of a Christian."[60] Luther clearly intends this dogmatic construct to serve as an analytic help in reading Galatians well. Before God's sight, we are righteous for Christ's sake—his imputed righteousness is our proper righteousness, wherein we do not live, but Christ lives. Before others, however, we are righteous by imitation of Christ—his elicited righteousness is our active righteousness, wherein we do live by faith in the Son of God. The logic of Galatians 2:20 shoots through the whole construct.

## Reformed Federal Theology

In the Reformed churches, the Lutheran teaching on two kinds of righteousness has been upheld and affirmed. Yet Reformed theologians tried to provide a

---

59. Robert Kolb, "Contemporary Lutheran Understandings of the Doctrine of Justification: A Selective Glimpse," in *Justification: What's at Stake in the Current Debates*, ed. Mark Husbands and Daniel Treier (Downers Grove, IL: InterVarsity, 2004), 165–66.

60. Luther, *Lectures on Galatians (1535)*, trans. Middleton, 325–26 (5:13); "The Freedom of a Christian," in *Martin Luther's Basic Theological Writings*, ed. Timothy Lull, 2nd ed. (Minneapolis: Fortress, 2005), 401, 404, 406.

wider covenantal framework within which these forms of righteousness would make sense. Thus, Reformed theologians made use of another schematic overlaid upon the Lutheran distinction of two kinds of righteousness: the distinction between the covenant of works and the covenant of grace. Made famous by the Reformed federal theologians, this distinction was meant to provide historical context for the moral and legal categorizations latent in the Lutheran schema.

The Reformed affirm the existence of a covenant of works. The Westminster Larger Catechism illustrates this doctrine well.

> The providence of God toward man in the estate in which he was created, was the placing him in paradise, appointing him to dress it, giving him liberty to eat of the fruit of the earth; putting the creatures under his dominion, and ordaining marriage for his help; affording him communion with himself; instituting the sabbath; entering into a covenant of life with him, upon condition of personal, perfect, and perpetual obedience, of which the tree of life was a pledge; and forbidding to eat of the tree of the knowledge of good and evil, upon the pain of death.[61]

Adam sinned, though, and rendered a public and representational death to his posterity: "The covenant being made with Adam as a public person, not for himself only, but for his posterity, all mankind descending from him by ordinary generation, sinned in him, and fell with him in that first transgression."[62]

In the face of sin, the triune God pledges grace. Indeed, from eternity past God has determined to provide for his people amid their failure to keep the covenant of works. Thus the good news of salvation takes the form of a promise that God will fulfill the covenant of works and make its fruits available to those yoked to Christ by faith. Again, the Westminster Larger Catechism illustrates this well: "God does not leave all men to perish in the estate of sin and misery, into which they fell by the breach of the first covenant, commonly called the covenant of works; but of his mere love and mercy delivers his elect out of it, and brings them into an estate of salvation by the second covenant, commonly called the covenant of grace."[63] There are rights and responsibilities in this covenant: "The grace of God is manifested in the second covenant, in that he freely provides and offers to sinners a Mediator, and life and salvation by him; and requiring faith as the condition to interest them in him."[64]

61. Westminster Larger Catechism 20.
62. Westminster Larger Catechism 22.
63. Westminster Larger Catechism 30.
64. Westminster Larger Catechism 32. Use of the language of "rights," of course, is taken analogically to human treaties, inasmuch as God unilaterally condescended to initiate the first

Thus, there are two conditions for Christian salvation, and they are not equal: Christ's filial obedience secures our standing before God, but Christian faith grasps hold of Christ and unites us to him. Reformed theologians affirm, of course, the Augustinian tenet that even such faith exercised by the Christian is itself a gift of God.[65] Indeed, the very faith that grasps Christ is itself a gift enjoyed by the elect due to the merits of Christ himself—it and all other spiritual blessings are theirs only in him (Eph. 1:3; cf. 1:18). But his faithful obedience to his Father really does generate Christian faith in the lives of the redeemed.[66] Here Francis Turretin is instructive.

> Again, these two conditions are proposed because they are necessary to the salvation of the sinner: perfect obedience in Christ to fulfill the righteousness of the law (to dikaiōma tou nomou), without which the justice of God did not permit life to be given to us; faith however in us that the perfect obedience and satisfaction of Christ might be applied to us and become ours by imputation. Thus what was demanded of us in the covenant of works is fulfilled by Christ in the covenant of grace. Nor is it absurd that in this way justification takes place by works and by faith—by the works of Christ and by our faith.[67]

The Reformed base this covenant theology on the "representational motif" in Scripture, and they seek to affirm both the singular divine act in pledging such covenantal grace and the mutual obligations intrinsic even to the covenant of grace: Christ is fully faithful in our place before God's law, while Christians must believe (imperfectly).[68] Christ does work on our behalf, we

---

covenant and, even more so, this second covenant. God would very well have been justified in demanding obedience without rendering any reward. That life and blessedness is promised (in the first covenant) is of God's kindness; that grace is offered (in the second covenant) is really grace upon grace. See Mark J. Beach, "Christ and the Covenant: Francis Turretin's Federal Theology as a Defense of the Doctrine of Grace" (PhD diss., Calvin Theological Seminary, 2005), 88, 127, 129, 165, 226–28.

65. One of the most curious charges raised against Reformed Protestant theology by Douglas Campbell involves the identification of a semi-Pelagian anthropology (manifesting Campbell's lack of awareness that these Reformed Protestants are the most ardent Augustinians, attributing any human act of goodness to nothing but God's grace); see Deliverance of God, 212–13, 818–19. Any confessional Protestant in the Lutheran, Reformed, or Anglican tradition could affirm his statements regarding the necessity of Word and Spirit (819); indeed, they have done so in numerous confessional documents, exegetical commentaries, and dogmatic treatises.

66. Somehow Campbell believes that "justification theory" renders the life of Christ unimportant (Deliverance of God, 210–11, 987n86). Yet Turretin demonstrates a Reformed (and Lutheran) consensus regarding the lifelong fulfillment of the law of works by Christ (to dikaiōma tou nomou).

67. Francis Turretin, Institutes of Elenctic Theology, ed. James T. Dennison Jr., trans. George Musgrave Giger (Phillipsburg, NJ: P&R, 1997), 268 (12.12.22).

68. Beach, "Christ and the Covenant," esp. 381–82.

do trust in his person—and that trust necessarily, organically leads to lives of selfless obedience: "the obedience of faith" (Rom. 1:5; 16:26).[69]

## Conclusion

One mode of analysis too little practiced today is comparative dogmatic analysis. Paul's words are not those of the Lutherans and the Reformed. But these two Reformational traditions seek to honor Paul's word of gospel with these corresponding words. Both schemes make sense of grace and freedom in non-competitive fashion. Both schemes manage to hold the christological and the anthropological together in a generative order. Both schemes, therefore, might serve contemporary Pauline scholars well, inasmuch as they are exegetically impelled and theologically pliable, capable of upholding Pauline emphases that seem to fall by the wayside in the battle between "christological" and "anthropological" approaches, or sociological and apocalyptic reading modes.[70]

We can conclude by turning to the testimony of one who in his own contemporary way has followed the Lutheran and Reformed forebears to witness to Paul's apostolic testimony about grace. George Hunsinger's "Chalcedonian pattern" serves as yet another dogmatic construct capable of proving helpful in making sense of the ins and outs of Pauline exegesis. Hunsinger's point is clear and compelling.

> Grace that is not disruptive is not grace—a point that Flannery O'Connor well grasped alongside Karl Barth. Grace, strictly speaking, does not mean continuity but radical discontinuity, not reform but revolution, not violence but nonviolence, not the perfecting of virtues but the forgiveness of sins, not improvement but resurrection from the dead. It means repentance, judgment, and death as the portal to life. It means negation and the negation of the negation. The grace of God really comes to lost sinners, but in coming it disrupts them to the core. It slays to make alive and sets the captive free. Grace may of course work silently

---

69. Again Campbell misconstrues classical Protestant teaching regarding Christian faith: it is unequivocally not construed as a work (contra Campbell, *Deliverance of God*, 1138–39n113). The early Reformers made this point emphatically (see, e.g., Luther, "Two Kinds of Righteousness (1519)," where only one sort of righteousness is a work—namely, that "passive righteousness" of Christ; cf. *Lectures on Galatians (1535)*, trans. Middleton, 71, 90, 128–30, 133), and the later confessional traditions adopted it wholeheartedly (see, e.g., Heidelberg Catechism 61–63).

70. The failure of such approaches is evident in the inconsistency latent in Campbell's project, where he opposes any conditionality premised on human action (*Deliverance of God*, 101, 187–88) yet points to two groups of people whose repudiation is premised on their failing to meet a conditional human action—namely, sole reliance upon the apocalyptic grace of Jesus (810–11). Furthermore, Campbell continues to find a place for faith as a condition for Christian assurance, even if not for the application or appropriation of salvation in Christ (821).

and secretly like a germinating seed as well as like a bolt from the blue. It is always wholly as incalculable as it is reliable, unmerited, and full of blessing. Yet it is necessarily as unsettling as it is comforting. It does not finally teach of its own sufficiency without appointing a thorn in the flesh. Grace is disruptive because God does not compromise with sin, nor ignore it, nor call it good. On the contrary, God removes it by submitting to the cross to show that love is stronger than death. Those whom God loves may be drawn to God through their suffering and be privileged to share in his sufferings in the world, because grace in its radical disruption surpasses all that we imagine or think.[71]

Grace really does disrupt us from the outside—it kills to make alive. But it does make us alive, and we do thereby enjoy freedom from captivity. The apocalyptic and christological proposals of late focus on the decisive action of Jesus and the invasive, counterintuitive nature of the gospel. One only wishes that—following any of these Reformational interpreters of Paul—they could equally affirm that salvation really brings life, that Christ's faithfulness really brings faith, that redemption really delivers us to freedom that must be lived. Galatians 2:20 and the full splendor of its confession—"it is no longer I who live, but Christ who lives in me"—demands such testimony, if we are to honor its two claims and the jolting "but" that joins them, if we are to affirm union with Christ and the imputation of his righteousness, if we are to make sense of his life for us and his reign in us. The totality of this text startles us and overturns our expectations of agency and gift. That is as it should be. Grace is disruptive—it disrupts us so we can live by it.

71. George Hunsinger, *Disruptive Grace: Studies in the Theology of Karl Barth* (Grand Rapids: Eerdmans, 2000), 16–17.

# PART 3

# CHRIST IN US

# 5

## "Freedom for Love"

### Justification and Sanctification

The most frequent objection to the traditional Protestant doctrine of justification remains the antinomian charge—namely, that this belief undercuts the moral life. It is a serious charge. Jesus calls his followers to discipleship, transformation, and obedience. Any doctrine of justification that somehow denigrates this biblical priority is clearly wrongheaded. So we must consider the objection.

Perhaps we should back up one step, locating this charge in a wider context. The charge of "legal fiction" has often been heaped upon the Protestant doctrine. If one's vindication is based on an imputed righteousness, then God's verdict tells a false tale or fails to reflect lived reality in an accurate way. But more is involved. Two charges are latent here: first, a claim that imputed righteousness renders God a less than equitable judge; second, a suggestion that justification *extra nos* results in libertinism and stunts moral growth. The first charge (regarding the relationship of justification and the doctrine of God) was considered in chapter 1. It is a crux, inasmuch as the apostle Paul shows a passionate concern to link justification by faith alone with the justice of God (Rom. 3:25–26). In this chapter, however, the second concern deserves attention. What can we say to the charge that justification in Christ alone leads to or encourages antinomianism and libertinism? Is the judgment of one recent

Luther scholar accurate, that "at times [Luther] makes it sound as if grace accomplishes nothing substantive in the Christian life"?[1]

Surely the logic of this charge can be appreciated. If eternal acceptance is already granted by God, then a certain feverish pursuit of acceptance will not follow. Consider an analogy. If a driver is immediately pardoned by a law enforcement officer for a driving infraction, let off the hook right away for no other reason than the officer's laxity and mercy, then the driver is unlikely to have motivation to correct his or her driving in the future. If, however, his or her record were to be expunged only on the basis of future good driving, there would be an immediate motivation for zeal in carefully following the rules of the road. The moral logic appears obvious. Or so it has seemed to generations of Christians in Roman Catholic and holiness traditions. Nevertheless, we must ask if this really gets to the issue at hand and accurately reflects the way the biblical text speaks of obedience and its motivation.

Douglas Campbell has reiterated this claim in his polemics against what he calls "justification theory." "Faith does not 'put itself into effect' through love in Justification theory. It has no need to do so, and neither can it. That is, it makes no sense to suggest . . . that the state of faith is a more effective *ethical* state, in the sense of being more 'powerful' than either circumcision or uncircumcision. Justification theory is not initially concerned with ethical capacity per se, and it ultimately makes little contribution to the Christian's capacity, as we have already seen at some length; it is ethically anemic."[2] This charge that justification by faith alone (construed in the traditional Protestant sense) is "ethically anemic" arises in his discussion of Galatians 5:5–6. He suggests that in the way faith is construed by Luther and others in this Protestant tradition, it simply cannot provide incentive or enlarge capacity for love. Elsewhere he says,

> Justification theory cannot, in strictly theoretical terms, generate a responsible ethical state within the Christian at all. From a very early point, the theory launches a scathing attack *on* ethical behavior. This attack, which provides such effective leverage on the unsaved individual, also condemns empty "religion" and potentially oppressive ecclesial institutions. . . . After reducing the condition of salvation from ethical perfection to faith alone, the theory cannot then consistently expect self-interested individuals to undertake further ethical behavior!

1. Jesse Couenhoven, "Grace as Pardon and Power: Pictures of the Christian Life in Luther, Calvin, and Barth," *Journal of Religious Ethics* 28 (2000): 63–88, quote on 73.

2. Douglas Campbell, *The Deliverance of God: An Apocalyptic Rereading of Justification in Paul* (Grand Rapids: Eerdmans, 2009), 887. The first part of Campbell's massive book analyzes "justification theory" and finds it wanting in a host of ways (see esp. 932, 934 for his assessment). For analysis of its sizable flaws in historical and theological argumentation, see chap. 2 above.

Their sins are forgiven and they are saved, so no further leverage on them can be generated through self-interest (which previously came principally from the prospect of hell, but that problem has now been resolved).[3]

Campbell even says that the traditional Protestant approach to justification *sola fide* (which he casts into this theoretical construct "justification theory") contradicts and undermines the logic of sanctification, and vice versa. Not only does justification not precede sanctification, but the way the two have been conceived (forensic declaration and moral transformation, respectively) is also logically incoherent and arbitrary. So we can state the objection bluntly: if justification is given by faith alone, then sanctification not only need not follow but also will most likely not follow. All things being equal, the traditional Protestant will appropriate justification by faith alone as a good reason to live like hell, for heaven is already assured.

In discussing evangelical obedience—more specifically, the relationship between justification and sanctification—I will focus on the theme of freedom. Jean-Luc Nancy has said, "If nothing is more common today than demanding or defending freedom in the spheres of morality, law, or politics . . . , then nothing is less articulated or problematized, in turn, than the nature and stakes of what we call freedom."[4] Yet it is precisely this often misunderstood idea of freedom or liberation that links justification and sanctification. Eberhard Jüngel says,

> By now it should be self-evident that from such faith deeds of gratitude proceed quite spontaneously. These are deeds freely performed. Yet they arise of necessity from the gratitude of faith; they cannot help coming out of persons who are grateful to God. In thankfulness, freedom starts to press the issue. Faith, which is nothing other than receiving, is a taut coil springing creatively into action for the common good. For believers know that since God has done enough for our *salvation*, we can never do enough for the *good* of the world. . . . There is no more liberating basis for ethics than the doctrine of justification of sinners by faith alone.[5]

Jüngel starkly opposes the antinomian charge and does so by asserting that Christian freedom impels obedience. Indeed, he goes further, saying that justification by faith alone frees one for obedience. This seems strange—freedom

3. Ibid., 81.
4. Jean-Luc Nancy, *The Experience of Freedom*, trans. Bridget McDonald (Stanford: Stanford University Press, 1993), 1.
5. Eberhard Jüngel, *Justification: The Heart of the Christian Faith*, trans. Jeffrey F. Cayzer (London: T&T Clark, 2001), 259.

impelling something—so we must consider this argument over against the antinomian charge leveled by Campbell and others.[6]

At this point, theological reason has moved from the realm of mere biblical commentary to the work of dogmatic analysis. Such reflection relies on the work of commentary, and succeeds inasmuch as it remains tethered to the prophetic and apostolic witness, but it moves into a new idiom: the categories of dogmatic theology.[7] Before turning to a dogmatic sketch of justification's relation to sanctification, a few words about the nature and need for a dogmatic approach are due.

First, dogmatic theology seeks to honor the breadth of the canon's teaching on a given topic. Whereas individuals are inclined to fix their eyes upon their "canon within a canon," a dogmatic approach must always ask how such texts are shaped and supplemented by other biblical teaching. In other words, dogmatic theology attempts to confess the "whole counsel of God." With respect to justification debates, this suggests that we ought to look beyond the Pauline texts around which the debates seem to circle so insistently. The Pauline teaching will be considered, but it must be viewed within its canonical orbit. Given the nature of Paul's theological argumentation as reasoning from Scripture, this is all the more apparent.[8] Paul reasons about the proper way to read texts in light of the Christ event. Thus, to grasp the totality of his teaching, we should turn to the texts of Israel's Scriptures and then read Paul as an apostolic commentator on these texts.

Second, dogmatic theology attempts to emphasize that which the Bible emphasizes, allowing its priorities to shape the passions of reason itself. We should note the way various points may be articulated and affirmed, yet with differing levels of priority. Paul speaks of some matters being "of first importance" (1 Cor. 15:3). Presumably, other issues are "of secondary importance," likely some issues addressed in that very letter. In regard to debates about justification, we might note the way that various biblical texts emphasize different parts of the covenant relationship. Furthermore, many things may be affirmed without being emphasized as "of first importance." So we require a dogmatic analysis to get not only the breadth of Scripture right but also the balance and priorities of Scripture.

6. For suggestive reflections similar to my own, see Michael Weinrich, "Justified for Covenant Fellowship: A Key Biblical Theme for the Whole of Theology," in *What Is Justification About? Reformed Contributions to an Ecumenical Theme*, ed. Michael Weinrich and John Burgess (Grand Rapids: Eerdmans, 2009), 17–20.

7. This distinction is clearly made in John Webster, "Biblical Reasoning," *Anglican Theological Review* 90, no. 4 (2008): 749–50.

8. Indeed, Francis Watson has shown that Paul's reflections on torah are largely readings of a text (Pentateuch); see *Paul and the Hermeneutics of Faith* (London: T&T Clark, 2004).

Third, dogmatic theology pursues the intelligible articulation of the ways these various biblical teachings cohere, insofar as this is possible for creatures with limited knowledge. It would be presumptuous to claim that we can describe precisely how all biblical truths hang together, inasmuch as they all center on the ways and works of a holy God in our midst. His ways are not ours; his identity exceeds our categories. Herman Bavinck rightly notes that "mystery is the lifeblood of dogmatics."[9] A large part of dogmatic work involves locating mystery at the right place, tracing the distinct lines of biblical teaching to the furthest expressible coherence that we can muster and no further.[10] Two errors loom: first, the slothful tendency to punt too early, claiming that God's works are mysterious and their logic cannot be traced; and second, the prideful assertion that we can hem in the nature and acts of God. God has spoken, and we must think carefully about the coherence of his words; *yet* we must realize that at some point we will come to the end of our reason and view the precipice of mystery. "The secret things belong to the LORD our God, but the things that are revealed belong to us and to our children forever" (Deut. 29:29). It is the dogmatic task to ask these questions of coherence. That is why dogmatics is so frequently referred to as "systematic theology"—not that it teases out a host of beliefs based on some foundational tenet or central dogma, but that it seeks to articulate the systematic coherence of the Christian confession as far as the Bible allows.[11]

With respect to the debates about justification, we need dogmatic analysis of God's redemptive activity as it relates to humanity's ethical calling. These are questions of coherence and fittingness and, thus, fall within the work of dogmatics.

To show that freedom and justification are related and, more important, that forensic declaration before God fuels lives of service and good works, I will trace three cycles of biblical teaching: the exodus narrative, the Ten Commandments, and key Pauline texts. I will seek to show that Karl Barth is right when he argues, "Faith is not obedience, but as obedience is not obedience without faith, faith is not faith without obedience. They belong together,

9. Herman Bavinck, *Reformed Dogmatics*, vol. 2, *God and Creation*, ed. John Bolt, trans. John Vriend (Grand Rapids: Baker Academic, 2004), 29.

10. Here it is important to remember that we confess what we cannot always explain; see Michael Weinrich, "Die Ökumene in der Rechtfertigungslehre in evangelischreformierter Perspektive," in *Von Gott angenommen—in Christus verwandelt: Die Rechtfertigungslehre im multilateralen ökumenischen Dialog*, ed. Uwe Swarat, Beiheft zur Ökumenischen Rundschau 78 (Frankfurt: Otto Lembeck, 2006), 125–54.

11. For analysis of what systematic theology surely cannot be, see Karl Barth, foreword to *Dogmatics in Outline*, trans. G. T. Thomson (New York: Harper & Row, 1959), 5–6.

as do thunder and lightning in a thunderstorm."[12] In so doing, I will engage narrative, torah, and epistolary material from across the Bible, showing the breadth and canonical relation of various scriptural texts.

## The Exodus: Freedom and Service

The exodus is event, text, pattern—all of these at once. The exodus refers to an event, in which Yahweh freed the Israelite slaves from their toil in Egypt. The exodus also refers to the biblical text that describes this epic battle between Pharaoh and Yahweh, culminating in the establishment of Israel as God's own people, "a kingdom of priests and a holy nation" (Exod. 19:6). Throughout the canon, however, the exodus functions as a type or figure of salvation itself. Whether in Isaiah 40–66, the Psalms (e.g., Ps. 106:47), the Gospel of Mark, the Acts of the Apostles, or other texts, the restoration of God's fallen people is depicted as a new exodus.[13]

The exodus is all about deliverance. Slaves are set free from oppression. Burdens are relieved. Exile in a foreign land ends. The Israelites are taken out of Egypt, as the prophet Hosea says (Hos. 11:1). Indeed, this delivery follows from the conquest of Yahweh over Pharaoh and all his might. The plague narrative recounted in Exodus 7–12 shows the supremacy of the God of Israel, in contrast to the feebleness and futility of the gods of Egypt and, ultimately, her pharaoh. Comparative studies illuminate this observation, showing that the various plagues mock the pagan gods of the Egyptians.[14] Whereas the locals believed the Nile possessed divine power of a life-giving sort, Yahweh turns it dead, portrayed as a river of shed blood. This plague cycle shows that freedom involves the triumph of the true God over the false gods of the Egyptians. Feigned claims of lordship and sovereignty are rendered null and void; so the God of Israel, having slain the very lifeblood of Pharaoh's house, can demand, "Let my people go!" Indeed, James Barr has shown that Israel's *Magnificat*, the

12. Karl Barth, *Church Dogmatics*, vol. 4/2, *The Doctrine of Reconciliation*, ed. G. W. Bromiley and T. F. Torrance, trans. G. W. Bromiley (Edinburgh: T&T Clark, 1958), 538.

13. See Brevard S. Childs, *Isaiah: A Commentary*, Old Testament Library (Louisville: Westminster John Knox, 2000), 110–11; as well as a number of studies on the intertextual use of the exodus in Isaiah and then in the New Testament, e.g., Joel Marcus, "Mark 1:2–3: The Gospel according to Isaiah," chap. 2 in *The Way of the Lord: Christological Exegesis of the Old Testament in the Gospel of Mark*, Studies of the New Testament and Its World (Edinburgh: T&T Clark, 1992); Rikki E. Watts, *Isaiah's New Exodus in Mark*, Biblical Studies Library (Grand Rapids: Baker Academic, 2000); David Pao, *Acts and the Isaianic New Exodus*, Biblical Studies Library (Grand Rapids: Baker Academic, 2002).

14. See John Currid, *Ancient Egypt and the Old Testament* (Grand Rapids: Baker Books, 1997), chap. 6.

Song of the Sea in Exodus 15:1–21, mentions neither freedom nor slavery but focuses entirely on the exodus event as Israel's God triumphing over Pharaoh.[15]

Why does Yahweh care so passionately about freedom? Why does God contest Pharaoh's sovereignty? If we let the immediate narrative set the parameters for the question, an answer is consistently, but surprisingly, offered: Yahweh frees Israel so that it might serve him. This purpose is first revealed to Moses at Horeb, when God says, "But I will be with you, and this shall be the sign for you, that I have sent you: when you have brought the people out of Egypt, you shall serve God on this mountain" (Exod. 3:12). What serves here as a sign of authorization is quickly revealed to be the very purpose of deliverance, for time and again Moses demands the freedom of the Israelites so that they might go serve or worship their God in the wilderness (e.g., Exod. 3:12, 18; cf. 5:1; 7:16; 8:1, 20; 9:1, 13; 10:3). Pharaoh and his servants realize that the demand is not for independence or autonomy, but for space to serve God rather than Pharaoh and his empire (e.g., Exod. 10:7, 11, 24; 12:31).

May we summarize the theology of the exodus? Surely efforts to do so can become reductive. Witness, for example, the various liberationist approaches to the exodus, suggesting that this represents God's universal and (seemingly timeless) "preferential option for the poor." Jon Levenson has reminded us, however, that the exodus was embedded within a covenantal history and remains a witness amid a canonical framework.[16] While Amos 9:7 suggests that the exodus does serve as a paradigm for understanding common grace, Levenson has shown that "the exodus thus cannot justly be taken to authorize liberation in the sense of freedom from external constraints or the attainment of self-determination," two pillars of so much political theology in the liberationist strain.[17] Thus, we cannot deny that attempts to summarize the meaning of an event, a text, or a canonical paradigm like the exodus can easily go awry. Yet misuse does not preclude proper use. It remains worthwhile to plumb the depths for the meaning of the exodus. In fact, Levenson has provided a useful paradigm for understanding what is going on in the exodus. He sees three meanings: enthronement, covenant, and dedication.[18] Furthermore, he suggests that all three emphases are illustrated in the Song of the Sea (Exod. 15).

15. James Barr, "The Bible as a Political Document," in *The Scope and Authority of the Bible* (Philadelphia: Westminster, 1980), 107–8.

16. Jon Levenson, "Exodus and Liberation," in *The Hebrew Bible, the Old Testament, and Historical Criticism: Jews and Christians in Biblical Studies* (Louisville: Westminster John Knox, 1993), 133–37.

17. Ibid., 150. For analysis of Amos 9:7, see Walter Brueggemann, "Exodus in the Plural (Amos 9:7)," in *Texts That Linger, Words That Explode: Listening to Prophetic Voices* (Minneapolis: Fortress, 2000), 89–103.

18. Levenson, "Exodus and Liberation," 144.

These three themes are foretold earlier in the exodus account: "Say therefore to the people of Israel, 'I am the LORD, and I will bring you out from under the burdens of the Egyptians, and I will deliver you from slavery to them, and I will redeem you with an outstretched arm and with great acts of judgment. I will take you to be my people, and I will be your God, and you shall know that I am the LORD your God, who has brought you out from under the burdens of the Egyptians. I will bring you into the land that I swore to give to Abraham, to Isaac, and to Jacob. I will give it to you for a possession. I am the LORD'" (Exod. 6:6–8). The promise climaxes with the demonstration that Yahweh is the Lord, enthroned over all. Indeed, the manner of triumph mocks the claims of Pharaoh, for the Egyptians pictured Pharaoh's potency and sovereignty residing in his "outstretched arm." So Yahweh brings "great acts of judgment" upon the false gods of Egypt. But this sovereignty is exercised on Israel's behalf and at the behest of her prayers. God's freedom is displayed in the deliverance of the slaves. Finally, this liberation brings covenantal relationship and responsibility: the redeemed will be God's people, his possession and prize. James Mays says that "the first commandment is the true meaning of the exodus."[19]

The exodus narrative does not depict Israel as a model of spiritual vitality. Immediately after hearing the promise of Exodus 6:6–8, we read that "Moses spoke thus to the people of Israel, but they did not listen to Moses, because of their broken spirit and harsh slavery" (v. 9). Their obstinate response is echoed throughout the whole narrative, well after the decisive liberation wrought at the Red Sea. Indeed, they grumble time and again, as described in Exodus and considered by both Paul (1 Cor. 10:1–11) and the anonymous author who wrote to the Hebrews (Heb. 3:7–19). By noting the lessons gleaned by Paul and the Hebrews account, we can see a link between unbelief and idolatry. In other words, Paul says that the freed slaves failed to please God because they went after other gods or idols (1 Cor. 10:7, 14); speaking of the same events, Hebrews points to unbelief as their sin (Heb. 3:19). We might ask how these two charges relate to each other: do Paul and the author of Hebrews speak of discrete sins or of the same wrongdoing from different angles?

## Trust and Having a God, or Unbelief and Idolatry: The Ten Commandments

The key principle to seeing these sins as part of a larger whole is that unbelief involves idolatry. We see this notion expanded upon in the Ten Commandments,

19. James Luther Mays, *Psalms*, Interpretation (Louisville: Westminster John Knox, 1994), 267.

manifest in the hermeneutical role the first commandment plays in properly appreciating the other nine commandments.

We can grasp this best by reflecting on a claim made by Augustine and viewing it within the orbit of Old Testament teaching about sin. Thinking about the various vices, Augustine suggests that pride is the root of all sin. In *City of God*, he traces the power of pride behind the fall of angels and of humans.[20] In *Confessions*, he depicts the slavery of sin as the power of pride and lust.[21] Paul Griffiths summarizes the Augustinian position in this way: "Sin's characteristic mark is self-serving aversion: sinners turn their faces away from God and attempt, narcissistically, to look only at themselves."[22] At first glance, Augustine's analysis may seem speculative or removed from the biblical portrait of sin, wherein idolatry, not pride, is the chief culprit. Indeed, the Old Testament consistently depicts idol worship as the enduring problem of humanity. Not surprisingly, the first commandment addresses this very challenge: "You shall have no other gods before me" (Exod. 20:3). The famed *shema* puts it another way, positively, we might say: "Hear, O Israel: The LORD our God, the LORD is one. You shall love the LORD your God with all your heart and with all your soul and with all your might" (Deut. 6:4–5). Augustine's maxim may seem detached from the warp and woof of the biblical teaching on sin: whereas he focuses on pride and the New Testament fixes on unbelief, these Old Testament texts seem to portray idolatry as the greatest and most dangerous sin.

Yet we must ask how idolatry is unpacked within the Bible's own categories. Idolatry is identified with self-love or other-love apart from the triune God. When we reflect on the nature of the first commandment and ask what it means to have another god, we see that pride is always involved in idolatry, and further, that unbelief is also implicated in such misdeeds. Martin Luther grasped this more clearly than perhaps anyone.

That is, you are to regard me alone as your God. What does this mean, and how is it to be understood? What does "to have a god" mean, or what is God?

*Answer:* A "god" is the term for that to which we are to look for all good and in which we are to find refuge in all need. Therefore, to have a god is nothing else than to trust and believe in that one with your whole heart. As I have often said, it is the trust and faith of the heart alone that make both God and an

20. Augustine, *Concerning the City of God against the Pagans*, trans. Henry Bettenson (New York: Penguin, 1984), 471–73 (12.1), 571–74 (14.13), and 649 (16.1).

21. Augustine, *Confessions*, ed. Maria Boulding, trans. John E. Rotelle, Works of St. Augustine 1/1 (Hyde Park, NY: New City, 1997), 123–24 (5.15).

22. Paul J. Griffiths, *Lying: An Augustinian Theology of Duplicity* (Grand Rapids: Brazos, 2004), 55.

idol. If your faith and trust are right, then your God is the true one. Conversely, where your trust is false and wrong, there you do not have the true God. For these two belong together, faith and God. Anything on which your heart relies and depends, I say, that is really your God.[23]

Idols are objects of affection and sources of satisfaction, whether religious, political, sexual, economic, psychological, or otherwise. They can include any number of things, good things, given an importance and a weightiness (or glory) that they do not deserve and cannot carry. They are pursued for what they offer the idolater; yet this process results in the idolater serving the idol. For example, Jesus says you cannot serve God and mammon (Matt. 6:24). Mammon is not served by having its needs met; rather, it is served by being approached as the supplier of the deepest needs of others, assuring them of surety and security.[24] In so doing, however, idolaters show a self-love and pride insofar as they place their affections and root their identity in that idol. Doing so demonstrates that their opinion or suspicions carry more weight than do the revealed words of God, who calls us to flee idols. So other idols always point to the idol of the self. Idolatry is pride.[25] The pursuit of satisfaction and fulfillment in things other than God is a pursuit of one's identity, one's vindication and justification, apart from the will and design of God.

Luther considers the first commandment to be the key to the whole Decalogue, indeed, to the whole of the Scriptures. In his 1520 "Treatise on Good Works" he says,

> This is the work of the first commandment, which enjoins, "Thou shalt have no other gods." This means, "Since I alone am God, thou shalt place all thy confidence, trust, and faith in me alone and in no one else." For you do not have a god if you just call him God outwardly with your lips, or worship him with the knees or bodily gestures; but only if you trust him with your heart and look to him for all good, grace, and favor. . . . This faith, this trust, this confidence from the heart's core is the true fulfilling of the first commandment. Without such faith no work at all can satisfy this command. And because this commandment is the very first of all commandments and the highest and the best, the one from which all others proceed, in which they exist and by which they are judged and assessed, so its work (that is, the faith or confidence that God is gracious at all times) is the very first, highest, and best from which all

---

23. Martin Luther, "The Large Catechism (1529)," in *The Book of Concord: The Confessions of the Evangelical Lutheran Church*, ed. Robert Kolb and Timothy J. Wengert, trans. Charles Arand (Minneapolis: Fortress, 2000), 386.

24. Matt. 6:25–33 serves as commentary on the principle enunciated in Matt. 6:24.

25. R. R. Reno, "Pride and Idolatry," *Interpretation* 60, no. 2 (April 2006): 166–80.

others must proceed, in which they must exist and abide, and by which they must be judged and assessed.[26]

Dependent submission to God requires that we have no other gods or benefactors.[27] Again, to put it in terms of the exodus account of which the Ten Commandments are a part, freedom *from* masters other than Yahweh is for the sake of freedom for service to Yahweh. Luther finds faith and worship directed solely at Yahweh present in the first commandment of the Decalogue, as noted above. He also observes that this commandment is the pathway to the others. Indeed, without obeying the first commandment (trusting God), it is impossible to obey the others.

The New Testament witnesses echo this requirement. "Without faith it is impossible to please him, for whoever would draw near to God must believe that he exists and that he rewards those who seek him" (Heb. 11:6). The sequence of faith and pleasing God is not like that of a relay race, in which one moves from a time of faith (conversion) to a period of obedience (the Christian life). Rather, as becomes clearer in a different text, faith must impel every action, or else the action cannot please God. Paul tells us, "For whatever does not proceed from faith is sin" (Rom. 14:23). Here he speaks of the need for specific actions to be rooted in trust, that is, overflowing from a belief that Christ's work is sufficient to save and to meet one's needs. Unless one knows that one's deepest need is met in Jesus, one will not be freed to serve others selflessly and sacrificially.[28]

Tracing the argument thus far: in the exodus God frees Israel so it may worship (serve) God. In the Ten Commandments trust is the necessary first step to any real service (worship) of God. How these two statements cohere takes us to the apostle Paul's biblical reasoning. Paul links them and does so by applying the exodus framework to Christian experience in Jesus.

26. Martin Luther, "Treatise on Good Works (1520)," in *The Christian in Society I*, ed. James Atkinson, Luther's Works 44 (Philadelphia: Fortress, 1966), 30. The Westminster Assembly tried to articulate this claim in their confession of faith: "They who, upon pretense of Christian liberty, do practice any sin, or cherish any lust, do thereby destroy the end of Christian liberty, which is, that being delivered out of the hands of our enemies, we might serve the Lord without fear, in holiness and righteousness before Him, all the days of our life" (Westminster Confession of Faith 20.3).

27. See Patrick D. Miller, *The God You Have: Politics, Religion, and the First Commandment*, Facets (Minneapolis: Fortress, 2005); Karl Barth, "The First Commandment as an Axiom of Theology," in *The Way of Theology in Karl Barth: Essays and Comments*, ed. H. Martin Rumscheidt (Allison Park, PA: Pickwick, 1986), 63–78.

28. Rowan Williams points to the so-called peace dividend here as an illustration of this principle: at the end of World War II, the Allies spoke of a "peace dividend" that could be spent on other nonmilitary projects now that this epic battle was concluding (*Tokens of Trust: An Introduction to Christian Belief* [Louisville: Westminster John Knox, 2007], 81–104).

## Paul on Vindication and Freedom

Why has a chapter on justification and sanctification spent the lion's share of its time on the book of Exodus? The notion of freedom relates directly to justification, as Martin Luther declared, and freedom involves obedience. Thus the redemption of slaves from Egypt—and the obedience to which they are summoned—is of great importance in thinking about the doctrine of justification in biblical perspective. We must make the move, however, to talking about the apostle Paul, who writes about justification more than anyone else in the Scriptures. But grasping the force of Paul's theology here involves reading him as a biblical thinker, a theologian tethered to the interpretation of Israel's Scriptures in light of the gospel of Jesus.[29] Paul's exposition of justification makes plain this biblical connection between freedom and justification before God.

We see this conceptual link made in Paul's words to the Ephesians. "In him we have redemption through his blood, the forgiveness of our trespasses, according to the riches of his grace, which he lavished upon us, in all wisdom and insight making known to us the mystery of his will, according to his purpose, which he set forth in Christ as a plan for the fullness of time, to unite all things in him, things in heaven and things on earth" (1:7–10).[30] The key phrase for our purposes is "in him we have redemption through his blood" (v. 7). Paul describes an exodus or liberating event in terms of a slave being redeemed at the auction block. The instrument of freedom is described in two ways: "through his blood," that is, "through . . . the forgiveness of our trespasses." Christ's blood ensures forgiveness; forgiveness frees the captives. The context (in fact, the letter as a whole) does not mention justification, yet the notion cannot be far from this author's mind as he talks of forgiveness. Remember that Paul so frequently links justification with the forgiveness of sins (e.g., Rom. 4; 2 Cor. 5).[31]

---

29. The literature here is vast and ever growing. The most pertinent texts are Francis Watson, *Paul and the Hermeneutics of Faith*; and Richard Hays, *The Conversion of the Imagination: Paul as Interpreter of Israel's Scripture* (Grand Rapids: Eerdmans, 2005).

30. For argument in favor of Pauline authorship of Ephesians, see Peter S. Williamson, *Ephesians*, Catholic Commentary on Sacred Scripture (Grand Rapids: Baker Academic, 2009), 15. The cumulative case argument against Pauline authorship is admittedly weak on every individual point and no more conclusive when considered together; see its most lucid exposition in Ernest Best, *A Critical and Exegetical Commentary on Ephesians*, International Critical Commentary (London: T&T Clark, 1998), 6–36, esp. 35–36.

31. Indeed, it is because of Paul's frequent use of forgiveness to stand in as a synonym for all that is going on in justification that the Heidelberg Catechism can move back and forth between talking of forgiveness and referring to justification, including the imputation of our sins to Christ and the imputation of his righteousness to us (so Heidelberg Catechism 60).

Furthermore, links can be found between the language in Ephesians 1 and the next chapter. Indeed, 1:7–10 offers a summary of the two key points in chapter 2. First, God redeems. He rescues and saves sinners from sin, evil, and death. Lexical and thematic continuities cross 1:7–9 and 2:4–9, both of which depict the work of God in Christ saving. Second, God unites his people. This sanctifying of a people for unity across typical racial and social boundaries appears in 1:9–10 as well as 2:11–22. In 4:2–3, this unity is depicted as a work of love. Ephesians 2 offers the very same dynamic theologically, as does Galatians 2, although without using the terminology of justification. Because the work of Christ for us (*pro nobis*) and outside us (*extra nos*) reconciles us to God, nothing should divide us socially. Galatians 2 depicts reconciliation via the notion of justification (vv. 11–21), whereas Ephesians 2 describes salvation as the engine for reconciliation. Each term brings with it some unique conceptual background and nuance. The same logic, however, resides behind both concepts.[32]

Too often exegetes and theologians alike have allowed lexical distinctions to foreshorten conceptual expansion and discussion. Especially with regard to justification, we must remember that the doctrine need not be directly tied to certain Hebrew and Greek word groups.[33] Ephesians 2 should play a part in discussion of justification, inasmuch as it relates to key issues (faith, salvation, Christ, sin, grace, works) that are everywhere appearing when justification is discussed. Again, this is not to say that Paul did not have particular shades of meaning in mind when he used the terminology of salvation over against justification. Rather, it is to say that realms of semantic overlap and, more important, dogmatic relations are clear here. So Ephesians 2 and its logical argument from salvation by grace alone to racial reconciliation parallel Paul's argument via justification by faith alone in Galatians 2. In both cases the gospel of Jesus is described as work accomplished, organically applied to the practice of ethnic reconciliation. If this conceptual link of salvation in Ephesians 2 and justification in Galatians 2 is accepted, then the former text can inform our theology of justification more broadly. Indeed, it augments the tie to forgiveness of sins in Ephesians 1:7 and suggests that Paul is linking redemption (v. 7) with God's justifying action—or, more narrowly construed, God's forgiving action in Christ.

That this is not an exegetical stretch is made more apparent when one notes that Colossians 1:13–14 also connects redemption with forgiveness:

32. See the discussion in chap. 2 regarding the biblical and dogmatic realms of discourse as it pertains to the use of "justification" and other soteriological terms.
33. See the discussion in chap. 2 under the heading "The Forensic Entryway of the Gospel," as well as Michael Allen and Daniel J. Treier, "Dogmatic Theology and Biblical Perspectives on Justification: A Reply to Leithart," *Westminster Theological Journal* 70, no. 1 (2008): 105–10.

"He has delivered us from the domain of darkness and transferred us to the kingdom of his beloved Son, in whom we have redemption, the forgiveness of sins." The contextual point, amid Paul's broader argument in the chapter, is to encourage "endurance and patience with joy" (v. 11). To walk in such a way, the Colossians are in need of strength, and Paul turns to explain the effects and outputs of their redemption in Christ as a means of providing such vigor. Deliverance and redemption are theirs (v. 13). Identified with Christ ("in whom"), they are freed for life with God. Surely, the reference to the "beloved Son" points back not only to the transfiguration and the baptism of Christ (when he was called God's "beloved") but also to the long tradition of the "beloved Son" within Judaism.[34] Jesus is put forward in place of his people, just as the ram was provided by Yahweh for Abraham's offering. His *akedah* ("sacrificial binding") brings "the forgiveness of sins" (v. 14), freeing those enslaved to the claims of the "domain of darkness." Again, forgiveness terminology (rooted in the same theological realm as justification language and occasionally paired with it—e.g., Rom. 4:7) is used to depict the means of freedom and the pathway to endurance, patience, love, and joy. Not only that, but Paul is also surely alluding to the restoration of the exiles and, behind that prophetic idea, the liberation of the original exiles from Egypt.[35] Paul is reading the exodus and applying it figurally to the church. Obedience comes from freedom, and freedom is somehow grounded in forgiveness (the sacrifice of the beloved Son).

Assuming that these two strands of evidence make sense, or at least that it is obvious that Paul speaks straightforwardly about forgiveness of sins redeeming the captives, we still need to ask why this is true. How is it that forgiveness of sins or justification before God somehow frees slaves? We will see that being declared just before God's judgment frees and empowers obedience, inasmuch as it renders moot and futile the accusations of sin. Romans 6 offers help in approaching this question.

As we consider Romans 6 in context, a preliminary point must be made. It is not simply the case that the traditional Protestant doctrine of *sola fide* can muster some ethical implications. Arguments thus far have shown this to be the case; however, we can go a step further and turn the tables on the interlocutor.

---

34. Jon D. Levenson, *The Death and Resurrection of the Beloved Son: The Transformation of Child Sacrifice in Judaism and Christianity* (New Haven: Yale University Press, 1993). Cf. R. W. L. Moberly, "Genesis 22: Abraham—Model or Monster?," in *The Theology of the Book of Genesis*, Old Testament Theology (Cambridge: Cambridge University Press, 2009), 187–89.

35. Douglas J. Moo, *The Letters to the Colossians and Philemon*, Pillar New Testament Commentary (Grand Rapids: Eerdmans, 2009), 103–4. Moo rightly argues that there is likely a two-step allusion here: first to the exile and then, via that exile tradition, to the original exodus.

When reading Paul's Epistle to the Romans, the rhetorically sensitive reader must ask, why does the antinomian objection arise in Romans 6? Remember that the chapter begins with, "What shall we say then? Are we to continue in sin that grace may abound?" (v. 1).

That Paul must address this objection suggests that the preceding chapters must have included doctrinal reasoning that would lead to the raising of this question. Paul's epistles are not replete with esoteric or speculative flights of fancy, so the presence of a rhetorical question here likely suggests that Paul's earlier instruction will be misconstrued as antinomian. To put it more bluntly, a faithful exposition of Romans 1–5 had better sound such that people will ask if this is not antinomianism. To the degree that one's doctrine of justification, as described in these earlier chapters, does not raise that objection, it is out of sync with Paul's thinking.[36]

Paul does rebut the antinomian charge, however, and sharply defends the moral integrity of his gospel. Indeed, "we were buried therefore with him by baptism into death, in order that, just as Christ was raised from the dead by the glory of the Father, we too might walk in newness of life" (6:4). Identification with Christ, in death and in life, symbolized by baptism, ought to lead to a new lifestyle or "walk." Why? Paul explains the reason for this new obedience a few verses later, in Romans 6:6–7. To grasp the doctrinal argument that he makes, we need to attend to two issues regarding translation and logical argument.

First, we must consider the translation of verse 7. The NRSV renders Romans 6:6–7 as follows: "We know that our old self was crucified with him so that the body of sin might be destroyed, and we might no longer be enslaved to sin. For whoever has died is freed from sin." A verb has been rendered anachronistically, however, and this translation misleads in an important regard. This is the only occasion where the verbal "justify" (*dedikaiotai*) is not translated "justify" or some variant. Commentators and translation committees, no doubt, have had difficulty making sense of the phrase "has been justified from sin" in verse 7. It is an odd phrase, to be sure, but it is worth considering a way to make sense of it. Indeed, reading *dedikaiotai* as "has been set free" should only be considered if "has been justified" cannot make sense at all. Fortunately, however, consideration of the immediate context as well as the full breadth of Scripture's teaching offers a bit of clarity that allows one to maintain the most likely lexical rendering.

If one remembers that sin can be personified—spoken about in cosmic, social, and powerful terms—then sin can be considered a force with which we

---

36. A similar rhetorical analysis should affect interpretation of Rom. 9:14, 19, where two rhetorical questions are brought to Paul's account of divine predestination.

must reckon. The Scriptures go further than that, however, in personifying sin as the Accuser, who attacks or battles by means of false accusation (e.g., Rev. 12:10). Job was the object of such slurs: "Does Job fear God for no reason? . . . But stretch out your hand and touch all that he has, and he will curse you to your face" (Job 1:9, 11). False charges are meant to disrupt fellowship between the faithful and their Lord. Sin entangles so frequently by leading the believers to view themselves as outside the realm of grace, alienated and apart from God's good graces.[37]

Against that background, we can make perfect sense of saying that one, united with Christ in baptism, "has been justified from sin." Indeed, identification with Christ Jesus relocates one's own identity. His death is for you. His life is your hope.[38] Paul elsewhere explains this by saying that "I have been crucified with Christ. It is no longer I who live, but Christ who lives with respect to me" (Gal. 2:20, my translation).[39] Christ has already been vindicated by the Father, shown to be righteous in his resurrection glory. Though maligned while on earth and falsely accused even to the point of his death (when he was killed as an alleged blasphemer), Jesus was vindicated by God on the third day. Those united with him share in that vindication, shown righteous before all the mockery of the scoffers. Paul later commands believers to remember their identity in Christ: "For the death he died he died to sin, once for all, but the life he lives he lives to God. So you also must consider yourselves dead to sin and alive to God in Christ Jesus" (Rom. 6:10–11).

The second crucial facet to interpreting Romans 6:6–7 involves the logical relationship between the two verses. The primary point of these verses is located in verse 6c: "so that we would no longer be enslaved to sin." This claim addresses the broader question of Romans 6: "What shall we say then? Are we to continue in sin that grace may abound?" (v. 1). So far from supporting libertinism, Paul's teaching maintains that justified Christians are no longer under the power of sin; that is, they are not enslaved by its snares. The syntactical link between this main point in verses 6c and 7 is crucial: that the

37. Note that sin alienates one from God primarily. There are surely other manifestations of alienation: from self, society, and the like. But it cannot be severed from the need to relate rightly to God, which many attempts to translate justification into a search for "meaning" fail to affirm. For analysis of this unfortunate trend, see Hendrik M. Vroom, "'Meaning' as a Replacement for 'Justification': On the Consequences of Secularization and Pluralization," in Weinrich and Burgess, *What Is Justification About?*, 248–61.

38. For recent reflection on personal identity and being "in Christ," see David H. Kelsey, *Eccentric Existence: A Theological Anthropology* (Louisville: Westminster John Knox, 2009), chaps. 20A and 20B.

39. Interpretation of Gal. 2:20 hangs on rightly understanding the prepositional phrase *en emoi* as "with respect to me" or "with regard to me," rather than "in me" or "within me." See chap. 4 for discussion of this text.

"one who has died has been justified from sin" (my translation) grounds the reality that "we would no longer be enslaved to sin." In other words, verse 7 explains why verse 6c is true. Verse 7 is offered as a reason or explanation for the reality of verse 6c, a syntactical link made clear by the conjunction beginning verse 7 (*gar*). To translate a syntactical point into dogmatic terms, vindication from sin's condemnation leads to freedom from the enslaving power of sin. Justification frees one for love and service.

As if the logical link between Romans 6:6 and 6:7 were not clear enough, Paul reiterates exactly the same argument in 6:10–12. As mentioned above, verses 10 and 11 state that Christ offers a sufficient life and death for all and mention that these Roman believers "must consider yourselves dead to sin and alive to God in Christ Jesus." Conscious self-identification with the person of Jesus is mandated. Paul then extrapolates a moral imperative: "Let not sin therefore reign in your mortal body, to make you obey its passions" (v. 12). Again, justification frees one from the power of sin—it is a declaration that makes real what it affirms.[40] On the basis of identification with Christ and all the blessings enjoyed therein (vv. 10–11), one can therefore obey God rather than sinful passions (v. 11).

So justification fuels sanctification. Not only is this a possibility but the Scriptures go further and pressure us to say that sanctification will organically follow from justification. In Romans, the apostle Paul says, "As one trespass led to condemnation for all men, so one act of righteousness leads to justification and life for all men" (5:18). Reflecting on this passage, Herman Bavinck notes that "justification brings life in its train."[41] Justification is decisive, yet it is purposive and certainly not the end of the Christian story. As we saw in chapter 2, justification is a necessary event that opens up new vistas of communion with God, but it is the fellowship in God's house that is the very point of the whole journey. When the Son has returned and the curtain falls, justification will be an instrumental enjoyment relative to the glory of the divine presence itself. As Michael Horton says, "The status being settled once and for all, our new relationship to God and the promised inheritance is a *terminus a quo* (starting point) of divine accomplishment and not a *terminus ad quem* (goal) of our striving."[42]

40. Michael Horton, "'Behold, I Make All Things New': The Verdict That Does What It Says," in *Covenant and Salvation: Union with Christ* (Louisville: Westminster John Knox, 2007), 243–66; and Bruce L. McCormack, "What's at Stake in Current Debates over Justification? The Crisis of Protestantism in the West," in *Justification: What's at Stake in the Current Debates*, ed. Mark Husbands and Daniel J. Treier (Downers Grove, IL: InterVarsity, 2004), 106–17.
41. Herman Bavinck, *Reformed Dogmatics*, vol. 4, *Holy Spirit, Church, and New Creation*, ed. John Bolt, trans. John Vriend (Grand Rapids: Baker Academic, 2008), 249.
42. Horton, "'Behold, I Make All Things New,'" 248.

Paul Tillich interprets the Protestant doctrine of justification as a denial of any inherent righteousness or growth, but this is not the Pauline and Protestant approach. Tillich rightly sees that justification involves a vindication "in spite of" what we are: imperfect, law-breaking, unclean, covenant-breakers. He says that "justification brings the element of 'in spite of' into the process of theology. It is the immediate consequence of the doctrine of atonement and it is the heart and center of salvation."[43] However, the fact that justification is not based on our intrinsic righteousness does not mean that justification precludes such transformation and growth.

In fact, we must say that the salvation wrought in eternity past, accomplished in Christ's finished work and applied in our own time, will be completed eventually at the resurrection of the body. God promises to move his children by acceptance into maturity. Christians do not go beyond acceptance, as if they cease to need the atoning work of Christ or become individually sufficient on their own merits. But Christians do progress beyond the point of initial acceptance; indeed, acceptance itself creates forward momentum, stirring the hearts of the redeemed in gratitude. By "considering" themselves "dead to sin and alive to God in Christ Jesus," "death no longer has dominion" over them (Rom. 6:11, 9). Conscious appropriation of one's justification in Christ (v. 11) grounds one's freedom (v. 9). More important, though, the same God who justifies also promises to conform these redeemed ones to the image of his Son and, eventually, to glorify them as the Son is glorified. The logic of Romans 8:29–30 must not be undercut: "For those whom he foreknew he also predestined to be conformed to the image of his Son, in order that he might be the firstborn among many brothers. And those whom he predestined he also called, and those whom he called he also justified, and those whom he justified he also glorified." The chain culminates not merely in some sanctification, but in glory itself; indeed, from the beginning these recipients of divine grace are elected "to be conformed to the image of his Son."

The link between justification and sanctification, then, is maintained primarily by divine promise. We must avoid the temptation to manipulate and ensure obedience by means of loading the theological deck, defining sanctification somehow into the basis for justification itself. We should resist the urge to somehow out-theorize sin. In this we can be instructed by, perhaps, a surprising figure. John Wesley has been interpreted by many as a critic of the traditional doctrine of justification by faith alone, as an opponent of the Reformed perspective in particular. Yet Wesley summarizes *sola fide* well and

43. Paul Tillich, *Systematic Theology*, vol. 2, *Existence and the Christ* (Chicago: University of Chicago Press, 1957), 178.

explains its connection to sanctification in succinct and helpful ways. Wesley was asked, "But do you not believe inherent righteousness?" He responded, "Yes, in its proper place; not as the ground of our acceptance before God, but as the fruit of it; not in the place of imputed righteousness, but as consequent upon it. That is I believe God implants righteousness in every one to whom he has imputed it."[44] We need not manipulate the doctrine of justification so that sanctification happens by fear of hell. Rather, we must confess that the God who cancels the penalty of sin upon us also breaks the power of sin in us. Indeed, canceling sin's penalty—and our conscious appropriation of that finished work—frees us for self-sacrificial love and service. As James Gustafson says, "Christianity is no less moral simply because it is not primarily moral."[45] Justification frees one from the task of securing one's place with God—but it also frees one for the task of honoring God and doing good to one's neighbor.

Jüngel argues that the modern notion of freedom encourages a "sham existence."[46] What is he attacking, and how does this definition of freedom relate to justification's ethical implications? Start with John Stuart Mill's portrayal of freedom as autonomy.

> The human faculties of perception, judgment, discriminative feeling, mental activity, and even moral preference, are exercised only in making a choice. He who does anything because it is the custom, makes no choice. He gains no practice either in discerning or in desiring what is best. The mental and moral, like the muscular powers, are improved only by being used. . . . He who lets the world, or his own portion of it, choose his plan of life for him, has no need of any other faculty than the ape-like one of imitation. He who chooses his plan for himself, employs all his faculties.[47]

Mill furthers the project of Jeremy Bentham, who opposes any notion of "natural rights" as "nonsense upon stilts," effectively removing the whole category of nature from the realm of ethics.[48] The crux is to be a self-made man, one who "chooses his plan for himself" and determines his own identity. Clearly Mill believes that a denial of "nature" thereby removes the restrictive schematics of so much authoritarian dogma in the realm of ethics. In this vein

---

44. John Wesley, *The Works of John Wesley*, vol. 1, *Sermons I, 1–33*, ed. Albert Outler (Nashville: Abingdon, 1984), 458.

45. James Gustafson, *Christ and the Moral Life* (New York: Harper & Row, 1968), 183.

46. Jüngel, *Justification*, 262–66.

47. John Stuart Mill, *On Liberty*, ed. Stefan Collini, Cambridge Texts in the History of Political Philosophy (Cambridge: Cambridge University Press, 1989), 59.

48. See, e.g., Jeremy Bentham, *Introduction to the Principles of Morals and Legislation*, ed. J. H. Burns and H. L. A. Hart (New York: Oxford University Press, 1996).

the polemic of Mill is very similar to Kant's famed argument against submitting to authority in "What Is Enlightenment?"[49] There is no creation—all are creators. The moral person shirks social pressure and religious tradition in the name of self-government and self-constitution according to the tenets of reason alone.

An equation of the Protestant doctrine of justification and its concomitant belief in Christian freedom with the modern notion of freedom as autonomy has raised massive ethical questions.[50] Justification *sola fide* will leave the door open for libertines, it is feared, and will allow God's grace to be mocked. Bavinck describes the effects of this fear. "All the sects that arose in Protestant churches more or less proceeded from the idea that the confession of justification by faith was, if not incorrect, at least defective and incomplete *and had to be augmented with sanctification.*"[51] Managing moral transformation becomes a central concern. Gabriel Fackre says that "the temptation to sever justification from justice is unrelenting."[52] Therefore many liberals or progressives express concern that *sola fide* encourages an otherworldliness that fails to question the structural injustices of present-day societies. Faith alone is not a rigorous-enough requirement to bring about the kingdom of Christ; something else must be added, whether the "brotherhood of mankind," the pursuit of social justice, or a "preferential option for the poor."[53]

It is useful to think of this approach to ethical action as managerial. It flows from a concern that good works will not occur unless the system of doctrine, the faith and practice of the Christian communion, requires it for future progress. The logic of this view can be depicted in economic terms: unless payment is required, free riders will take God's services without contributing to his economy. To out-theorize such behavior, then, they reframe the categories themselves

49. Immanuel Kant, "An Answer to the Question: What Is Enlightenment?," in *Practical Philosophy: Cambridge Edition of the Works of Immanuel Kant*, ed. Mary J. Gregor (Cambridge: Cambridge University Press, 1999), 17–22.

50. For a historical and ethical analysis of how later Protestant thought equated justification by faith alone with the gift of autonomy, see Stanley Hauerwas, "History and Fate: How Justification by Faith Became Anthropology (and History) in America," in *Wilderness Wanderings: Probing Twentieth-Century Theology and Philosophy*, Radical Traditions (Boulder, CO: Westview, 1997), 32–47.

51. Herman Bavinck, *Reformed Dogmatics*, vol. 4, *Holy Spirit, Church, and New Creation*, ed. John Bolt, trans. John Vriend (Grand Rapids: Baker Academic, 2008), 245 (emphasis added).

52. Gabriel Fackre, "Affirmations and Admonitions: Lutheran and Reformed," in *The Gospel of Justification in Christ: Where Does the Church Stand Today?*, ed. Wayne C. Stumme (Grand Rapids: Eerdmans, 2006), 25.

53. John Burgess describes the way this frequently leads to battles regarding the necessary shape of just/holy life (now seen as essential to salvation itself), whether it involves social activism, fiscal and sexual restraint, or other forms of moral passion; see "Justification and Sanctification," in Weinrich and Burgess, *What Is Justification About?*, 57–87, esp. 84–85.

by including moral transformation within justification itself, suggesting that the Protestant doctrine of *sola fide* points to distinctions not found in Paul.[54] Brian K. Blount expresses this approach well when he says, "There is no real separation for Paul between justification and sanctification. Sanctification, which is usually identified with ethics, is not a follow-up to justification, but an integral part of it."[55] If justification prior to sanctification cannot guarantee an ethic of obedience, then we had better make justification somehow equivalent to sanctification, including ethics from the very beginning.

In such approaches, justification is seen as needing modification via sanctification. That is, *sola fide* is viewed as the gift of autonomous freedom, a dangerous prospect if not immediately paired or somehow mixed with a healthy dose of moral rigorism.[56] Legal emphases may focus primarily on issues of individual spiritual experience and conservative moral shibboleths, or they may lean heavily on efforts to work justice, mercy, and righteousness in sociopolitical spheres. In such a case, though, the radically free vindicating work of God is viewed as a threat to order and morality. Because vindication ushers in autonomous freedom, these approaches suggest that justification by faith alone undermines any sustained basis for moral zeal.

We have seen that it is not merely the case that justification by faith alone does sustain obedience but also that any doctrine of justification that forfeits this radical grace in Christ will not sustain obedience. In his study *Counseling and Theology*, Wilhelm Hulme observes,

> When a person's justification is dependent upon his sanctification it is not only justification that is jeopardized but sanctification as well. Since both the meaning of and the power for sanctification reside in the motive of love and this motive is created in the justification experience, it follows that if my sanctification is motivated also by the desire to earn or deserve, I have undercut sanctification at its incipiency because I have corrupted the love motive. There is a subtle temptation—a particular danger in counseling—for an individual to become egocentric in his endeavors toward growth. Having experienced a certain amount

54. Rom. 2:14–26 can also be read to suggest that justification may be by faith but that it is also by works. Yet there are a number of ways this passage may be read and related to Paul's teaching elsewhere (e.g., Rom. 3:21–27). See Dane Ortlund, "Justified by Faith, Judged according to Works: Another Look at a Pauline Paradox," *Journal of the Evangelical Theological Society* 52 (2009): 323–39.

55. Brian K. Blount, *Then the Whisper Put on Flesh: New Testament Ethics in an African-American Context* (Nashville: Abingdon, 2001), 139.

56. John Webster relates this construal to a failure to maintain a focus on the character of God when thinking about justification: justification then quickly moves from covenantal and ethical to existential concern; see "*Rector et iudex super omnia genera doctrinarum?* The Place of the Doctrine of Justification," in Weinrich and Burgess, *What Is Justification About?*, 35–56, esp. 39.

of progress, he may become enthusiastic in his efforts to gain more. Unknow-
ingly he may assume an activist role that is doomed to defeat. He falls into the
error of "trying too hard" and becomes tense in his efforts to overcome irrita-
tion, moods, and among other things, tension. Finally, he may break down in
complete frustration. *What has happened is that self-improvement has become
its own motive under the disguise of religious endeavor.* . . . Sanctification is
also by grace through faith. . . . It is the Holy Spirit himself that is to be sought,
rather than his fruits. Growth is growth in grace.[57]

Hulme suggests that good works truly flow only from those who are con-
vinced and confident that their future is secured by God; love flows only from
freedom—the rest is Nietzsche's will-to-power or the Serpent's temptation
in the garden. The key to liberation, then, is grasping salvation *extra nos*
and *en Christo*. As Thomas Chalmers says, "The freer the gospel, the more
sanctifying the gospel."[58]

The grand irony is that efforts to move sanctification into justification not only
morph the latter but also make the former problematic. Obedience to God is not
a self-generating thing. Rather, Paul points to the roots of transformation in the
gift of freedom found only and fully in Christ. Paul speaks of being controlled
by the "love of Christ" (2 Cor. 5:14). In other words, Paul's moral activity and
self-sacrifice for the sake of working reconciliation among humans is impelled by
the gospel. This gospel logic is teased out in his many statements that describe
the reconciling work of Christ followed by a logical implication. For example,
"He died for all, that those who live might no longer live for themselves but for
him who for their sake died and was raised. From now on, therefore, we regard
no one according to the flesh" (2 Cor. 5:15–16). The death of Christ is not
equated with racial reconciliation; rather, the meaning of the death of Christ
and its saving effects, savored by faith, fuels a new perspective and a desire for
racial reconciliation that is apparent in Paul's missionary activity. The logic of
justification leading to transformation can also be found in Galatians, when
Paul speaks of "faith working itself out in love" (5:6, my translation). Should
faith and love both ground justification, this reduces to mere tautology. Unlike
references in Romans to "the obedience of faith"—where the term "faith" might
plausibly (though not likely) be construed epexegetically as a clarification of what
obedience consists in—Galatians 5:6 will not allow an epexegetical rendering.
Somehow faith and love are being differentiated yet linked.

57. William E. Hulme, *Counseling and Theology* (Philadelphia: Fortress, 1956), 180, 193, 194
(emphasis original). My thanks to Dane Ortlund for pointing me to this text.
58. Thomas Chalmers, "The Expulsive Power of a New Affection," in *The Complete Works
of Thomas Chalmers* (Philadelphia: Towar, Hogan & Thompson, 1833), 387.

Titus 3:7–8 provides another instance of this spiritual link between justification in Christ alone and real moral transformation. Recounting the mystery of salvation, the apostle says that "being justified by his grace we might become heirs according to the hope of eternal life. The saying is trustworthy, and I want you to insist on these things, so that those who have believed in God may be careful to devote themselves to good works." Paul wants believers to be doers: "that those who have believed in God may be careful to devote themselves to good works." So he arms Titus with a "trustworthy saying" that is worth "insisting" on over and over again. It is not a new exhortation, and it is not even a moral imperative at all. It is the liberating word of the gospel: "being justified by his grace we might become heirs according to the hope of eternal life." Paul tells Titus that Christians need the gospel insistently pressed into their hearts and minds—that freeing reminder that their inheritance was won by Jesus, their vindication given by grace, and, best of all, that all of this is an already-experienced reality (for they are not "soon to be justified" or "later to be justified" but are addressed as those who are now "justified by his grace"). The insistence of the gospel inspires the good works, for it is only when we know that our future is secure in Christ that we are free to give our present away in serving our neighbors and selflessly taking up our cross. To go further toward the goal of good works, Paul goes deeper into the grace of the gospel's ground.

The apostle is not the first to speak this way. It has been learned, no doubt, from the hermeneutical tradition of Jesus. In Luke 7, Jesus identifies obedience (love) as the fruit of belief (faith). He clearly cares about both faith and love, but they are two discrete realities between which he sees a logical and spiritual connection. When the sinful woman shows love toward him by anointing his feet, the religious naysayers denounce Jesus's willingness to be identified with a shady character. But Jesus notes that the woman expresses deep love and devotion, because she has been forgiven much (Luke 7:41–42). "I tell you, her sins, which are many, are forgiven—for she loved much. But he who is forgiven little, loves little" (v. 47). Jesus makes an observation about forgiveness by pointing to its symptom: love. Love is not the linchpin, of course, as Jesus makes clear in specifying what saved the woman. "And he said to the woman, 'Your faith has saved you; go in peace'" (v. 50). Faith has yoked her to him, such that she enjoys deep peace with God. Knowing such peace, she is free to give herself away in devotion to him. Jesus does not conflate faith and love, and yet he shows that they are anything but separate; rather, these discrete realities are spiritually yoked and ordered.

Of course, there is a danger that justification and transformation—that is, sanctification or good works—might be rent asunder. Richard Hays rightly

observes that "there is no meaningful distinction between theology and ethics in Paul's thought, because Paul's theology is fundamentally an account of
God's work of transforming people into the image of Christ."[59] Connections
are made by Paul, and they pressure faithful interpreters to inquire after their
logic and implications. Dogmatics cannot divide the biblical proclamation
of the gospel. Yet it would be unfortunate if Hays's warning led us to avoid
drawing distinctions. Indeed, understanding certain distinctions fuels the
flourishing of one element or the other.

A recent example of blurring distinctions can be found in the work of
Michael Gorman, *Inhabiting the Cruciform God: Kenosis, Justification, and
Theosis in Paul's Narrative Soteriology*. Gorman rightly argues that the doctrine of justification relates to vertical and horizontal relationships, that is,
one's life before God and among other humans. Thus, he believes (and ex-
plicates in the final chapter of the book) that justification impinges on our
understanding of doing justice in the world.[60] Well before we get to the radical proposal regarding justice and "the end of violence," a problem arises
in Gorman's book: relationship has morphed into identity. Justification no
longer implies something about justice; rather, justification is making justice among our fellow creatures. For this reason, Gorman will criticize the
definition of justification given by Michael Bird, who points to its nature as
an event in which God creates a people with a new status: "Although this is
generally a very fine description, the word 'status' is a bit troublesome, since
it may be heard as an echo of certain theologies that wish to minimize the
transformative character of justification that reconciliation and new covenant
require."[61] Gorman goes on to argue that "2 Corinthians 5:14–21 suggests
that inherent within the very notion of reconciliation/justification are both
participation and transformation."[62] Note that he has worked in the idea of
transformation being "inherent within" justification, which goes beyond the
more obvious claim that justification somehow relates to moral change (in this
textual context, specifically, efforts at human reconciliation). Gorman makes
his case most plainly when discussing Romans 5–8. "The realities narrated
in these chapters . . . are constitutive of, not consequences of, justification."[63]
Never mind that Romans 5–8 does not tell a story and, thus, cannot properly

59. Richard B. Hays, *The Moral Vision of the New Testament: A Contemporary Introduction
to New Testament Ethics* (San Francisco: HarperSanFrancisco, 1996), 46.
60. Michael J. Gorman, *Inhabiting the Cruciform God: Kenosis, Justification, and Theosis
in Paul's Narrative Soteriology* (Grand Rapids: Eerdmans, 2009), 46–47.
61. Ibid., 54n41.
62. Ibid., 56.
63. Ibid., 73.

be narrating anything. More substantive is the concern that Gorman glosses over the transition in Romans 5:1, which begins with the clause "Therefore, since we have been justified by faith." The text itself moves from justification to its organic enfleshments: peace and endurance (vv. 1–5), newness of life and freedom from sin (6:4–14), delight in the law and life in the Spirit (7:22–8:17). Gorman can offer no textual reason for suggesting that these are "constitutive" rather than "consequential" with respect to justification.

Gorman and others, fortunately, express themselves in logically inconsistent ways. Whereas Gorman will say that "for Paul, Romans 6 does not supplement justification by faith or merely explain its effects or consequences; rather, it *defines* justification by faith,"[64] he will then cite with approval the words of Robert Tannehill: "When Paul shifts to participatory language in Romans 5:12–21 and 6:1–7:6, . . . he has not moved on from soteriology to a new topic but is deepening his soteriology, providing further insight into how redemption in Christ Jesus has taken place and explaining its implications."[65] Something cannot be identical with another thing and yet, at the same time, have the latter thing be an implication of it. Realities cannot be both identical and implied one by the other. Fortunately Gorman's hyperbolic statements—which are plainly at odds with Paul's teaching in Romans 5–8—are contradicted by his endorsement of Tannehill, who sees that redemption implies obedience and is not based upon or identified with it.

Campbell and others have charged the Protestant doctrine of justification with undermining the process of discipleship and the ethical life. We have considered the ways that the Bible describes redemption, freedom, and justification, with respect to their ethical implications. In so doing we have found the charges of Campbell to run aground of the evidence and instead have found G. C. Berkouwer to be right in his historical assessment that "the Reformation, in its defense of the forensic, declarative justification that points us always to the free favor of God, has not endangered, but rescued the confession of true sanctification."[66] Just as the exodus was unto service, so justification is unto obedience and conformity to Christ while itself being completely free from such activities. What God has distinguished, let no one conflate; what God has joined, let no one rend apart.

64. Ibid., 74.
65. Robert C. Tannehill, "Participation in Christ: A Central Theme in Pauline Soteriology," in *The Shape of the Gospel: New Testament Essays* (Eugene, OR: Cascade, 2007), 235, quoted in ibid.
66. G. C. Berkouwer, *Faith and Justification*, trans. Lewis B. Smedes, Studies in Dogmatics (Grand Rapids: Eerdmans, 1954), 100.

# 6

## "The Church's One Foundation"

### *The Justification of the Ungodly Church*

The doctrine of the church has taken first chair within twentieth-century theology in both Protestant and Roman Catholic manifestations. Whereas ecclesiology arrived late on the dogmatic scene, taking shape as a distinct locus only in the last century, it quickly came to dominate ecumenical and theological discussions.[1] As debates regarding soteriology and bibliology failed to combat secularism and denominational disarray, the theology of church praxis moved to center stage: by focusing on a common sacramental life, divided communions forged a unity worth celebrating; by emphasizing the earthly work of the churches, Christianity might be made more compelling to human aspirations.

The doctrine of justification by faith alone offers pertinent judgments regarding the extrinsic and gracious nature of the salvation found in Jesus Christ; thus, this soteriological image must continually shape the doctrine of humanity—individual,

---

1. There are very few precursors (e.g., James Bannerman's two-volume *The Church of Christ*, published in the nineteenth century) to ecclesiological reflection as a distinct locus prior to the twentieth century. For the absence of extended reflection on the doctrine of the church in the patristic era, see Brian Daley, "Old Books and Contemporary Faith: The Bible, Tradition, and the Renewal of Theology," in *Ancient Faith for the Church's Future*, ed. Mark Husbands and Jeffrey Greenman (Downers Grove, IL: IVP Academic, 2008), 56.

social, ecclesial.[2] While avoiding the overblown characterization of justification as *articulus stantis et cadentis ecclesiae*, I will nonetheless show the extensive pressure it exerts on the whole of dogmatics. In particular, the doctrine of imputation testifies to the externality of human being and, thus, its gracious roots in the person and works of Jesus Christ. In this chapter I will consider the pilgrim nature of the church, suggesting that the doctrines of God, salvation, and eschatology must all shape our view of the people of God. I will consider classical and Reformational tools that can be employed to honor these connections, pointing to the truth that the church—by the grace of Christ—is both justified and sinful while on her journey homeward to God. I will conclude by analyzing some of the typical moments in the Christian liturgy, showing that they, each in their own way, rehearse the gospel message by pointing the church beyond herself to life and flourishing founded upon and fueled by her Lord Jesus Christ.

## The Justification of the Ungodly Church

*The church is a pilgrim people, founded upon and fueled by the triune God of love; therefore, our thinking about the church must be rightly based on our Christology and pneumatology, each befitting the economy of salvation and the eschatological shape of the kingdom of God.*

Theology reflects on the God of the gospel and his relation to all things. In so doing, it listens to the canonical testimony of Christ's prophets and apostles and seeks to provide an orderly account of their full scope and sequence. Crucial to this expository task is refusal to lose the dynamism of its shape as a sequence. Thus, most Christian theologians have felt compelled to follow the pattern of teaching used in the Bible and the ecumenical creeds.

The doctrine of the church is affirmed in the creeds as part of Christ's work by his Holy Spirit. Indeed, the church is a key part of the third article of the creeds—having confessed belief in the Holy Spirit, we also confess that we believe this church of Christ.

*The church is a pilgrim people.* The dynamism of the church's life is rooted in the biblical witness in both an explicit and an implicit way. In the apostolic writings we find Christianity described explicitly as "the Way" (Acts 9:2; 19:9, 23; 24:14, 22).[3] The terminology is not technical by any means, but it is regular and appears in various writers and settings. Crucial to understanding

---

2. Carl E. Braaten has recently suggested the importance of reflecting on the link between the doctrine of justification and the church; see *That All May Believe: A Theology of the Gospel and the Mission of the Church* (Grand Rapids: Eerdmans, 2008), 58.

3. Other phrases are closely linked: "the way of salvation" (Acts 16:17); "the way of the Lord" (18:25); "the way of God" (18:26); and "this Way" (22:4).

it, though, is its basis in Old Testament teaching on the two ways (Ps. 1:1–6; Isa. 30:21; 35:8).[4] The Old Testament presented a dynamic view of the life of God's people: they were journeying toward the fulfillment of his promises to them. The apostles identify themselves and their fellow Christians with these sojourning Israelites of old (1 Cor. 10:1–6; Heb. 3:12–19).

This life of the church in a dynamic sequence, however, is also unveiled in implicit ways. The apostle Paul, for example, speaks to the church as those with a "new self" and yet a continuing need to put off their "old self" (Col. 3). He follows Jesus in so doing, for his Lord had taught that the kingdom of God was like a mustard seed. Paul also likens Christians to their ancestor in the faith, Abraham. He was a serial sojourner, a man on the go. His story does not merely happen to involve travel, but the journey is constitutive of his life of faith: the first command being, "Go from your country and your kindred and your father's house to the land that I will show you" (Gen. 12:1); the first submission being, "So Abram went" (v. 4). Faith follows, and it does so most poignantly on the road of life. Not only does Paul make use of Abraham as the paradigm, but Hebrews 11 also does so. The most extended discussion of an Old Testament saint in that chapter regards Abraham and his willingness to depart (Heb. 11:8), to journey (vv. 9–10), to anticipate the promise of a seed (vv. 11–12), even to believe that the seed would be provided again on the far side of death (vv. 17–19). In the midst of this paradigmatic account, the author steps back and reflects on the many examples of faith in this earlier epoch. "These all died in faith, not having received the things promised, but having seen them and greeted them from afar, and having acknowledged that they were strangers and exiles on the earth. For people who speak thus make it clear that they are seeking a homeland" (vv. 13–14). It is not for nothing that these summarizing remarks appear amid the specific account of Abraham (showing that he is paradigmatic), nor is it merely accidental that they portray faith as a journey of trust (showing that the gospel involves a dynamic movement of daily provision from God and persevering dependence on God). The Christian—like Abraham here, and later like Jesus (Heb. 12:1–3)—is defined as one "seeking a homeland," still on that journey and presently short of heaven.

Later Christians have found great power in this imagery. Thomas Aquinas speaks analytically of our knowledge of God as that of the wayfarer (*viator*), not the blessed (*comprehensor*).[5] The Protestant scholastics followed suit,

4. For analysis, see William P. Brown, *Seeing the Psalms: A Theology of Metaphor* (Louisville: Westminster John Knox, 2002), chap. 2.

5. Augustine affirms that the church is spiritually located in the wilderness and desert, rather than the promised land of Canaan; see "Homily 28," in *Homilies on the Gospel of John 1–40*,

distinguishing pilgrim theology (*theologia viatorum*) from beatific theology (*theologia beatorum*). Most famously, John Bunyan makes use of the pilgrimage as the grand allegory for the Christian life in his remarkable *Pilgrim's Progress*. In each respect, the goal is to honor the biblical teaching: "So we do not lose heart. Though our outer self is wasting away, our inner self is being renewed day by day" (2 Cor. 4:16).

The Christian life is just that—a life—and, as such, it is a journey with all its perilous temptations and distressing turns. What hope do we have amid such constant upheaval? How can we, with Paul, not lose heart if this is our story and situation? Unfortunately, hope cannot be found in ourselves or our own projects, which are flimsy and fading. Still further, hope cannot be premised upon the spiritual efforts of Christian communities. Our Christian persons and churchly projects are too absorbed in themselves and mired in sin to be an inviolable source of hope. As Michael Horton says, "A community 'living the gospel' is not good news, especially when we know ourselves—and the community of which we are a part—all too well. Jesus came to serve the church because the church too is part of the problem. Only Jesus Christ is the solution. With the disciples on the Mount of Transfiguration, all we see is Jesus."[6]

The point is not that the church is especially pernicious, of course, or even that the church is untouched by grace. The church does demonstrate the reality of grace, and it does so precisely by God's life-giving Spirit, "the power from on high" promised and delivered by Jesus himself (Luke 24:49). Nonetheless, the church is not untrammeled by sin in this life. It remains a weak vessel containing the water of life. To put it another way, the gracious Word of the gospel comes as a "treasure in jars of clay" (2 Cor. 4:7).

How can we express this dynamic life of the church and its continuing dependence upon not only the Spirit but also the ongoing work of the Son? *The church is a pilgrim people, founded upon and fueled by the triune God of love.* The link between justification and ecclesiology is especially apt, inasmuch as justification highlights the extrinsic basis of one's life and holiness. Justification by faith alone in Christ alone serves to accent the finished, external basis for Christian assurance—namely, the settled status of the Christian "in Christ Jesus" before the Father's judgment seat. Various idioms may be used to describe such justifying activity—for example, sacrifice, redemption, salvation—and we dare not allow divergent linguistic categories or metaphorical realms to segment our theological categories.

---

ed. Allan Fitzgerald, trans. Edmund Hill, Works of St. Augustine 1/12 (Hyde Park, NY: New City, 2009), 485–86 (9).

6. Michael Horton, "The Weight of Glory: Justification and Theosis," in *Covenant and Salvation: Union with Christ* (Louisville: Westminster John Knox, 2007), 307.

The Westminster Confession of Faith addresses it in this way: "The purest churches under heaven are subject both to mixture and error: and some have so degenerated as to become apparently no churches of Christ. Nevertheless, there shall be always a Church on earth, to worship God according to his will."[7] There is realism here as well as profound hope. The realism addresses the mixed nature of God's people. Not only do some churches degenerate terribly, but even "the purest churches under heaven" are a mixed bag. The church is no collection of saints cut from the holy cloth and unstained by sin. The church is a group reconciled in Christ and on the way to renewal in his grace by his Spirit. The hope acknowledges an external promise: a word from above and beyond, "according to his will." The church will remain: amid tumult without and within, it endures and continues, though not of her own power. The pairing bespeaks the theme of this chapter—the justified yet ungodly church, that is, the church founded upon and fueled by one outside it: Jesus Christ.

The hope flows from the reality that the gospel promise involves not only a christological center but also an ecclesiological shape. This dual focus becomes apparent when we see the lesson in evangelical hermeneutics that Jesus gives to his disciples in Luke 24. After giving a brief initial synopsis of the teaching of the Law and the Prophets (24:26–27), he offers an extended summary.

> Then he said to them, "These are my words that I spoke to you while I was still with you, that everything written about me in the Law of Moses and the Prophets and the Psalms must be fulfilled." Then he opened their minds to understand the Scriptures, and said to them, "Thus it is written, that the Christ should suffer and on the third day rise from the dead, and that repentance and forgiveness of sins should be proclaimed in his name to all nations, beginning from Jerusalem. You are witnesses of these things. And behold, I am sending the promise of my Father upon you. But stay in the city until you are clothed with power from on high." (vv. 44–49)

The Old Testament Scriptures are about his passion—death and resurrection—but they are also about his presence to and through the church. Proclamation of his Word will go forth to the nations, precisely because his witnesses will be clothed with "power from on high," the "promise of my Father" whom Jesus sends. His gifts will keep the church—his grace will sustain her mission. The gospel is not merely about the accomplishment of redemption but also the good news that the divine Word will apply that redemption through the church's witness and by his Spirit's power. Grace leaves nothing to chance. Christ, as the Good Shepherd and the gracious Lord, ensures every step of the way.

---

7. Westminster Confession of Faith 27.5, in *Constitution of the Presbyterian Church (U.S.A.)*, Part One: *Book of Confessions* (Louisville: Geneva, 1996), 205.

Other texts emphasize this extrinsic promise. The Gospel according to Matthew contains that famous pledge that "the gates of hell shall not prevail" over Christ's church (Matt. 16:18). The context makes quite apparent that this is not due to the cunning or competency, much less the moral consistency or fidelity, of Peter. Though he has made the good confession at this point, his failures to come are made evident by the gospel writer. No, the promise cannot hang upon Peter's power or purity. And it is certainly not a promise made as a result of the lack of threats against the church: she has already been tried from without and tested within, and Matthew's account will only heighten its exposure to such efforts in the final dozen chapters. The promise simply cannot derive its force from the power of the disciples or the lack of threats from their enemies.[8] From where, then, does it derive its force? It is a promise made good only in its saying by Jesus. He pledges its fulfillment, and he commits himself to its satisfaction. Thus, it is not at all surprising that Matthew's account of the gospel concludes as it does. Most readers remember the supposed "great commission" of Matthew 28:19–20 as its finale, an exhortation to the disciples to spread the good news. However, this calling is enclosed by an announcement of Christ's presence and a promise of his staying power: "All authority in heaven and on earth has been given to me. . . . And behold, I am with you always, to the end of the age" (Matt. 28:18, 20). The gospel's declaration to the nations is sustained by Christ's presence and his authority. This man is King of kings and Lord of lords, and he wills to be with them and to be for them: they will be his people, and he will be their Lord.

The apostle Paul picks up on this gracious foundation of the church's life in his writing to the Christians in Ephesus when he says,

> Grace was given to each one of us according to the measure of Christ's gift. Therefore it says, "When he ascended on high he led a host of captives, and he gave gifts to men." (In saying, "He ascended," what does it mean but that he had also descended into the lower regions, the earth? He who descended is the one who also ascended far above all the heavens, that he might fill all things.) And he gave the apostles, the prophets, the evangelists, the shepherds and teachers, to equip the saints for the work of ministry, for building up the body of Christ, until we all attain to the unity of the faith and of the knowledge of the Son of God, to mature manhood, to the measure of the stature of the fullness of Christ. (Eph. 4:7–13)

8. Augustine interprets Ps. 121:1—"I have lifted up my eyes to the mountains, from where help will come to me"—as a statement about our need to learn from the evangelists and apostles (the "mountains" or "lofty ones"). However, he highlights the psalm's immediate shift to locate this help beyond the humans themselves, as v. 2 says: "My help is from the Lord, who made heaven and earth" (*Homilies on the Gospel of John 1–40*, 42–43 [1.6]).

Paul here quotes and adjusts the language of Psalm 68, a cry of victory over Israel's foes. In the psalm, the Lord assumes his throne atop the royal mountain and then receives gifts to mark his triumph. This is what newly inaugurated rulers or recently victorious warriors do: rest and receive the gifts of those hoping to buy their security. But not here in the Epistle to the Ephesians. Here the ascended King Jesus assumes the throne, not to receive gifts, but to give grace: "the apostles, the prophets, the evangelists, the shepherds and teachers." The ministers of the church are the gift of Christ, so that he ensures that the saints are equipped "for the work of ministry, for building up the body of Christ." Jesus does not run a lap and then pass the missional baton to his followers, as if to say that it is up to them now to finish the job; he continues to carry them along the track of life and ministry. As the ascended Lord, he gives good gifts and reigns as head of the church, his body. Thus, her maturity, unity, and stature are owing to the "fullness of Christ," that is, the overflowing life that he has and shares with her by grace. Her life is centered outside herself, in the living promise of her alive and authoritative head.

These texts do not directly speak of justification, of course, so some will suggest that they have no pertinence to that doctrinal topic. Yet we must keep in mind two things. First, topics in theology can be expressed in a variety of conceptual idioms. We must always push through various terms to the specific theological claims they render, realizing that varying jargon can express the same judgment. Second, these texts do share a common theme: the identity of God's people as sustained and, yes, justified not by their own competence or character but by God's promise and Christ's action to fulfill that divine pledge.

Further, we are compelled to say that this external Word does change us— sanctifying as well as justifying—but change occurs slowly in this life and always imperfectly before the return of Christ. Only when we see him face to face will we become like him. The church is already being sanctified and will then be glorified. There is a whole doctrine of transformation or participation in God through Christ Jesus that can and must be articulated to fully describe the gospel's impact on human society and selves. Indeed, there is a hope that is portrayed in Scripture as blessed, largely because everything sad—as Lewis would put it—will come untrue, whether our ills and failures or our jealousies and divides. The church militant shall be the church triumphant in that day. Meanwhile, though, this church remains east of Eden and can be described as a "chaste harlot" or a "justified sinner."[9]

9. For the former, see Hans Urs von Balthasar, "Casta Meretrix," in *Explorations in Theology*, vol. 2, *The Spouse of the Word* (San Francisco: Ignatius, 1991), 193–288. For the latter, see Martin Luther, *Lectures on Galatians (1535), Chapters 1–4*, ed. Jaroslav Pelikan, Luther's Works 26 (St. Louis: Concordia, 1963), 109 (2:11). These images for the church are a result of biblical

Three doctrines are engaged here: theology, soteriology, and eschatology. We should consider them briefly before turning to look at classical tools employed by patristic and Reformational churches to highlight these doctrines.

First, the justification of the ungodly church sits coherently with a theological point of great prestige: the Trinity alone is Lord and intrinsically alive, while all others are created and only alive by grace.[10] *Our thinking about the church must be rightly based on our Christology and pneumatology.* The church's life and blessing, therefore, cannot be grounded within or guarded by her own wherewithal. "In him we live and move and have our being" (Acts 17:28)—this is true for the church surely, as well as for the individual or the cosmos.

Second, the justification of the ungodly church extends a profound soteriological feature of biblical teaching: the reality that sinners' life with God occurs only by way of reconciliation in Christ. *Our thinking about the church must be rightly based on our Christology and pneumatology, each befitting the economy of salvation.* We must confess with St. Gregory the Great, "Let the Church cry out, 'I am black but beautiful,' black by your judgment, but beautiful through the radiance of grace . . . black by merit, beautiful by grace . . . black by myself, beautiful by gift, black from the past, beautiful through what I am made to be in the future."[11] God's declaration of his justifying word—this word of grace—sustains our very life.

Third, the justification of the ungodly church jibes with the eschatological shape of the Christian life—namely, the dynamic form of redemption now and not yet. The church has been reconciled and even changed, but not yet fully glorified. The assurance of its eventual arrival at this hope of glory is located outside itself in God's Word. Indeed, this is the fulfillment of the

---

reasoning pressured by texts like Rev. 11:3, where the authoritative witnesses of God to his church must speak "clothed in sackcloth" due to the sinfulness and ongoing struggle of God's people. See the insightful comments on the church in Joseph Mangina, *Revelation*, Brazos Theological Commentary on the Bible (Grand Rapids: Brazos, 2010), 136–38 (cf. helpful comments on the danger of a doctrine of the church's indefectibility on 156–58); and Oecumenius, "Commentary on the Apocalypse," in *Greek Commentaries on Revelation*, ed. Thomas Oden, trans. William Weinrich, Ancient Christian Texts (Downers Grove, IL: IVP Academic, 2011), 13 (second discourse on Rev. 2:12–17).

10. The doctrine of divine aseity plays a considerable role, then, not just in describing God but also in showing how the shape of salvation is set by the trinitarian being of God; see John Webster, "Life in and of Himself: On Divine Aseity," in *God without Measure: Essays in Christian Doctrine* (London: T&T Clark, forthcoming); and idem, "In the Society of God: Some Principles of Ecclesiology," in *God without Measure*. See discussion of this link between God's life in himself and his giving of life to others in the economy of grace in chap. 1.

11. St. Gregory the Great, *Canticle of Canticles*, Patrologia Latina 79, ed. J.-P. Migne (Paris, 1862), 486–88 (1.5).

Abrahamic promise not only to give many descendants but also to bless them, that is, to preserve, prosper, and eventually perfect them.[12] Thus, *our thinking about the church must be rightly based on our Christology and pneumatology, each befitting the economy of salvation and the eschatological shape of the kingdom of God.*

In all these ways, then, it is systematically crucial to allow theology, soteriology, and eschatology to inform our ecclesiology. More specifically, we must avoid thinking of the church as anything but a creaturely, reconciled, and gradually renewed people, yet a people sure to share in the glory of the triune God. To speak of the justification of the ungodly church highlights these very dogmatic commitments.

## Three Classical Tools

Having seen the implications that the doctrine of the Trinity and the justification of the ungodly lead to in the realm of ecclesiology, we now consider three ways in which Christian theology seeks to express and honor this connection. As mentioned above, the doctrines of God, salvation, and eschatology are in play at this point. We can point to one doctrinal fixture used to highlight each of these three facets. Other tools could be employed to make these theological judgments, but these are tools with great prestige in the catholic and Reformational traditions. Though their function and intent is too little known today, they can serve to point us to the deep mystery of the church's life in Christ. For those of us trying to claw our way out of the empirical naturalism of contemporary thinking about the church—so dominated by the categories of the marketplace and of religious phenomenology—these tools might help us find a more theologically imaginative view of the church's pilgrimage through this spiritual wilderness on her way to glory.

### We Believe One, Holy, Catholic, and Apostolic Church

The Nicene Creed states that Christians believe in the triune God and believe the church. Herman Witsius understands the difference and its ecclesiological ramifications.

When we affirm, therefore, that we believe the Church, we profess, that there has existed from the beginning of time, still exists, and will continue to the end

12. Luther makes the connection between the church's life and the Abrahamic promise in *Lectures on Genesis, Chapters 6–14*, ed. Jaroslav Pelikan, trans. George Schick, Luther's Works 2 (St. Louis: Concordia, 1960), 257, 265 (12:2, 3).

of the world to exist, a society of men chosen by God to salvation, called by the Gospel and the Spirit, professing faith and piety with the mouth, and practicing them in the conduct. We declare also, that neither the machinations of the world that lieth in wickedness, nor the gates of hell, shall ever prevail against this society: For it is utterly impossible that the decree of God should fail; that the promises of God should come to nought; that the word of salvation should be preached in vain; that the prophecies respecting the perpetuity of Christ's kingdom should fall to the ground; or that Christ should lose the reward of his labor, and become a Master without disciples, a King without subjects, a Bridegroom without a bride, a Head without a body.[13]

The key phrases speak of the inviolability of the church, which has existed, does exist, and will exist to the end of the world. The strongest furies of the world and the gravest efforts of hell itself will not overcome this society of God. Why? Witsius offers a number of reasons (prefaced by the term "for"), all pertaining to the planks of God's economy of salvation: his decree, his promise, his word of salvation, his prophecy, Christ's labor, and so forth.

The Heidelberg Catechism states the theological basis for the church's life profoundly.

Q. What do you believe concerning "the Holy Catholic Church"?

A. I believe that, from the beginning to the end of the world, and from among the whole human race, the Son of God, by his Spirit and his Word, gathers, protects, and preserves for himself, in the unity of the true faith, a congregation chosen for eternal life. Moreover, I believe that I am and forever will remain a living member of it.[14]

The issue involves the nature of the church's life as rooted in its particular basis. Because it is based outside itself in God's promise, it is by definition not fundamental but dependent, not in itself but fully in Christ. Martin Luther says, "Therefore even though the church was never at peace, it nevertheless weathered the fiercest tempests of its trials."[15]

---

13. Herman Witsius, *Sacred Dissertations on What Is Commonly Called the Apostles' Creed*, trans. Donald Fraser (Glasgow: Khull, Blackie, & Co., 1823), 2:362. Cf. John Calvin, *Institutes of the Christian Religion*, ed. John T. McNeill, trans. Ford Lewis Battles, Library of Christian Classics (Philadelphia: Westminster, 1960), 4.1.2.

14. Heidelberg Catechism 54, in *Reformed Confessions of the Sixteenth Century*, ed. Arthur C. Cochrane (Louisville: Westminster John Knox, 2003), 314.

15. Luther, *Lectures on Genesis, Chapters 6–14*, 235 (11:14–26). Luther later notes that the strife of the church was not merely external but also internal. On Nimrod's heresy, he says, "We observe that not only the collateral branches among the patriarchs fell into error and idolatry but even the very root of the church, Terah and Abraham. . . . The Scriptures reveal that even

The God of the gospel has all life in himself, and thus he is capable of giving fully to others. This one—the resplendent triune God of glory—can be the object of faith and the material basis of our hope. This one, inasmuch as he needs nothing from us and has all beauty and good within himself, can be the inviolable foundation for our faith. The church, though, lives by the will of another and has her being not in herself but in Christ Jesus. Thus, the church cannot give fully to others and meet their every need and, as such, cannot be the final basis for creaturely reliance. The church is essential, due to God's determination alone, but it serves an instrumental or penultimate role. Thus, we believe in God while we believe the church, and the two are not unrelated. That we believe the church is a miracle owing fully to the fact that we believe in this God who gives her life.[16]

### The Creature of the Word

The first of the Theses of Berne is as clear as can be: "The holy, Christian Church, whose only Head is Christ, is born of the Word of God, abides in the same, and does not listen to the voice of a stranger."[17] The claim identifies the creaturely status of the church: not a natural entity with an existence of its own doing but with roots "born of the Word of God." The thesis goes still further and points to this gift of life as an ongoing reality, inasmuch as the church "abides in the same" Word of God that birthed it.

The Reformers spoke at length about the marks of the church: public identifiers of the true church. Having professed belief that there is a holy catholic church, the question naturally arose, where is it? So the Reformers pointed to the church's marks: the reading and preaching of the Word, the right administration of the sacraments, and, at least in certain corners of the Reformed world, the right administration of church discipline.[18] But it is crucial to see that this list (even the longer version) really involves only one mark in several forms: the presence of the Word. This focus on the Word is evident in the Geneva Confession of 1536 as it addresses the issue. "We believe that the proper mark by which rightly to discern the Church of Jesus Christ is that his holy gospel be purely and faithfully preached, proclaimed, heard, and kept, that his sacraments be properly administered, even if there be some imperfections

---

the greatest heroes of the church were human beings, that is, that they often fell, often sinned, and nevertheless were received back into grace by a merciful God" (240 [11:29–30]).

16. Cf. Oswald Bayer, *Martin Luther's Theology: A Contemporary Interpretation*, trans. Thomas H. Trapp (Grand Rapids: Eerdmans, 2008), 278–79.

17. Ten Theses of Berne 1, in Cochrane, *Reformed Confessions of the Sixteenth Century*, 49.

18. For discipline as the third mark of the church, see Belgic Confession 29, in Cochrane, *Reformed Confessions of the Sixteenth Century*, 210.

and faults, as there always will be among men."[19] Notice that the confession speaks of "the proper mark" in the singular, even as it goes on to speak of two aspects of that mark: preaching and the sacraments. A fundamental tenet of Reformational theology is found here—that is, the notion (following Augustine) that the sacraments are primarily to be considered as visible words. One could go still further and say that, if one accepts discipline as a third mark of the true church, it is only because discipline is the Word enacted in congregational life. "The keys have an indissoluble bond with the Word, which has been destroyed from among them."[20] Neither the sacraments nor discipline are autonomous activities; rather, they are the shape that the Word takes in the concrete life of his people.

The sole dependence upon the Word of God is seen in two ways. First, the sacraments and discipline are defined in such terms that they are fundamentally identified as forms of the Word. Second, the Word is called the sole mark of the true church, even amid discussions that clearly refer to the sacraments (and sometimes also to discipline). Luther is willing to point to the first mark (right reading and preaching of the Word) as the only necessary mark of the true church in his 1539 treatise "On the Councils and the Church."[21] The only way that theologians like Luther or Martin Bucer can hold these tenets together is to suggest that the single Word upon which we depend does take various forms (oral or visibly administered in the sacraments or even enacted by church discipline).

The dependence on the Word can be clearly seen in Paul's reflections on the ascended ministry of Jesus in his Letter to the Ephesians. When he describes the gifts of the ascended king to his church, they all involve the ministry of the Word: "the apostles, the prophets, the evangelists, the shepherds and teachers" (Eph. 4:11). The function of these officers is "to equip the saints for the work of ministry, for building up the body of Christ" (v. 12). Some of these offices are initial gifts to a church (for example, evangelists who help begin a church) while others are sustaining gifts to a church (for example, shepherds and teachers who continue to guide a church). Crucially, though, the beginning and the continuing are both sustained by officers whose primary task is marked out by their service of the Word. Evangelists share the word of good news, while teachers seek to deepen their pupils' knowledge of that same Word. "Put briefly, the entire authority (*maiestas*) of

---

19. Geneva Confession 18, in Cochrane, *Reformed Confessions of the Sixteenth Century*, 125.

20. Calvin, *Institutes* 4.2.10.

21. Martin Luther, "On the Councils and the Church," in *The Church and Ministry III*, ed. Eric W. Gritsch, trans. Gordon Rupp, Luther's Works 41 (Philadelphia: Fortress, 1966), 150.

the Gospel collapses unless we know that the living Christ speaks to us from the heavens."[22]

Whether in Ephesians or other Pauline writings, the being of the church is also spelled out in terms of election. Gary Badcock argues that "the biblical idea is that it is *God* who chooses us rather than *we* who choose God. Thus the church does not exist because people elect to join it for reasons relating to personal fulfillment, but because God reaches out to the world in love, calling a people into existence as his own."[23] Deuteronomy makes this plain, inasmuch as the choice of Israel is not based on her perfection or prowess (7:6–8). Indeed, after pointing to the unrighteousness of the Israelites again (9:4–5), the author is compelled to illustrate their unfaithfulness by pointing to archetypal events in her history: the wilderness murmurings and the golden calf incident (vv. 6–29). They are not allowed to interpret their looming occupancy of a rich and fertile land as an achievement or ascent of their own. Paul finds this of compelling, ongoing significance for the church as well. Before telling the Ephesians that they have the gifts of Christ, he reminds them that their spiritual identity is finally owing only to the glorious word that "he chose us in him before the foundation of the world. . . . In love he predestined us for adoption as sons through Jesus Christ, according to the purpose of his will" (Eph. 1:4–5). The very root of the church's life is just as external and gracious as the eternal fount of salvation, located principally in divine election, wholly by God's grace and "according to the purpose of his will."[24]

John Webster emphasizes the point of this description: "The Word is not *in* the church but announced *to* the church through Holy Scripture. The church is therefore not first and foremost a speaking but a hearing community."[25] The church lives on borrowed breath and depends on God's sustaining grace.

P. T. Forsyth confesses this truth as clearly as anyone.

> The Church rests on the grace of God, the judging, atoning, regenerating grace of God which is his holy love in the form it must take with human sin. Wherever that is heartily confessed and goes on to rule we have the true Church. Insofar as the Church is a creature, it is the creature of the preached gospel of God's grace,

---

22. John Calvin, *Commentary on Acts 1–13*, Calvin's New Testament Commentaries 6 (Grand Rapids: Eerdmans, 1995), 124. Note the present tense in the dependent clause: "the living Christ *speaks*."

23. Gary D. Badcock, *The House Where God Lives: Renewing the Doctrine of the Church for Today* (Grand Rapids: Eerdmans, 2009), 170 (emphasis original).

24. Eberhard Jüngel, "The Church as Sacrament?," in *Theological Essays I*, ed. and trans. John Webster (Edinburgh: T&T Clark, 1989), 208.

25. John Webster, "The Visible Attests the Invisible," in *Confessing God: Essays in Christian Dogmatics II* (London: T&T Clark, 2005), 190 (emphasis original).

forgiving, redeeming, and creating us anew by Christ's cross. The Church was created by the preaching of that solitary gospel and fortified by the sacraments of it which are, indeed, but other ways of receiving, confessing and preaching it. The Church is the social and practical response to that grace.[26]

The church rests as the church receives. God loves as he rules. That is the miracle of life by grace. Genesis 1 is matched by John 1: life was given *ex nihilo*, and new life is given no less gloriously from above. The gospel creates; the creature glories in this new creation "by Christ's cross."

## The Visible Church and the Invisible Church

The churches of the Reformation speak of the church as visible and invisible (following Augustine again).[27] They do not speak of two churches, but of the one church of Christ with two aspects. The First Helvetic Confession of 1536 speaks to this unity and difference: "And although this Church and congregation of Christ is open and known to God's eyes alone, yet it is not only known but also gathered and built up by visible signs, rites and ordinances."[28] The distinction is not meant to suggest that the real church is somehow ethereal or nonbodily, over against the tangible, material communities we encounter on a regular basis. No, as John Webster observes, "The issue is not whether the church is visible, but what *kind* of visibility is to be predicated of the church."[29]

Hans Urs von Balthasar has articulated a similar commitment. "As a concrete community of believers, the Church always exists in this tension, and so concretely she looks in two directions. . . . She is always both 'spotless Church' and 'disfigured Church,' always both 'virgin' and 'harlot,' for 'the whole, through the diversity of its parts, can get conflicting names.'"[30] Looking at the biblical imagery employed for the church—as sinful, in Eve, and now as righteous, in Mary—Balthasar will yet say, "True, the Church has her grounding in Mary, but in her members she constantly tends to lapse back into being Eve, or at best to strive upward from Eve to Mary."[31] He also speaks plainly when he says,

26. P. T. Forsyth, *Lectures on the Church and the Sacraments* (London: Longmans, Green, 1917), 31.

27. For further reflection on ecclesial invisibility, see Michael Allen, "The Church and the Churches: A Dogmatic Essay on Ecclesial Invisibility," *European Journal of Theology* 16, no. 2 (2007): 113–19.

28. First Helvetic Confession 14, in Cochrane, *Reformed Confessions of the Sixteenth Century*, 105.

29. Webster, "Visible Attests the Invisible," 179.

30. Balthasar, "Casta Meretrix," 227.

31. Ibid., 243.

"The seriousness of the issue dawns on us when we stop seeing the bride's infidelity as something largely outside her, in heresy, and realize that it exists inside her. At this point the Church cannot avoid confronting the Jerusalem texts of the Old Testament."[32]

There is spiritual wisdom here, for too many interpret the church as the response to Israel, or the New Testament era as an epoch entirely divorced from and juxtaposed to the Old Testament era.[33] Surely there are epoch-dividing factors—"if anyone is in Christ, he is a new creation" (2 Cor. 5:17)—though they occur amid a covenantal plot that has not been rejected.[34] The church is Eve and Mary in this time: two-faced in these overlapping ages, at war not only with the world but also with herself. Whereas so many focus on sin, death, and the devil as the great dangers to the church's life and flourishing, it is a breath of fresh air to hear Balthasar's reminder that the churchly Eve is ecclesial Mary's own worst enemy.

Yet Protestants can and must go beyond Balthasar. Indeed, I believe we must go beyond what even the Westminster Confession asserts explicitly. The invisibility of the church is not merely a correlate of the sinfulness of her nominal members but also of the indwelling sinfulness of her genuine members. Luther's Large Catechism makes the point clearly in its unpacking of the creedal phrase "the communion of saints": "Forgiveness is constantly needed, for although God's grace has been acquired by Christ, and holiness has been wrought by the Holy Spirit through God's Word in the unity of the Christian church, yet we are never without sin because we carry our flesh around our neck."[35] Calvin agrees: "The church is holy, then, in the sense that it is daily advancing and is not yet perfect: it makes progress from day to day but has

32. Ibid., 244–45.

33. At this point the Baptist doctrine of regenerate church membership surely comes to mind. For the most cogent argument to this effect, see Henri Blocher, "Old Covenant, New Covenant," in *Always Reforming: Explorations in Systematic Theology*, ed. Andrew McGowan (Downers Grove, IL: IVP Academic, 2007), 240–70. Cf. Stephen Wellum, "Baptism and the Relationship between the Covenants," in *Believer's Baptism: Sign of the New Covenant in Christ*, ed. Thomas Schreiner and Shawn Wright, New American Commentary Studies in Bible and Theology (Nashville: Broadman & Holman, 2007), 97–162. Both accounts suffer from their underappreciation of the ongoing process of the old covenant's obsolescence (as described in Heb. 8:13) as well as the eschatological descriptions by Jesus of the mixed church (e.g., Matt. 25:31–46) and his explicit instructions not to separate wheat and chaff now (e.g., Matt. 13:24–30). Augustine's writings against the Donatists (e.g., his matchless *Homilies on the First Epistle of John*) presciently address the key issues of Baptist hermeneutics.

34. That the plot has not been rejected and rescripted is surely the point of Rom. 9–11, a necessary argument offering assurance that any of the promises given in Rom. 8 are worth our trust.

35. Martin Luther, "The Large Catechism (1529)," in *The Book of Concord: The Confessions of the Evangelical Lutheran Church*, ed. Robert Kolb and Timothy J. Wengert, trans. Charles Arand (Minneapolis: Fortress, 2000), 438. Cf. Luther, "On the Councils and the Church,"

not yet reached its goal of holiness."[36] The church is and remains in this life simultaneously justified yet sinful.

Balthasar offers a critical qualification here. "All Christians are sinners, and if the Church does not sin as Church, she does sin in all her members, and through the mouths of all her members she must confess her guilt."[37] A distinction has been drawn between the church as church and the church as her members—while the latter can be sinful and righteous, the former is only righteous.[38] Charles Journet summarizes well when he says, "The church is not without sinners, but she herself is sinless."[39] Matthew Levering has offered the most nuanced defense of this approach in his recent work on the priesthood and hierarchy of the church. Levering does argue successfully that the church must be viewed theologically as sharing by grace in God's gifts and God's own life, yet he does not trace out the soteriological and eschatological shape of this participation.[40] It is this latter issue that must be engaged satisfactorily to mount a defense of the Roman Catholic distinction. Without such a defense, the distinction between a holy essence and sinful members hangs in midair.

Can such a distinction be maintained? At times, at least, Luther himself makes such a distinction. For him, when clarified, it is seen that the distinction is not between the essence of the church and her members, but between the actions of the church and the specific action of the preaching of the church (which he identifies as God's activity and not the church's).

---

165–66. For a Reformed parallel, see the Geneva Confession of 1536 (in Cochrane, *Reformed Confessions of the Sixteenth Century*, 122).

36. Calvin, *Institutes* 4.1.17. Calvin then proceeds to say that it is fitting that "forgiveness of sins" follows reference to the "communion of saints" in the creed. The saintliness of the church cannot be said with a straight face unless one also affirms that God is in the business of forgiving his sinful people (cf. 4.1.21).

37. Balthasar, "Casta Meretrix," 245. Cf. Pope Pius XII, "Mystici Corporis," §66, in *Foundations of Renewal: Four Great Encyclicals of Pope Pius XII*, ed. Gerald C. Treacy (Glen Rock, NJ: Deus, 1961), 31; and *Lumen Gentium: Dogmatic Constitution of the Church*, in *Decrees of the Ecumenical Councils*, ed. Norman P. Tanner (London: Sheed & Ward, 1990), par. 8. For further reflection on the teaching of the Second Vatican Council, see Karl Rahner, "The Sinful Church in the Decrees of Vatican II," in *Theological Investigations 6: Concerning Vatican Council II*, trans. K. H. Kruger and B. Kruger (London: Darton, Longman & Todd, 1969), 270–94.

38. *The Catechism of the Catholic Church*, 2nd ed. (Vatican City: Libreria Editrice Vaticana, 2000), 218.

39. Charles Journet, *Théologie de L'Église* (Paris: Desclée de Brouwer, 1958), 236. Cf. Joseph Ratzinger, "The Church's Guilt: Presentation of the Document *Remembrance and Reconciliation* from the International Theological Commission," in *Pilgrim Fellowship of Faith: The Church as Communion*, ed. Stephan Otto Horn and Vinzens Pfnür, trans. Henry Taylor (San Francisco: Ignatius, 2005), 274–83.

40. Matthew Levering, *Christ and the Catholic Priesthood: Ecclesial Hierarchy and the Pattern of the Trinity* (Chicago: Hillenbrand, 2010), 282–94.

A preacher should neither pray the Lord's Prayer nor ask for forgiveness of sins when he has preached (if he is a true preacher), but should say and boast with Jeremiah, "Lord, thou knowest that which came out of my lips is true and pleasing to thee" (Jer. 17:16); indeed, with St. Paul and all the apostles and prophets, he should say firmly, *Haec dixit dominus*, "God himself has said this" (1 Cor. 1:10). And again, "In this sermon I have been an apostle and prophet of Jesus Christ" (1 Thess. 4:15). Here it is unnecessary, even bad, to pray for forgiveness of sins, as if one had not taught truly, for it is God's word and not my word, and God ought not and cannot forgive it, but only confirm, praise, and crown it, saying, "You have taught truly, for I have spoken through you and the word is mine." Whoever cannot boast like that about his preaching, let him give up preaching, for he truly lies and slanders God.[41]

Luther has not merely affirmed that the preaching of the Word of God is itself the Word of God but also stated that this mandates the purity and perfection of that preaching (even if not of any other part of the church's activity).

Whether in the Roman or the Lutheran form, the implications seem insurmountable: a separation of church and community (in Rome) or a separation of preaching and normal churchly activity (in Luther). Yet neither portrayal accurately fits the biblical picture, wherein the same church is both holy and sinful.[42]

The New Testament portrays a community continuing to deal with strife and struggle, coming from outside and from within. Looking at Acts 6:1–6, John Calvin testifies: "Now we learn from this story, first of all, that the Church cannot be formed all at once in such a way that nothing remains to be corrected; and that an edifice of such a massive size cannot be finished on the first day so that nothing needs to be added to make it perfect."[43] "Furthermore we learn that there is no institution of God so sacred and praiseworthy that it is the case that it is not corrupted or rendered less useful by the fault of men."[44] In

41. Martin Luther, "Against Hanswurst," in *Church and Ministry III*, 216. For a related, though less specific, claim by Luther, see thesis 61 in "Theses Concerning Faith and Law," in *Career of the Reformer IV*, ed. Lewis Spitz, Luther's Works 34 (St. Louis: Concordia, 1960), 113.

42. Cf. Nicholas M. Healy, *Church, World, and the Christian Life: A Practical-Prophetic Ecclesiology*, Cambridge Studies in Christian Doctrine (Cambridge: Cambridge University Press, 2000), 10: "The eschatological 'not yet' reminds us that until the end of the church's time it remains imperfect and sinful, always *ecclesia semper reformanda* or *semper purificanda*. . . . As Christians, then, we have not only to fight against the power of sin in the fallen world, but we must fight against it in the midst of our ecclesial body and within ourselves." See also Mangina, *Revelation*, 156–58. "'Mother church' does not stand over the individual Christian; rather 'mother church' *is* Christians as they belong together through the Word of God and derive from the Word of God" (Jüngel, "The Church as Sacrament?," 208).

43. Calvin, *Commentary on Acts 1–13*, 157.

44. Ibid., 158.

this case, social distinction—whether one is a Hebrew or a Hellenic widow—has led to social injustice within the church; the diaconate is introduced as a solution. On top of this flaw in the shape of the community's life together, moral failures creep into the earliest Christian communities. The Corinthians are a hotbed of such conundrums, whether in the form of sexual impropriety (1 Cor. 5) or the misuse of Christian freedom (chaps. 8–9) or consumeristic excess (11:17–22).

Other texts point toward doctrinal inconsistency. Indeed, it would be difficult to find a New Testament epistle that did not in some way address doctrinal imprecision or worse, whether in the form of the Judaizers' teaching or the denial of the resurrection. New Testament accounts also witness to lapses in unity. The Corinthian correspondence points to factionalism that has crept into the community. Immediately after saying "we have the mind of Christ" (1 Cor. 2:16), Paul then says that he "could not address you as spiritual people, but as people of the flesh" (3:1). Some follow one apostle, others another—jealousy and strife have taken hold of their community. Disunity and division do not render them outside Christ, though they are called "infants in Christ" (v. 1) and are told that they "are still of the flesh" (v. 3).

Whether in the form of social injustice, ethical failure, doctrinal inconsistency, or lapses in unity, the earliest Christian communities were mixed multitudes.[45] The texts considered here could easily be multiplied, putting the lie to any notion of a pure core of the Christian community. The New Testament never employs such narratives or makes such observations about the sinfulness of the church to insist that "these persons are not the church."[46] Rather, the New Testament identifies the same people as sinful in the flesh (still) yet holy in Christ (already).

In the later language of the creed, we are reminded that we must believe there is a church that is one, holy, catholic, and apostolic. These Nicene marks are not obvious or straightforward in an empirical sort of way. Each of them is true

45. Augustine, *City of God*, 1.35; Jüngel, "The Church as Sacrament?," 210–11.
46. The text that might come immediately to mind here is 1 John 2:19—"They went out from us, but they were not of us"—perhaps suggesting that those who sin are not genuinely the church. First John does present a stark polarity between holiness and sin (see, e.g., 3:6–10), but it clearly does not refer to sinless perfection and patently points to ongoing imperfections (see the mention of the pangs of conscience in 3:20 and the explicit declaration that brothers do sin, though not the sin that leads unto death, in 5:16–17). Indeed, the epistle insists, "Beloved, we are God's children now, and what we will be has not yet appeared; but we know that when he appears we shall be like him, because we shall see him as he is. And everyone who thus hopes in him purifies himself as he is pure" (3:2–3). Here it is plain that adoption as God's child is a present reality, even though perfect purity is an ongoing task. While apostasy does lead some to show they are not genuine members of God's people (2:19; 5:16–17), even genuine sons and daughters do sin until they are perfected in the presence of the returning Christ.

of the church in Christ Jesus, but not yet true insofar as the church continues her journey away from sin and into holiness. Ephesians 4:4–6 speaks of the real unity enjoyed by Christians, even though it follows the call in Ephesians 4:1–3 to seek and maintain unity. Indeed, this issue can serve as a litmus test for the doctrine of the church's invisibility. The divisions of the church serve as a reminder of the church's brokenness.

Ephraim Radner has pointed to the biblical figure of church as Israel.[47] Both Israel and the church are to be understood in light of the Christ: broken and disfigured. Israel divided, struggled, and eventually was sent into exile. The prophets witness to her sinfulness; the law foretold her eventual failings; the Psalms lament the indwelling sin and social strife of her daily grind. But the Christian and the church cannot reflect upon this scriptural witness from a safe distance, as if they were divorced from or superior to such struggle.[48] Radner argues that Christ recapitulates those struggles in the economy of the gospel, and that his ecclesial body will likewise be called to bear burdens and to carry a cross. There is a scriptural matrix within which the church must be viewed, and it enables us to appreciate the cross-shaped discipline required of Christian communities.

Some respond by arguing that the true church is holy and united. Impostors may be separated, but they are simply false claimants to the title of the church. The invisible church is pure even now, but with nominal believers and errant parishes or denominations mingled throughout. In much interdenominational polemic, this approach dominates.[49] Perhaps this approach is politically help-ful—hoisting blame on others rather than one's own interest group can sell tickets and gain donations—but it is akin to the malaise so poignantly de-scribed long ago by Blaise Pascal: "Being unable to cure death, wretchedness, and ignorance, men have decided in order to be happy, not to think about such things."[50] Radner sees this willful lack of reflection as obscuring the church's real scriptural location. "The obviousness of the judgment on the divided

47. See esp. Ephraim Radner, *The End of the Church: A Pneumatology of Christian Division in the West* (Grand Rapids: Eerdmans, 1998); and idem, *Hope among the Fragments: The Broken Church and Its Engagement of Scripture* (Grand Rapids: Brazos, 2004). Cf. Bruce Marshall, "The Divided Church and Its Theology," *Modern Theology* 16, no. 3 (July 2000): 377–96.

48. See the language of exile still in use in 1 Pet. 1:1.

49. Peter Leithart recounts the ways in which commentary on 1 and 2 Kings took this form in both Roman Catholic and Reformational polemic of the sixteenth century, noting instead an evangelical way of reading the church as the whole broken body of Israel, that is, of Christ Jesus (*First and Second Kings*, Brazos Theological Commentary on the Bible [Grand Rapids: Brazos, 2006], 24, 92–95). Paul Avis traces this move to a more exclusionary reading of Israel's history and, by extension, of sixteenth-century ecclesiology in Reformers after Calvin (*The Church in the Theology of the Reformers* [Atlanta: John Knox, 1981], pt. 1).

50. Blaise Pascal, *Pensées*, trans. A. J. Krailsheimer (New York: Penguin, 1966), 37 (no. 133).

church's lack of integrity has been obscured by a novel unwillingness, over the last few centuries, to view the Christian church as figured prophetically in the people of Israel."[51] As Rusty Reno has argued, "You and I need to avoid recoiling from that suffering as if it were evil. We need to draw ever nearer to the reality of Christian faith and witness in our time, however burdensome, however heavy with failure, limitation, and disappointment. The reason is simple. Our Lord Jesus Christ comes to us in the flesh. We can draw near to him only in his body, the church. Loyalty to him requires us to dwell within the ruins of the church."[52]

Radner argues that the church must be viewed figurally in relation to the exiled Israelites and the crucified Christ. Jeremiah 14:2 is paradigmatic: "Judah mourns, and her gates languish; her people lament on the ground, and the cry of Jerusalem goes up." The division, diminishment, and eventual exile of Israel have been recapitulated in Christ's passion and are now experienced in the life of the church. This figural reading raises a seemingly contradictory reflection—namely, that "it is very difficult to believe that the church is the light of the world, ordained by God as the champion of his holy Word, and at the same time to face the fact that it is in ruins. To deny the former entails a massive repudiation of the plain sense of Scripture. To deny the latter requires an equally massive act of self-deception."[53]

Thus, the Christian community is called to a cruciform existence, whereby holiness is worked out amid the difficulties of life and the disappointments of communion. Joseph Mangina suggests that this focus on the cross-shaped life of the church has been the most glaring absence in recent ecclesiology.[54] Indeed, recent ecclesiology has struggled to surmount the divides of the Reformation era. Perhaps the most crucial theological maneuver for a time such as this would be a recovery of the Reformational ecclesiology that allows us to subsist within an Israel-like church: broken yet hopeful. The beginnings of such cross-shaped existence involve ecclesial self-awareness—of our divisions, our ruins, our sin. The hope of this cruciform path will be found only outside ourselves: in the promise of our Lord, our Christ, our Jesus. The broken body dies, but it really does rise again.

---

51. Ephraim Radner, "The Cost of Communion: A Meditation on Israel and the Divided Church," in *Inhabiting Unity: Theological Perspectives on the Proposed Lutheran-Episcopal Concordat*, ed. Ephraim Radner and R. R. Reno (Grand Rapids: Eerdmans, 1995), 135.

52. R. R. Reno, *In the Ruins of the Church: Sustaining Faith in an Age of Diminished Christianity* (Grand Rapids: Brazos, 2002), 14.

53. Ibid., 16.

54. Joseph Mangina, "The Cross-Shaped Church: A Pauline Amendment to the Ecclesiology of *Koinōnia*," in *Critical Issues in Ecclesiology: Essays in Honor of Carl E. Braaten*, ed. Alberto L. García and Susan K. Wood (Grand Rapids: Eerdmans, 2012), 68–87, esp. 70–71.

Precisely because of that resurrection promise, a Christian may grieve when faced with these and other failures of the church, yet not as those without hope. Jaroslav Pelikan summarizes the Lutheran appraisal of such problems in this way:

> According to Lutheran theology, it would seem that history is the conditioned bearer of the activity of God. This applies alike to the church and to the church's witness. For this reason, Lutheranism is not fearful of historical criticism, for it does not pin its faith on the infallibility of the historical church. But when such criticism discovers that the historical church is indeed historical and that it has not managed to escape the corruption that affects all things historical, Lutheran theology does not discard its regard for the historical church. . . . It devotes itself to the study of patristic theology, not with authoritarian reverence, nor yet with supercilious contempt, but with a deep regard and a healthy suspicion.[55]

Why is this distinction crucial? Not because the gospel fails to have material impact on lives, relationships, communities, and society. And certainly not because there are two churches in need of separation—at least not yet. No, the distinction honors the one community of God, genuinely concrete and social, which will yet undergo that judgment foretold by Jesus (see, e.g., Matt. 25:31–46), whereby those truly in him will be separated from those only superficially identified with him and wherein those truly in him will see him in glory and in so doing be transformed from two-faced inconsistency to full-throated confession of him alone as their way, truth, and life.

Looking at the church, one can be neither optimistic (for there is too much indwelling sin) nor pessimistic (for there is a Savior coming to her aid); one must be hopeful. Heinrich Heppe articulates this approach well. "Consequently, while the Church is indeed not without lack of knowledge and of life, still, preserved by grace she cannot completely lose the righteousness of Christ bestowed on her, deny the basic doctrines of the Gospel and sin against God with really deliberate disobedience and persistently; so that at any time she therefore remains in essential possession of grace and of sanctifying knowledge."[56] The church does not remain or recede; she rests.

Perhaps recent focus on the eucharistic nature of the church can be turned to highlight not simply the concrete nature of the church's practices (as is popular today) but also the invisible nature of the promised presence of God. Gary Badcock makes this link when he says, "Just as the body of Christ is contained in heaven, so also the church awaits its own fulfillment, when it will

55. Jaroslav Pelikan, *Obedient Rebels: Catholic Substance and Protestant Principle in Luther's Reformation* (New York: Harper & Row, 1964), 40–41.

56. Heinrich Heppe, *Reformed Dogmatics*, ed. Ernst Bizer, trans. G. T. Thomson (New York: HarperCollins, 1950), 662–63.

be made wholly one with the risen Lord. Thus does the idea of the church as the body of Christ ultimately represent what is present to faith and hope rather than to sight and to our experience."[57] Badcock points to the New Testament language of the Holy Spirit as "down payment" as suggesting such an eschatological anticipation (2 Cor. 1:22; 5:5; Eph. 1:14).

The invisibility here is not one of ethereal disengagement from concrete practices. Think of Augustine's maxim regarding baptism: "Take away water, there is no baptism; take away the word, there is no baptism."[58] Just as the Eucharist involves material objects in the arena of spiritual fellowship, so Badcock suggests that the church points beyond its visible self. The claim that there is invisible grace rendered in the visible words of the sacrament simply means that more is going on than is evident to the naked eye. Similarly, the invisibility of the church speaks of the depth of the church's being, exceeding her empirical reality and taking into account the ongoing pledge of eschatological perfection.

The church is a pledge inasmuch as it is the temple of the Holy Spirit. The church dwells within the overlap of the ages: Christ has brought the end, yet the fallen ways of the sinful world continue on, both outside and inside the church.

In one sense it is obviously the church's realization of her limits that marks out her distinction from the world. The novelist Flannery O'Connor understood this paradox that holiness and awareness of sinfulness are bound up with each other—as any reading of the apostle Paul or Martin Luther makes plain. In her tale *Wise Blood*, she writes of a female character, a skeptic, who confides to a believer, Mr. Motes: "'For myself,' she continued, '. . . I believe that what's right today is wrong tomorrow and that the time to enjoy yourself is now, so long as you let others do the same. I'm as good, Mr. Motes,' she said, 'not believing in Jesus as a many a one that does.' 'You're better,' he said, leaning forward suddenly. 'If you believed in Jesus, you wouldn't be so good.'"[59]

How then do we know the real church? "Accordingly, knowledge of the church cannot be derived in a straightforward way by deduction from its visible phenomenon and practices. . . . Rather the church is visible to the perception of faith, for it is to faith that the church steps out of the obscurity and indefiniteness of an historical phenomenon and becomes fully and properly visible as the creature of the Spirit. . . . The visibility of the church is thus spiritual event, spiritually discerned."[60] The real church is an object of faith,

---

57. Badcock, *House Where God Lives*, 101.
58. Augustine, *Homilies on the Gospel of John 1–40*, 277 (15.4). Cf. Martin Luther, "The Private Mass and the Consecration of Priests (1533)," in *Word and Sacrament IV*, ed. and trans. Martin Lehmann, Luther's Works 38 (St. Louis: Concordia, 1971), 202.
59. Flannery O'Connor, *Wise Blood* (New York: Farrar, Straus & Giroux, 2007), 225.
60. Webster, "Visible Attests the Invisible," 182.

precisely because it is spiritually visible now, evident only to those who grasp the promise of Christ's Word. This is a three-stranded cord: it is no doubt a lot to grab hold of, but it is sturdy enough to sustain a journey upward to God.

These doctrinal concepts (believing the church; the creature of the Word; the invisible church) all point to two things: the church's intrinsic limits and the promised life outside herself that sustains this justified yet sinful people amid their journey homeward to God. Each in its own way accents the grace of the gospel and, more specifically, the way in which God's people always receive life with God only in this one: Jesus the righteous. Each in its own way points to the profoundly trinitarian and deeply evangelical shape of the church's life.[61]

## Conclusion: Reflection on the Gospel, Rehearsing the Church's Identity in Christ

The church lives by good news not of its own doing—in other words, the church lives on borrowed breath. This posture of faith and receptivity does not merely mark the entrance into life with God, but it goes all the way down and continues throughout life. The church enjoys the presence of God's glory, not because she is pure but on the basis of Christ's mediatorial work.

Perhaps nothing makes this point more powerfully than an excerpt from Martin Luther, which so moved Karl Barth that he included it in lieu of a foreword to the second part-volume of his famed *Church Dogmatics*.

> It is not we who can sustain the Church, nor was it our forefathers, nor will it be our descendants. It was and is and will be the One who says: "I am with you always, even unto the end of the world." As it says in Hebrews 13: "Jesus Christ, yesterday, today, and forever." And in Revelation 1: "Which was, and is, and is to come." Verily He is that One, and none other is or can be.
>
> For you and I were not alive thousands of years ago, but the Church was preserved without us, and it was done by the One of whom it says, "Who was," and "Yesterday."
>
> Again we do not do it in our life-time, for the Church is not upheld by us. For we could not resist the devil in the Papacy and the sects and other wicked folk. For us, the Church would perish before our very eyes, and we with it (as we daily prove), were it not for that other Man who manifestly upholds the Church and

---

61. "Only through the same Spirit is the church visible. . . . This rooting of the doctrine of the church in the doctrine of the Spirit has one crucial effect. It makes clear that the third element of the economy of salvation—the making real of reconciliation in human life and history—is as much a divine work as the first element (the Father's purpose) and the second element (its accomplishment by the Son)" (ibid., 181).

us. This we can lay hold of and feel, even though we are loth to believe it, and we must needs give ourselves to the One of whom it is said, "Who is," and "Today." Again, we can do nothing to sustain the Church when we are dead. But he will do it of whom it is said, "Who is to come," and "Forever." And what we must needs say of ourselves in this regard is what our forefathers had also to say before us, as the Psalms and other Scriptures testify, and what our descendants will also experience after us, when with us and the whole Church they sing in Psalm 124: "If the Lord himself had not been on our side, when men rose up against us," and Psalm 60: "O be thou our help in trouble, for vain is the help of man."[62]

The church lives on borrowed breath indeed, and "were it not for that other Man who manifestly upholds the Church and us," it would cease to be. The link between justification and the church highlights the external basis of its very existence.[63] It is in Christ or not at all.

The moments of the Christian liturgy make this point powerfully. Each points behind and beyond the worshiping community to its source of life and blessedness, the gospel of Jesus and the promise of the triune God.

> *Invocation.* The community admits that a meeting with God cannot simply be demanded by creatures, much less manufactured by zeal or ritual. God must be invoked, asked to make himself present by the Holy Spirit. Descent from heaven must be sought immediately, for the prospect of ascending to heaven is sure to fail.

62. Martin Luther, *Schriften 1543/46, D. Martin Luthers Werke: Kritische Gesammtausgabe* 54 (Weimar: H. Böhlaus Nachf, 1968), 54:170, quoted in Karl Barth, *Church Dogmatics*, vol. I/2, *The Doctrine of the Word of God*, ed. G. W. Bromiley and T. F. Torrance, trans. G. T. Thomson and Harold Knight (Edinburgh: T&T Clark, 1957), xi.

63. Healy argues that "all good ecclesiologies are careful to set up blocks against glorying in the church rather than in Jesus Christ crucified" (*Church, World, and the Christian Life*, 11). Surely emphasis on the church as "body of Christ" can make this especially difficult to maintain; yet it is clear that "Christ transcends, is more than, his body and, as head of that body, cannot be considered a 'member' of the body in the same sense that the Christian is a member of the body" (Susan K. Wood, *Spiritual Exegesis in the Theology of Henri de Lubac* [Grand Rapids: Eerdmans, 1998], 145). For helpful reflections along these lines, see Ian McFarland, "The Body of Christ: Rethinking a Classic Ecclesiological Model," *International Journal of Systematic Theology* 7, no. 3 (2005): 225–45. Perhaps the key ecumenical theologian for whom the "body of Christ" image has done major work and seemingly led to a conflation of Christ and church is Robert W. Jenson (see *Systematic Theology*, vol. 2, *The Works of God* [New York: Oxford University Press, 1997], 211–27). More recently, Jenson has noted that a focus on church as body of Christ cannot be "undialectical," yet he does continue to define the church (and all creaturely being) as "not my persistence in what I am from the beginning and so am timelessly. . . . In Scripture, for me to be is to be drawn forward to what I will be when fulfilled in God, it is being *in via* à la Paul" ("The Bride of Christ," in García and Wood, *Critical Issues in Ecclesiology*, 2, 5). Jenson's affirmation of the dialectical nature of the church's being is surely apropos, yet he then offers an entirely eschatological definition of her being. One wonders if one is not missing the other end of the supposed dialectic.

*Confession and Assurance of Pardon.* The church affirms her sins "in thought, word, and deed; in what we have done, and in what we have left undone." The church points to her failures and owns them, turning to Jesus for a balm for these spiritual wounds and a comfort amid this moral disappointment.[64]

*Passing of the Peace.* In a world where typical greetings at a social gathering begin with "How are you doing?" as an opportunity to prove one's standing and status, a declarative word from above—"Christ's peace will be with you"—is given to the neighbor. Prior to any assessment of one's self-awareness, the self is reminded of God's gift of peace.

*Reading and Preaching of the Word.* The pastor brings a message founded not in his or her own ingenuity or intuition, but in an authoritative Word. Like John the Baptist, the pastor serves as a pointer to one of whom we can say, "He must increase, but I must decrease" (John 3:30). While this proclamation takes shape in new words, its authority hangs on the words read immediately prior. A rule is given just before the sermon for its adjudication: it must proclaim this text, displaying Christ's gospel via this portion of Holy Scripture, or it must be rendered a failure.

*Testimony.* The congregants offer profession of faith, either by confessing the common faith of the church of the ages in the form of a creedal text (e.g., the Apostles' Creed) or by speaking to the way God has graced an individual (e.g., the evangelical testimonial). Following the creeds, testimonial speaks of our stories only indirectly by locating our narratives within that grand unfolding of God's creational and redemptive purposes in Christ and by the Spirit.

*Sacraments as Visible Words.* The officiant addresses the congregation in the name of another: baptizing in the triune name, celebrating the Lord's (and not their own) table. The waters of creation, the bread from heaven, and the blood of our incarnate Lord are enlisted in these proclamations of God's consecrating and sustaining grace. We bring nothing but our need and hunger—God washes, gives life, and feeds us.

*Blessing.* The congregation disperses only after being promised the presence of the risen Lord. Just as Moses refused to take Israel along the journey unless God promised to accompany them, so the church cannot be scattered for the week until God's blessing is pronounced upon

64. To understand the importance of assurance in the time of the Reformation, it is crucial to understand the role of anxiety amid lay life; see esp. Stephen Ozment, "Lay Religious Attitudes on the Eve of the Reformation," in *The Reformation in the Cities* (New Haven: Yale University Press, 1975), 15–46. Relocation of anxiety from guilt to economic overwhelmedness or relational anonymity is no sign of anxiety's being overcome, but of its steady march forward.

them. The church's mission is given her from above (reminding us that, ultimately, we are not even competent to determine our course), just as her momentum must be supplied from outside (for we are surely not able intrinsically to mount any such campaign).

So the gospel is rehearsed.[65] The church's life is sure, precisely because it is dependent not upon her competency or character but upon the good news of the Christ. We believe in him, we are gathered by his Word, we are justified even if still journeying. So we do profess that the church's only foundation is Jesus Christ, in whom the sinful church is—miraculously, by grace—the justified church.

---

65. For wonderful reflection on the rehearsal of the gospel in the liturgy, see Bryan Chapell, *Christ-Centered Worship: Letting the Gospel Shape Our Practice* (Grand Rapids: Baker Academic, 2009).

# Subject Index

179

# Scripture Index